Anonymous

Expository Sermons And Outlines On The Old Testament

Anonymous

Expository Sermons And Outlines On The Old Testament

ISBN/EAN: 9783337087791

Printed in Europe, USA, Canada, Australia, Japan

Cover: Foto ©Lupo / pixelio.de

More available books at **www.hansebooks.com**

The Clerical Library.

THIS SERIES of volumes is specially intended for the clergy and students of all denominations, and is meant to furnish them with stimulus and suggestion in the various departments of their work. Amongst the pulpit thinkers from whom these sermon outlines have been drawn are leading men of almost every denomination, the subjects treated of being of course practical rather than controversial. The best thoughts of the est religious writers of the day are here furnished in a condensed form, and at a moderate price.

Six volumes in crown 8vo, cloth, are now ready (*each volume complete in itself*). Price, $1.50.

JUST READY—THE NEW VOLUME,

Expository Sermons on the Old Testament.

ALSO, NOW READY, NEW EDITIONS OF

1. Outlines of Sermons on the New Testament.
2. Outlines of Sermons on the Old Testament.
3. Outlines of Sermons to Children.
4. Pulpit Prayers by Eminent Clergymen.
5. Anecdotes Illustrative of New Testament Texts.

Copies sent post-paid on receipt of price, by publishers.

The Clerical Library.

EXPOSITORY SERMONS

AND OUTLINES

ON THE

OLD TESTAMENT.

New York:
A. C. ARMSTRONG AND SON,
714 BROADWAY.
1886.

AUTHORS OF SERMONS.

RIGHT REV. WILLIAM ALEXANDER, D.D., Bishop of Derry.
RIGHT REV. ALFRED BARRY, D.D., Primate of Australia.
VERY REV. G. G. BRADLEY, D.D., Dean of Westminster.
REV. STOPFORD A. BROOKE, M.A., London.
REV. PROF. A. B. DAVIDSON, D.D., LL.D., Edinburgh.
VEN. ARCHDEACON FARRAR, D.D., F.R.S., Westminster.
REV. CANON W. J. KNOX-LITTLE, M.A., Manchester.
REV. CANON H. P. LIDDON, D.D., St. Paul's, London.
REV. ALEXANDER MACLAREN, D.D., Manchester.
REV. GEORGE MATHESON, D.D., Mellar.
REV. JOSEPH PARKER, D.D., London.
VERY REV. J. J. S. PEROWNE, D.D., Dean of Peterborough.
REV. CHARLES STANFORD, D.D., London.
RIGHT REV. WILLIAM STUBBS, D.D., Lord Bishop of Chester.
VERY REV. C. J. VAUGHAN, D.D., Dean of Llandaff.

PREFATORY NOTE.

The following expositions are all gathered from fugitive or unpublished sources.

I. **Enoch.** GEN. v. 21–24. *"And Enoch lived sixty and five years, and begat Methuselah: and Enoch walked with God after he begat Methuselah three hundred years, and begat sons and daughters: and all the days of Enoch were three hundred sixty and five years: and Enoch walked with God: and he was not; for God took him."*

ENOCH is one of this world's representative men. It is written of him by the writer of Genesis, that he was not found amongst the dead; it is written of him by the writer to the Hebrews, that he was "translated that he should not see death." Such a contingency could never have befallen any man who was not essentially a representative of his race, could never have been attributed to any man who had not impressed his race with a sense of his representative character. In the world of literature, in the world of philosophy, in the world of morals, there are men who, spiritually speaking, may be said to have been translated that they should not see death, but these have all, without exception, been representative men. Time has not touched their fame, their eye is not dim nor their natural strength abated, but that is because their lives were universal lives. They were not men of a party, of a sect, of a school. They did not walk round the mere environments of their subject of study. They did not occupy themselves with the ephemeral and accidental questions which floated in their contemporaneous atmosphere; they laid hold of that element in their atmosphere which was to constitute the breath of every life and to form the being of every time. By that grasp of the universal in humanity, they being dead are yet speaking.

But just because the representative men of the world have refused to occupy themselves with the accidental questions of their own day, they have incurred the fate involved in Mr. Carlyle's aphorism; they have had short biographies. Let us look at this man Enoch as his figure looms down upon us through the mist of six millenniums. He stands amidst a group of antediluvians but his form is easily distinguishable from all beside. He is unquestionably and confessedly the hero of the band, the one life amongst them whom posterity has judged worthy to inherit everlasting youth; but this is on the heavenly side of his being. When we look at the earthly side we are impressed with a contrast between him and his contemporaries of a totally different kind. From the spiritual standpoint Enoch is the greatest man of the band, but from the earthly standpoint he is the least; he has a short biography. The test of earthly greatness in that day was the duration of years, and measured by that test, Enoch sinks far beneath his contemporaries. He cannot touch the longevity of the Adams, the Seths, the Cainans, the Methuselahs; his life embraces but a golden year of circling suns. The measurement of the man must be estimated on other grounds than those of duration, and his greatness must be determined by another standard than that of the world. His physical life is weaker than all the physical lives around him. The days of his earthly pilgrimage reach not to the days of those who went before nor of those who followed, yet he has an immortality that belongs not to them; he is not found among the dead.

Now in all this there is nothing accidental; it is the law of the spiritual life in every age. The leading men of the world have from the physical side had the least eventful lives. In the earliest recorded history of the human race the thought appears with marked emphasis. The opening chapters of Genesis contain the narrative of two contemporaneous orders of human life; they are called in that record respectively the Sons of God and the Sons of Men, but we of modern times should best describe them as the men of matter and the men of spirit. The one race is represented by Cain, the other is prefigured in Abel, and even in their first representatives their distinctive marks appear. "Cain" means possession; "Abel" signifies vanity; the one typifies the fulness of worldly gain, the other represents the sense of worldly emptiness. All down the stream of the antediluvian centuries the characteristics of these races are manifest. All the *historical* interest centres in the sons of Cain. They are the inventors of musical instruments, the forgers of brass and iron, the discoverers of a mode of architecture, the initiators of an art of poetry, the earliest builders of walled cities; they laid hold of the civilization of this world and therefore they have deservedly the higher place in the world's history.

With the order of Abel, on the other hand, it is all the reverse. The men of this school make no figure in the world and do not seek to make any figure. We know nothing about them but their names and genealogies. Whatever eventfulness belonged to their lives must have been an eventfulness of spiritual experience; it does not manifest itself on the surface. Their life is a hidden life; the changes and revolutions of their being are all within, and just because they are subsisting on that which is universal to humanity there is nothing in experience which can catch the historian's eye.

I. We have implied that in the lives of these representative men the absence of an outward eventfulness may be at once supplied and explained by an eventfulness of inward experience. Now, in the case of this man Enoch, it is emphatically so. Brief as is the record of his life it is long enough to give us a glimpse behind the scenes, and in the case of a representative man it is only behind the scenes that any one cares to see. The whole narration of his history is summed up in the simple words of a single sentence—" And Enoch lived sixty and five years and begat Methuselah; and Enoch walked with God after he begat Methuselah three hundred years and begat sons and daughters." Yet in that artless and primitive narrative, so simple, so compressed, so unadorned, there is revealed a volume of rich human experience. We are made to see that in the heart of this uneventful life there was indeed transacting one of the most marvellous events which the universe can ever witness—the birth of a human soul from darkness into light. It is by no accident that after the close of the first sixty-five years the words " Enoch lived " are changed into the words " Enoch walked with God ; " it is the expression of a great and solemn fact which sooner or later every spiritual man must learn.

It tells us that to this man there came that time which comes to every developed soul when the life of the vegetable is transformed into the life of the human, when the man ceases to be a mere living and breathing apparatus, and begins to manifest himself as a working force and power. For five and sixty years—the period, let us say, of an antediluvian youth—Enoch simply *lived*. He grew, as the plants grew, by the force of a spontaneous nature unconscious of its own native majesty. He entered into relation with the physical world, and had no glimmering of a suspicion that there was aught within him which had a right to transcend that world; through all these years he was but of the earth earthy. But at the end of these years there came a change, and from the manner in which the dates are marked we may infer that it was a sudden change. Had it been gradual it would have been no more possible to have fixed its year than it is possible to fix the year when the natural child becomes the natural man. How it came we know not; whether it was suggested by circumstances from without, or whether it arose incomprehensibly from within, we have not the data to determine. When a soul is ready to take fire a very slight external cause will be sufficient to ignite it—a cause which for any incombustible spirit would be simply non-existent.

Probably to the eyes of his contemporaries the change in the life of Enoch had that look of unaccountability which we call madness. It matters not; the important question is not its cause, but its nature. It is described in the narrative of Genesis as the transition into a new world, a spiritual world, a world incapable of being perceived by the merely physical life; for sixty-five years he had *lived*, for the next three hundred years he was to walk with God. He had been in union with the region of the five senses, and he had asked for nothing more, but now there were opening within him new senses leading into other regions —an eye that was cognisant of a light which never shone on land or sea, an ear which caught the sound of a music unutterable by earthly voices, a heart which had wakened into thoughts which the human imagination had not conceived. He was beginning to seek for objects beyond experience, to set his affections on things above, to look towards a life which was unseen and eternal. In that hour, though he knew it not, he had entered upon the process of vanquishing death; the beginning of his translation was the hour of his walk with God.

II. Here, then, was a mystery in the life of Enoch, a mystery which is repeated in every regenerated life. But let us look deeper into the narrative before us, and we shall find, if possible, a still greater mystery. Previous to that day on which Enoch became the subject of a great spiritual revolution he had already begun to discharge the ordinary duties of a householder; he had become the educator of a family. When the spiritual change passes over him we expect to hear that he has abandoned these commonplace cares. We expect to hear that, after the manner of Eastern devotees, his walk with God has become a desertion of man. We look for his translation out of the world even before his death. When we are told that at a definite period of life he walks with God, or strikes out into a spiritual pathway, we fully expect the sequel to be that he walks no more with men and participates no longer in the ways of men; that is the sequel which Brahmanism, which Buddhism, which the great mass of Eastern religions would have deemed imperative.

But this man reverses all our expectations. He is not of the East Eastern; he is no Brahman, no Buddhist, no ascetic. He goes up into the life of God, to walk in the spiritual regions, and we expect to see him vanish in the clouds of heaven, but presently he re-appears in the world of men and resumes the life of common day. He ascends up into the mountain, but it is only to come down again into the valley perfumed with the fragrance of the mountain air. When the great spiritual change first comes to him it finds him engaged in the duties of a householder; when the great spiritual change is completed it leaves him resuming those duties. The three hundred years of his walk with God are years of family life; he brings up sons and daughters. His life in its outward aspect in no respect differs from the lives of those around him. His walk with God lies not over a different road from the common walk with men; the difference lies not in the road but in the companionship, not in the steps taken but in the spirit with which they are taken. Before he saw God he had a sphere in a human family; after he saw God he had still the same sphere. But it was no longer the same man that filled it, and therefore it was no longer filled in the same way.

The walk with God leads through the paths of earth as well as the paths of heaven, but he who has entered upon that walk can no longer separate these paths; the atmosphere of heaven penetrates everywhere. It does not unsphere the lives of men; it purifies the old spheres. It makes better fathers, better sons. It makes the soldier a more loyal soldier, the philosopher a more true philosopher, the legislator a more just legislator; the triumph of eternity is the sublimation of time. That is the great truth which Enoch was the first to see, the great truth which he was to make the distinctive principle of the coming Jewish nation. This man standing at the head of the stream is at once the representative and the prophecy of that which constitutes the genius of Judaism.

That religion, almost alone amongst the faiths of the East, maintains from beginning to end that the sacred has its province in the secular. It is a protest against the Brahman, against the Buddhist, against the ascetic of every age. In opposition to all theories of mysticism and transcendentalism, it declares that the earth is the Lord's, and the fulness thereof. It claims for God all the kingdoms of the world and the glory of them: every government is His government, every law is His law, every political institution is an ordinance from Him. There is no difference between treason and impiety; there is no distinction between anarchy and atheism. God is not only the supreme ruler of the earth—He is the only ruler; He is without rival and without second. Therefore it is that to the Jew, that man who had most of the Divine life was the man who had the best right to fill the largest secular spheres.

Of all spheres that which he had most right to fill was the circle of family life, for the family was the beginning of the kingdom and the kingdom was the reign of the Theocracy. The goal of Jewish religion was morality, and the beginning of its morality was the life of home. The essence of Jewish religion was a *walk*, and the first steps of the walk were around the domestic altar. The sacred fire which illuminated the saints of the Old Testament burned not on the mountain-tops; it enshrined itself in the valleys of their lives. It lighted up the family circle, it warmed up the domestic duties, it irradiated the sphere of household commonplaces. It is not without significance that when we would describe in a single word the greatest leaders of that primitive age we call them by the one name of patriarch or father.

III. But there is one other point of significance in this brief narrative of Enoch's life, and a point in which, more than all others, he stands out as a representative of his nation. We have seen that in him is first revealed that great principle of Jewish faith—the identity of religion with morality. We have now to see revealed in him that other characteristic doctrine of his race—the connection between morality and immortality. That connection is expressed in one pregnant utterance: "he walked with God; and he was not." We have nothing to do here with that in the narrative which is miraculous; we are concerned with that which is non-miraculous, representative, universal. We wish to find what is that element in the life of Enoch which has constituted to posterity the fact of his immortality. When we read this fifth chapter of Genesis we seem to be walking through a cemetery perusing the inscriptions on the antediluvian tombstones. Each life contains a common epitaph—a record of birth, parentage, and length of years, closed by the one universal statement, "and he died."

But here, in the midst of the cemetery, there is a vacant space where a tombstone was meant to be, and instead of the common inscription of death there are found the words, "he was not, for God took him." He was not; he never became a thing of the past, it always can be written of him —he is: such was the deep significance of the primitive epitaph on Enoch. It tells us that he is not numbered amongst the things that have been, that he has not passed away with the shadows of a bygone time, that he lives in a perpetual present, in an everlasting now, in an eternity of immortal youth; and then it completes the picture by declaring that this immortality was to him no accident, no capricious destiny, no arbitrary fate; that he received immunity from death just because there was in him that which could not die—"he walked with God, and he was not."

Now here is the great truth which the world in general

has grasped, and which Judaism in particular has made her own—the connection between morality and immortality. To the consciousness of mankind the freshest and greenest thing in this world is the pure heart. It is independent of all time; it is independent of all space. When we meet it on the page of history we refer it to no age or clime; we accept it as a fact of humanity. The heroism of moral purity is never antiquated; it is always modern. The men who have walked through this world by the power of faith are, even in a spiritual sense, translated that they should not see death. They are not to us men of the past; we shake hands with them across the centuries as by the bond of a present continuity. They never recede with the years; they are as young to-day as they were a thousand years ago. The life which they lived was not the life of their time but the life of humanity. Their walk through the world was a walk with God, and the walk with God never becomes a beaten path; it is perpetually trodden, yet to every soul that treads it it is ever new. The man who treads that path is abreast of every age; it always can be said of him, he *is!*

Here, then, is the grand principle which Enoch bequeathed to the Jewish nation and to posterity—the power of morality to transcend the limits of time. He taught by his life, he illustrated by the survival of his life, that the evergreen element of humanity is conscience, that marvellous power which, call it by what name you will, issues the categorical imperative, "thou shalt; thou shalt not." The one life amongst the antediluvians which does not come to us as an echo of the past, is that life which is a walk with God. Seth, and Enos, and Cainan may have been greater men as the world counts greatness, and their lives may have been more eventful to their day and generation, but for that very reason they are less eventful to humanity. The distinctive merit of Enoch weighed against his contemporaries is the fact that his life laid hold of that which belonged not to his age, nor to any age, but which constituted the basis of human nature itself; by this, he being dead yet speaketh. He bequeathed to his countrymen a revelation of the truth that morality is man's hope of immortality. Judaism appropriated that lesson, and in theory never swerved from it. Of a future state in itself she speaks little, and of the nature of the future existence she does not tell. But the one point which this religion grasps is the message borne down to her by the life of Enoch, that the way to escape death is the walk with God.

"Who shall abide in His tabernacle, who shall dwell in His holy hill? He that hath clean hands and a pure heart, who hath not lifted up his soul unto vanity nor sworn deceitfully; he that doeth thus shall never be moved." The one eternal object in this world to the heart of the Jew was the life of God; the very name of Jehovah means the Eternal. The one hope of human immortality to the heart of the Jew lay in union with this life of God; to walk outside of Him was to die, to walk with Him was to live for evermore. Where was the place of the dead he knew not nor cared to inquire; all he knew was that even from that region the Divine Omnipresence was not excluded: "If I make my bed in Hades, Thou art there." The problem for Judaism was to get near to God, to touch the secret of that Divine holiness in which lay the Fountain of life. To be holy as He was holy, to be pure as He was pure; to meditate on His law day and night; to keep His commandments one by one: that was the sum of her creed, that was the substance of her hope. Her religion was a walk with God, and the walk with God was the road to immortality.

G. M.

II. **Noah.** HEB. xi. 7. *"By faith Noah, being warned of God of things not seen as yet, moved with fear, prepared an ark to the saving of his house; by the which he condemned the world, and became heir of the righteousness which is by faith."*

THE great servants of God, as a rule, share in a common stock of thoughts, feelings, resolves, efforts, sacrifices, which lift them, as a class, above the ordinary level of men, and make them what they are. They live in the world without being of it; they look beyond these narrow frontiers for their ruling interests and their deepest motives. In some shape or other, they give up what they see, for what they do not see; they feel beforehand that life is a thing at once blessed and awful; blessed in its opportunities, awful in its possibilities. They act as men who are in possession of the clue to its real meaning. They know and feel why they are here, and whither they are going; and in communion with the Author and end of their existence, and in doing His will, so far as they know it, by themselves and among their fellow-creatures, they realize the true scope and dignity of their being, and they fertilize the lives of all around them. "Blessed is the man that hath not walked in the counsel of the ungodly, nor stood in the way of sinners, and hath not sat in the seat of the scornful. But his delight is in the law of the Lord, and in His law will he exercise himself day and night. And he shall be like a tree planted by the waterside, that will bring forth his fruit in due season. His leaf also shall not wither, and look, whatsoever he doeth, it shall prosper." But over and above that which is common to them as a body, each among the servants of God has some distinguishing characteristic. As in nature, no two flowers, no two animals, no two human countenances, are exactly alike; so in grace, this reflection of God's exhaustless resources is even more apparent, and each who has a part, still more each who is eminent in the kingdom of grace, has in it a distinct place, and form, and working, which belongs to no other. His character, or circumstances, confer upon him a speciality, which makes him, at least in some respects, unlike any who have preceded him, unlike, we may dare to add, any who will follow him.

The great patriarchal figures who move before us in the earliest pages of the Bible are, as a class, naturally clouded in the dimness of a remote antiquity. Of the seven names which are contemporary with Noah, one only attracts a specific moral and religious influence. We pause at the holy life, at the glorious translation of Enoch. With this exception, there is little to arrest the attention beyond the length of years which was granted to these earliest generations of men. Strange, almost inconceivable, as such longevity may appear, when we contrast it with the existing limits of human life, it is in harmony, nevertheless, with the general scale of gigantic power, which, according to the most reliable evidence relating to the old world, was characteristic of it. Life in that earliest age was comparatively simple, regular, and free from the social mischief and wickedness which came along with a more organised society. The climate, the weather, and the natural conditions under which mankind moved, were probably very different from those which succeeded, and Paradise itself was still recent. So that although in the exercise of his great prerogative, man had forfeited the endowments with which he had been originally blessed, yet some of these, such as immortality, would abate but gradually, and thus it was that Enoch was translated into eternal life with God, without passing through disease and death. Five generations of ancestors, at least, must still have been living—Jared, Mahalaleel, Cainan, Enos, and even Seth; while Enoch's son, Methuselah, and his grandson, Lamech, had attained an age far beyond that of modern men. Of all the antediluvian life, from the time of the creation, only Adam had been taken to his rest, only Noah was not yet born. Sixty-five years elapsed between the translation of Enoch and the birth of Noah, and during that interval the moral atmosphere of human history had very rapidly darkened.

This result appears to be due to two main causes, beyond and above the constantly self-aggravating effects of the Fall. In the fourth and fifth chapters of Genesis, the development of the human race is traced through two entirely different lines—that of Cain and that of Seth. It would seem that notwithstanding the general sense of the phrase elsewhere in Scripture, the Sethites, and not any beings of a higher world, are on this occasion meant by the august title, "Sons of God;" and an inter-marriage between the Sethites, who had preserved the higher and better forms of religion, and the Cainites, who had entirely lost them, issued in the rapid moral degradation of the posterity of Seth.

Distinct from this, but contemporaneous with it, was the appearance of the giants; they were tyrants, it would seem, physical natural monsters—men who made the law of might to be the governing force in that primitive society. The corruption of the old world was therefore traceable to two causes, each in its way fatal to the moral well-being of man. It was traceable on the one hand to social oppression and cruelty; on the other hand to a reckless sensuality. Lamech felt the evils of his time; it all seemed to him to flow, as it did flow, from the sin which had been brought about, and from the curse which had been pronounced in Eden. He felt the burden of his labour upon the ungrateful soil; and when his son was born, we read of the father's melancholy, together with a profound presentiment of some brighter future, in the name of the infant, "and he called his name Noah, saying, This same shall comfort us concerning our work and toil of our hands, because of the ground which the Lord hath cursed." Noah's general and lofty piety is described by the same phrase as Enoch's— "He walked with God." This expression denotes more than that which was used in a Divine manner of Abraham. Abraham was to walk, and did walk before God. Still more carefully should it be distinguished from walking *after* God, the phrase by which Moses enjoins obedience to the commands given in the Divine law. To walk before God is to be ever conscious of His over-shadowing and searching presence; but to walk *with* God, is something higher and more blessed even than this; it is to be, as it were, constantly at His side, and admitted to His confidence; it is to be admitted to a close and intimate communion with Him as a dear personal friend. It is to be in spirit what the apostles were in flesh, when they shared day by day in the streets and lanes of Galilee, the Divine companionship of the Incarnate Son. It is St. John's "fellowship with the Father and His Son Jesus Christ." It is St. Paul's "being quickened and made to sit together in heavenly places with Jesus Christ." Once only besides does the phrase occur in the Old Testament, where the Prophet Malachi applies it, not to the Israelites generally, but specifically and distinctly to the conduct of the priests, considering that they stood in a closer relation to God than the rest of the ancient people, and could enter the Holy of Holies, and have intercourse with the Sacred Presence which was there veiled from the public eye.

Noah's piety, then, was of an exceptionably lofty kind; he is said to have been a religious man, and perfect in his generation, and in the midst of the general corruption he found favour in the eyes of the Lord. Of this temper his thankfulness after his deliverance is a sample; in order to express it he sacrifices some of the little store which he had saved from the general wreck, and a sentence in the

Prophet Ezekiel implies that he had special power as an intercessor with God. Yet his intercession is classed with that of Job and Daniel, and his thankfulness was both in form and the spirit of its manifestation, an anticipation of what is shown in other instances, as that of Moses; and Holy Scripture, with its wonted simplicity and truthfulness, describing his falling in his old age into an error, does not place him in this respect above the level of other servants of God. We have, then, still to ask, what it was wherein Noah's excellence more particularly shows itself. And this question is answered in the passage we are considering, in the Epistle to the Hebrews, which, omitting all else— and there is much which the history of this great patriarch suggests—bids us observe, that "By faith Noah, being warned of God of things not seen as yet, moved with fear, prepared an ark to the saving of his house; by the which he condemned the world, and became heir of the righteousness which is by faith."

Indeed, it is to this period in the life of Noah that all the allusions to him in the New Testament, with the one exception of that of our Lord in St. Luke's Gospel, consistently refer. In the mind not only of St. Peter, but of our Lord himself, the "days of Noah" were specially that most critical period of one hundred and twenty-five years which preceded the deluge. It is possible that the social or political interests of his life may have been greater at an earlier or at later periods, it is certain that the intensity of its moral interest centred in this.

In Noah's building the ark at the command of God, there are three main points to be considered. It implies, first of all, that he had an earnest conviction of the sanctity and greatness of moral truth—a conviction which, more than any other, is the basis of religious character. He was surrounded by a populace which had broken altogether away from the laws of God. Impiety, impurity, and licentiousness, were the order of the day. Every imagination of the thoughts of man's heart was only evil continually; the corruption was universal and profound. To numbers of men, this surrounding atmosphere of evil would be simply destructive to the moral sight. Those of us who know anything of our own hearts and characters must know this how easily we get accustomed to the sight of what is wrong—how soon we feel complacency, or something like complacency, towards it—how it undermines our sense of its own malignity, and makes us, if not exactly its captives, yet its tolerant apologists. " Neither did they abhor anything that is evil," is a severe and exceptional condemnation by the psalmist. It is not that evil triumphant, as in Babylon, crushes out the remaining righteousness in the land ; there it is, and we take it for granted in ourselves and others ; it is part of the actual sum of human life and activity—nay, it is a very large part; in our hearts, too, it finds something like countenance and sympathy. What is the good, we say to ourselves, of finding fault with the weather, or with an epidemic ? We may wish that things were otherwise ; we cannot but resign ourselves to take them as they are, and this acquiescence in evil, as inevitable, involves a something beyond ; it leads us to shut our eyes to what the deepest and truest of all human presentiment, apart from the revelation of God, points to as its certain consequences. It blinds us to the fact that it must be followed, at some time or other, by punishment. Could it be otherwise, God would not be God, a necessarily and intrinsically Moral Being. Could it be otherwise, the first and most earnest forms of belief in conscience would be untrustworthy. And yet we may by familiarity with this indolent sympathy with evil, learn first to forget that evil leads to punishment, and next, and not improbably, even to deny it. It is inconceivable, we say, that a world-embracing mass of evil should be punished : *its very universality is its safe-guard and its protection ; it might be punished if it were an exception, it must escape simply because it is the rule.* This is what we secretly say to ourselves. We shut our eyes to a first truth of morals, and we flatter ourselves that we naturally escape the effects.

It was against this tacit and fatal influence of a corrupt moral atmosphere that Noah's life was a protest of resistance. " He was," the Bible says, " perfect in " or among " his generations," and these generations were corrupt. He was a preacher of righteousness when righteousness was at a discount and peculiarly unpopular. He walked with God when mankind at large had forgotten Him. He did not think the better of evil, of its real nature or of its future prospects, merely because it was practised on a large scale and with considerable apparent impunity. To Noah, the eternal truths were more certain than the surface appearances of life; he was certain that evil was evil, and that it could not but be followed by chastisement, because God was God.

Such a moral conviction it must have been which fitted Noah to receive the Divine prediction of a coming deluge. God does not take the morally deaf and blind into His confidence. The words of Jesus Christ sound through all the ages of human history as the voice of a Divine and presiding Providence: " He that hath ears to hear, let him hear," he whose moral senses are really alive, let him listen to the proclamations of God's truth. To those only it will be made known. " He that willeth to do the will of God, shall know of the doctrine whether it be of God." . . . Noah was warned of God of things not seen as yet; he was the subject in some way—it were folly to attempt to determine in what way—of supernatural communications; it may have been some sensible voice from without, it may have been an unmistakably Divine operation, when God said unto Noah, " The end of all flesh is come before Me; for the earth is filled with violence through them; behold I will destroy them with the earth. Make thee an ark of gopher wood. . . . Behold I, even I, do bring a flood of waters upon the earth, to destroy all flesh, wherein is the breath of life from under heaven; and every thing that is in the earth shall die. But with thee will I establish My covenant." Why should Noah believe this prediction sufficiently to act upon that command? Because God had spoken; that was his reason, that was his conviction,—it was enough for him, he needed no more. But then his conviction of the unchangeableness of that truth, and of the moral laws of God, would have rendered such an announcement, under the circumstances, to him at least morally intelligible. It was true that what was foretold, was to come unprovided by any past experience. In the burning plains of central Asia, the idea of an universal deluge may well have seemed the wildest of imaginations. A thousand years, at least, had already passed, and there had been nothing like it. Nature seemed to be unvarying in her movements, the sun rose and set, the seasons succeeded each other, the generations of living beings appeared and passed away; there was a limit, so to call it, a regular period traversing this in a discernible and provided order, but as yet there was nothing that met the sense to warrant the expectation of a vast or overwhelming shock or catastrophe. Why should it be otherwise hereafter? why should this accumulated experience go for nothing? why should this sense of security, so amply warranted, be succeeded by apprehensions and distrust, for which, as yet, the annals of the world afforded no parallel? The answer was, that God had spoken. Who that believes in a real living God can plead observation in the divinity of nature against the avowed will of the Author of nature? After all, this invariability, so to call it, appeals rather to the imagination than to the reason; the imagination becomes so accustomed to it, so moulded by it, that it undergoes a certain distress at the very thought of its violent interruption; but reason, true reason, is ever mindful of the limits which must bound even our widest observations. Because we observe a continuous sequence of similar effects, it does not follow as an absolute certainty; it at most amounts to a very strong presumption, strong in proportion to the range of our observation, that these effects will continue. We are not really in possession of knowledge respecting any great necessity rooted in the nature of things, which makes it certain they must continue; and if we believe that the Almighty Author of nature is really alive, and that He is a Moral Being—and not merely an intelligence, still less merely a force—and that as a moral being He may have grave reasons for disturbing altogether this physical and social sympathy which encircles us, we shall not then distrust Him if He tells us that He means to do so. And so it was that Noah was moved, as the apostle says, with fear, with a fear most reasonable, as it was judicious; he did not treat the warning he had received as if it had been only some evil omen, appealing at best to his superstition, but he prepared an ark to the saving of his house.

This event, in which Noah believed before it came, was appealed to in a later age by St. Peter, as furnishing a reason for believing in a still, to us, future and greater catastrophe. St. Peter is writing at the very close of his life, and already a sufficient time had elapsed since the

Ascension of our Lord to allow for the foundation of systematic doubts respecting His second coming to judgment; doubts which were based upon the apparent endurability of the world and of the laws of life. Where is the promise of God's coming? men asked in that generation, too; all things continue as they were from the beginning of the creation. The apostle reminds those who argue thus, that Time has no meaning for the eternal God, and that to apply our notions of the difference between greater and lesser portions of it to His Majestic providences, is to forget that there is simply no such thing as succession in His unbegun, unending life. "Beloved, be not ignorant of this one thing—that one day is with the Lord as a thousand years, and a thousand years as one day."

But if Christ's delay meant nothing but His long-suffering, the unchanging order of the world could not be urged as a reason for this unbelief in the catastrophe of a future judgment, because the past history of the world contained at least one eminent example of such a catastrophe. "By the word of the Lord the heavens were opened, the earth standing out of the water and in the water, whereby the world that then was, being overflowed with water, perished." In other words, water had been the instrument by which the surface of the earth was moulded; water had been one of the constituent elements of its well-being and productiveness, yet at the creative word of God, from being a servant and blessing, it became an over-mastering force and scourge; and what had been, might yet, would yet, be. Another element had yet a work to do in God's Providence, and neither the lapse of years nor yet the observed regularity of nature were any real reasons for presuming that a final catastrophe would not come at last. "The heavens and the earth, which are now," says the apostle, " by the same word are kept in store, reserved unto fire against the judgment and perdition of ungodly men."

Nay, it is very possible that with a higher knowledge than that which we at present possess, we might be able to extend the argument by additional illustrations.

Some years ago it was usual to refer wholly to the time of the Deluge the more ancient animal remains which had been discovered in caverns or beneath the surface of the earth, but more recent science urges that these remains

C

simply imply, at least generally, a higher antiquity, and are found under circumstances for which no universal flood would sufficiently account. It may be so. But is there anything in the text of the Bible which obliges us to narrow down to 6,000 years, *or in any way whatever distinguish the measure of the earth's antiquity, short of admitting its absolute eternity?* On the contrary, between the original creative Act and the description of that gradual process, by which through successive periods (*days* they are called in the eastern idiom) this world was brought into its present state, there is room for a measureless interval, I should rather say for a *series* of intervals; and if this be so, who shall say that many of the animal, it may be some of the apparently human, remains, which are now pointed at as hostile to, or at least as damaging to, the faith of Christians, are after all only relics and records of bygone catastrophes of which, previous to the creation and present order of things, this globe has been the scene, and by which the ages of probation accredited to moral beings who have preceded us here, were by the judgment of the great Moral Ruler violently closed.

It is true that we are here altogether in a region of hypothesis, but I submit that there is at least nothing in Revelation which necessarily contradicts it; while if it be true, it yields support to the argument of the apostle, it justifies the generous faith of the patriarch. Not that Noah's faith had anything to do with such speculations; religious men may be glad to harmonize their convictions with the advancing and often inconsistent conclusions of human knowledge, but the foundation of their faith is one and invariable; they believe that He who made the world can control it, and when His purpose is clear to them, they do not allow themselves to lose sight of it simply because their imaginations are powerfully impressed by the spectacle of a settled and common order of continuance or execution. They are, therefore, in their deepest sympathies *independent* of scientific arguments, without being at all *indifferent* to them; they walk by faith and not by sight; they are certain that whatever difficulties may be urged against God's declared will at the moment, God will, in the long run, justify Himself to men, and will vindicate the wisdom of those who in days of trial or darkness have taken Him at His word.

A third point to be observed in Noah is his perseverance under difficulties. His faith was a practical principle, and it upheld him in the face of serious discouragements. He might have easily persuaded himself that there could be no real necessity for his personally exerting himself; that the threatened disorder would scarcely touch one who was already 480 years of age; that it would be enough to warn his children of what was coming, when he himself would probably have been laid in his rest. Why should he arouse himself in such advanced life to so great an effort as that required of him, instead of leaving it to be undertaken by younger hands? The answer in his conscience was, that it had been said to him, "Build thee an ark of gopher wood."

Again, he might naturally have dwelt upon the great mechanical and constructive difficulties of such an undertaking. It is not to be supposed that these were left to be found out for the first time by modern criticism. How could such an ark be built so as to secure at once sufficient space and safety? How could it be provisioned, lighted, and worked? How could the several representatives of the animal races be so gathered as to enter it? How would it be possible to preserve them under conditions of weather and temperature so unlike their own? And when the scourge had passed, how would it be possible to enter again upon the earth as solitary colonists, amid traces of so gigantic a desolation? Well may Noah's heart have sunk within him when God said to him, "Build thee an ark of gopher wood," yet he only lived to obey. Moreover, Noah had to begin his work and to continue it, not merely without active support and sympathy, but under the eye of public opinion which was not so much hostile as contemptuously cynical.

What was this extraordinary outlay of labour and skill for? what was its purpose and meaning? How was it other than the crotchet of a mere visionary fanatic? Did he really think that his fancies would become true, and that the settled order of nature, as well as the civilization and progress of human life, were going to be buried beneath the flood which he dreamt of? Was every one else wrong, while he was right? Was his private opinion to be weighed against the collective experience and judgment of mankind? How they must have mocked at the entire undertaking, how they must in their aversion to the awful idea have revenged themselves upon its form and details! What airy criticism must have been lavished upon it, and on each detail supplied to it, and on its complete structure what bitter comments must have been passed. Its uselessness, its ugliness, its utter opposition to the whole current of contemporary thought and feeling. How, too, to some of the more liberal critics would it have occurred to endeavour, as if in scornful and condescending pity, to enter, although only remotely and for a moment, into the strange hallucination that could have produced it, as if surveying from afar some mental curiosity, which only did not move anger because it ministered so largely to amusement. And then with what satisfaction, complacence, and confidence would they have betaken themselves anew to the life against which this ark was a protest and a warning, as to that which was warranted by the common sense and judgment of the time, and by a force of custom and of sentiment, which, as the world grew older, was daily gaining new strength.

Our Lord Himself has said that what took place then is an anticipation of what will be on the eve of the last judgment. "As it was in the days of Noe, so shall it be also in the days of the Son of man. They did eat, they drank, they married wives, they were given in marriage, until the day that Noe entered into the ark, and the flood came, and destroyed them all." Yet there was delay, a delay of 120 years, but the threatened judgment came at last, "the flood came, and destroyed them all." Whether it was a strictly universal or something less than a literally universal deluge; whether it covered Ararat without covering, for instance, the Himalayas; whether it can be possibly explained by any combination of known causes or only by simply natural ones—these are most important questions, but they do not touch the broad limits of the general fact, still less the moral interests of the narrative; they would only lead us away from it. What is important is, that the judgment *came*—it came to vindicate the morality and sovereignty of God; it came to justify Noah, and to contend with the generations which rejected him ; it came to demonstrate the folly and wickedness of the ancient civilization, the uncertainty of that nature which seemed at the time so well founded and so strong. There must have been upon that day a murmur—an outburst of surprise and alarm—a struggle—an agony—a despair—when this was realized. Poets and painters have endeavoured to portray it, but as the mind dwells on any such vast picture of human agony, the heart grows sick and the head giddy. In that very multitude, no doubt, there were degrees of responsibility and guilt, known to and weighed by the Eternal Justice. The apostle hints as, much in the significant expression which apparently implies, that on the descent of our Lord's human soul into the place of the departed, there was a preaching, at least, to some of the repentant spirits of the antediluvian world. But the general result is a contrast between an overwhelming judgment and a signal mercy—a judgment provoked by forgetfulness of the given law and knowledge of God—a mercy awarded to faith in His word—a faith which was not sacrificed to false and narrow views of duty, or to base misgivings, or to the current and corrupting opinions of the time. What Noah's work really and mainly foreshadowed would have been obscured in *his* day, but we Christians look back upon it from a vantage ground, which enables us to do it justice. We see that in the labour and temporal salvation of Noah, there is already the shadow of a greater toil and a more complete deliverance. Looking to our Lord Jesus Christ, may we not, in its wretchedness and yet in its hope, use in a true sense the word of Lamech, "This same shall comfort us concerning our work and toil of our hands." Like Noah, Jesus Christ was a preacher of righteousness—the preacher of a higher and brighter righteousness than man knew before. And as Noah built an ark for the saving of his house, so did our Lord build His Church to be the home of His followers, with the promise that against it the gates of hell should not prevail.

His teaching, His example, His works of mercy, His bitter death, His resurrection from the tomb, and His glorious ascension into heaven, all are steps in this mighty work. The Divine Architect shed His very life-blood in the labour of construction, and at length Pentecost came, and the eternal Spirit welded all into a consistent and enduring whole; and as the races and sexes and degrees of men passed within it, one after another, at the heavenly call, lo! there was to the eyes of faith neither Jew nor Greek, neither male nor female, circumcision nor uncircumcision, barbarian nor Scythian, bond nor free, but Christ was all and in all. And although since those earlier days, the passions and the errors of men have raised walls and partitions over and above the divinely-ordained stories within the Divine fabric, yet this most assuredly will not always last; they are but human, while the ark itself is Divine. Even now, too, it floats upon the waters, upon the vast ocean of human opinion and society, and we, without any merit of our own, but by His free grace and mercy, have been permitted to enter it. Over us, too, once was uttered the prayer that the everlasting God, who by His great mercy did save Noah and his family in the ark from perishing by water, would look upon and sanctify us, that, being delivered from His wrath, we might be received into the ark of Christ's Church, and, being steadfast in faith, joyful through hope, and rooted in charity, might so pass through the waves of this troublesome world, that in the end we might come to the land of everlasting life.

It would be useful to insist, before we end, upon one or two practical conclusions which are suggested by the life and work of Noah. It suggests, first of all, a particular form of duty which at certain times of the world's history may press very heavily on the consciences of public men, whether in Church or State, and at certain terms in life upon all of us, however retired and private our place and work may be—I mean, the duty which may arise on our seeing, or believing that we see, more or less clearly into the future, which has to be provided for or provided against. Indeed, to endeavour to look forward, or to provide in this way, is a part of the work of those who are charged with the maintenance and support of large public interests; it is their business to observe the direction in which things are moving, the forces which are coming to the front, the combination or separation of force which may fairly be anticipated, the general result that will apparently emerge from and succeed the state of things with which they are actually conversant. Here, as elsewhere, to seek knowledge is more or less to learn; and God teaches us through our natural powers of observation and reflection, as well as in other and higher ways. The prayer to know enough to be able to do His will, in our day and generation is answered. And it may be we have to deliberately anticipate very much, to which we would be willingly blind. Such a habit of looking forward, if its motive is something higher than mere speculative curiosity, will not interfere with the duties of the present hour, nor will it militate against that general temper of trustful resignation, which those who see furthest and deepest feel, and which is ever ready to leave its hopes and fears in the hands of God.

In private and worldly concerns, such foresightedness is not often undervalued. No man, for instance, continues to invest his money in an undertaking, recommended though it be by an imposing prospectus and an influential Board of Directors, if beneath its fair promises and apparent prosperity, he can clearly see at work the causes of a coming bankruptcy. But where the interests of others are only or chiefly concerned, it may be probable that the man himself will have passed away before his anticipations are realized; it is possible for him to find himself in Noah's moral position, to this extent, that he foresees a catastrophe which is hidden from the eyes of his contemporaries, and which imposes on him the plain duty of preparing to meet it. And then comes the trial; will he bestir himself to obey the behest of his conviction, or will he indolently fold his hands and let things take their course? Will he say to himself, "After all, this is no particular concern of mine, it is the concern of everybody; why should I in particular be compelled to put myself out of my way in a matter which interests hundreds of other people quite as much as it interests me? Why should I be taxed,—heavily taxed,—on the score of my far-sightedness, while others can go on easily and quietly, with a perfectly good conscience, only because they are too unobservant to see, or to try to see, beyond the next turn in the road of life? I will let things take their course; there is no necessity on my part for an interference which will be mocked at till it is justified, and then, even when it is justified, will soon enough be forgotten." Will he reason thus, or will he reflect that knowledge, insight, far-sightedness, if they really exist, and are known to exist, constitute responsibility; that he who as a man sees further and knows more than others, cannot merely be as others before his fellow-men or before God; that together with knowledge, at least of this kind, there comes, to a certain extent, the forfeiture of that particular species of liberty which is the moral bound of ignorance? Will he reason thus, and act upon his reason?

My brethren, this is a most critical question—possibly for the generation, for the country, for the Church to which he belongs, but certainly, under any circumstances, for himself. Can any one who has a heart at all, think without true sorrow of that king of France whose reign covers the greater part of the last century, who spans the interval which connects the great monarch with the Bourbon who died upon the scaffold. Few things in history are more piteous than the contrast of the youth of much interest and promise, and the advanced life of abject dissipation. Yet Louis XV. was not wanting in penetration. Even the gay revelries of Versailles did not wholly blind him to sights and sounds which might have convinced a less observant ruler, that the foundations of the great depth of national life were surely breaking up, and that a new order of things was imminent. Allowing for the difficulties of a traditional position such as his, may we not believe that an earnest and well-considered effort to improve the condition, and to assert the rights of the lower classes of the French people in the middle of the century, might have saved France from the torrents of blood in which the inevitable revolution was baptized. Yet Louis the Fifteenth passed away his time morally and physically in pleasures, which ministered only to the satisfaction of the hour, while the mutterings of the approaching storm were falling thick upon his dying ear, and his last and deepest conviction found expression in words, which were too surely to be fulfilled: "After us, the deluge."

H. P. L.

III. **Abraham.** GEN. xxv. 7, 8. "*And these are the days of the years of Abraham's life which he lived, an hundred threescore and fifteen years. Then Abraham gave up the ghost, and died in a good old age, an old man, and full of years; and was gathered to his people.*"

THE epitaph which the writer of Genesis inscribes upon the tomb of Abraham is this: An old man and full—we translate "full of years," but the addition weakens the sense of the inscription; the idea is not that of duration, but of ripeness. The truth is, that when we read this epitaph, we are made powerfully conscious of the fact that there has come into the world a new standard for the measurement of human life. Formerly the only standard had been that of extent or duration. Yet, measured by such a test, the life of Abraham was not long, and did not nearly reach to the days of his forefathers; one hundred and seventy-five years comprised the whole term of his earthly history. Nevertheless, the writer of Genesis has no diffidence in inscribing upon his grave the words, an old man, and he hastens to add the reason why he has no diffidence; he declares that Abraham's life was long because it was full. He was an old man, not because his life was extensive, but because it was intensive; not because it had many years, but because, within its comparatively few years, there were compressed large experiences. And this itself shows that in the view of that age there was already rising a new standard of the value of human existence. Enoch, as we have seen, had a short biography, but in his case the brevity of the earthly life is compensated by an exemption from the common law of mortality. In Abraham's case there is no such exemption, but we feel instinctively that it is not needed. We feel that no compensation is required for the brevity of his earthly years, for although few, they are already full. The shortness of the outward duration is compensated now and here by the intensity of every moment's experience. We see that the man is receiving a double portion of life in every instant of time. There are moments which seem to concentrate the value of years; one year of grief has silvered the hair and bowed the manly form. There are lives which come to maturity long before they have reached that conventional term of years which men call the coming of age. It is with such lives as with some American prairies, which at nightfall are colourless wastes and at morning are filled with beautiful wild flowers; they have sprung up in the hours of a single night. Even so there are seasons, and generally night seasons, in which the process of human growth is marvellously accelerated and the flowers burst prematurely into bloom. Such lives cannot be measured by duration, yet they do not really come short in quantity; there is less diffusion but there is more intense concentration; their years are not long, but they are full.

Wherein then consists the fulness of this life of Abraham? Manifestly in the fact that his is a complete life, embracing all the stages of human development. There are three great stages in the development of man. The first scene of existence is one of boundlessness, one in which the soul has sight of a great and glorious promise. The second stage is one of limitation: a cloud falls over the dream, and the glory of the promise seems to fade. Lastly, there comes a time when the second stage is reconciled with the first: the clouds which have gathered over the path of life are seen not to be really barriers to the fulfilment of the promise, but to be working out, under the semblance of adversity, the purpose and plan of our opening years.

Such is the natural and normal rhythm of human life—that is to say, of human life in its complete manifestation. It is not always that an individual existence is thus perfectly rounded; when it is, it is an exhibition of the fulness of being. Now such an exhibition of fulness is given in the earthly history of Abraham. Here the three stages are marked prominently and emphatically. We see, first, the youth in the boundlessness of hope looking out upon the prospect of his destiny, and beholding a promise of a kingdom. We see next a cloud falling over the promise of youth, and the prospect of the destiny threatened by the imminence of a great sacrifice. We see, lastly, the reconciliation between the cloud and the sunshine; the sacrifice is recognised as itself the fulfilment of the promise, and the element which seemed to be adverse is found to have been working out the prophetic ideal. Let us glance at each of these.

I. The first stage of Abraham's life is one of promise. He is introduced to us in an attitude of aspiration. There rises within him that desire which in one form or other animates the breasts of most young men—the longing for greatness. And with Abraham, as with most young men, the longing is accompanied by conviction. He feels that he has a destiny before him, that he has a name to make in the world. He interprets his aspiration itself as the voice, the prophecy of God within him, and his desire becomes the measure of his certainty. He is to become the founder of a great nation whose destinies are to influence the fate of the world; he is to be the progenitor of a vast multitude of descendants whose branches are to stretch through the whole earth, and by whose culture the whole earth is to be blessed : such is the vision of Abraham. And not the least strange feature of the vision is the occasion of its waking; it comes to him in the contemplation of nature. God brings him out to look at the stars and try if he can count their number, and it is in beholding the visible glory that he recognises his own glory. To a man in modern times the command to count the stars would have quite the opposite effect to that which it produced upon Abraham. There is nothing which so depresses the modern consciousness as the contemplation of the vastness of nature, nothing which so appals the soul with a sense of its own littleness. What the Psalmist said in wonder at a *fact*, we say in despair of a possibility : "When I consider the heavens, the work of Thy fingers, what is man that Thou shouldst be mindful of him ?" But then we must remember that the difference between us and the Hebrew mind lies deeper. Our different impressions of nature proceed from our different views of God. We come to nature to find God ; the Hebrew came to nature to commune with a God whom he had already found. The God of the Hebrew was in immediate contact with the soul. The human soul was the centre of His universe, and for its pleasure and profit were all things created. The mind of the ancient seer was not dismayed in looking abroad upon the world of visible beauty. He came to that vision with the knowledge that God was already in his own heart, and, therefore, he was exalted rather than depressed by it. He was inclined to say, in anticipation of the spirit of the Divine Teacher, "If God so clothe the grass of the field, shall He not much more clothe you ?"

So was it with Abraham. He came out to contemplate the expanse of the nightly heavens, but he had already heard within him a voice which had exalted him above the heavens. What he sought in the starry firmament was not so much a vision of the magnificence of creation as a reflex or mirror of that sense of expansiveness which he felt within himself. God had spoken to his soul, and had promised him great things; was it not natural that in his effort to picture the promise he should have cast his eye abroad over the bespangled dome of night? Nor to one already so impressed with the greatness of his own soul would the vastness and order of the spectacle be fraught with any depression; they would rather have the contrary effect. He would be disposed to argue from the less to the greater, from the clothing of the heavenly fields to the clothing of the yet more heavenly soul. In point of fact, Abraham did so argue. He retired from the contemplation of nature more confident than ever of his own splendid destiny. He felt that if there were such order in the laws of matter, there must be at least an equal order in the laws of human history. He felt that a single human soul had in it more of God than the united sum of all this visible glory. He felt anew that his own aspirations were the voice of God within him, the promises of God to his heart, and he was nerved by an impulse alike from without and from within to begin that great historic labour which was to produce a race of heroes like to the stars of the heaven in multitude.

II. The next time the curtain rises upon the life of Abraham the scene is entirely changed. A cloud has fallen over the promise of his youth. The Divine will has issued a command to his will. He is told to offer up as a sacrifice his only son Isaac. The command is tantamount to an abjuring of all his youthful expectations. These expectations had centred in one hope—the promise that he would be the progenitor of a race whose power and influence should fill the world. To render that hope vain, one stroke alone would suffice. The whole chain depended upon a single link—the life of Isaac; let that link be broken, and the entire fabric must fall to pieces. Abraham is commanded to break the link of the chain. He is not simply told that it must be broken, he is asked to make his own will the instrument in breaking it. Now, it is in the obedience to this command that Abraham comes before us as a distinctively religious man. The piety of his youth, beautiful as it undoubtedly was, had yet consisted mainly in a trust of the promises of God; he is now asked to trust God Himself, to trust Him not simply without any promises, but with the seeming reversal of all His promises. The star of hope which had been guiding him from the east to the place where Jehovah dwelt fades away as he draws near to the Invisible Presence. He is called to meet God alone, without the star, to come into the holy place as the Magi of an after day came into the manger and found cold and darkness where they expected to have seen a royal palace. Such is in spirit the trial of Abraham. He had accepted God for the sake of His gifts; he is asked to give up the gifts, and to accept God for Himself alone.

III. One other scene remains, and it is a very remarkable one, one which reconciles the days of Abraham's youth with the seeming contrast of his maturer years. Abraham yields himself up to the sacrifice, and immediately the hope of youth comes back to him. No sooner is the sacrificial act completed than Isaac, the child of promise, is restored, and along with him is restored the fulness of early expectation. It may seem strange that we have put it thus; in the popular view the sacrificial act was never completed. But the popular view is here an illusion. What was commanded was not really the sacrifice of Isaac, but the sacrifice of Abraham. It has been customary amongst theologians to regard Isaac as the type of Christ, but in truth, if there be any typology in the matter, it must be sought in the father and not in the son. Abraham himself is here the true foreshadowing of the Son of man, and he is so just because his sacrifice is essentially an inward one, a surrender of the will. His was, in the highest sense of the word, a completed offering; when He had willed to give up his son, the whole process was finished, nor would the consummation of the outward act have added anything to its completeness. But the point for us to observe here is that when the will had once been surrendered, the outward act was not required. When the man had yielded himself to the kingdom of God and His righteousness, he got back even the earthly things which he had consented to part with. And Abraham was in this the type of more than he knew. The scene of Mount Moriah was not simply an episode which interrupted for a time the promise of his youth, though doubtless to Abraham himself it appeared to be so. To us, who can look back from the height of a modern standpoint, the scene of Mount Moriah is not an episode, but a sequel; not an interruption of the promise, but a revelation of the mode in which the promise was to be fulfilled. The vision of Abraham's youth had revealed to him only the fact that he was to be the source of universal blessing; it had not told him the manner in which it was to be conveyed. The scene of Mount Moriah took up the vision of his youth, and supplied what it had left untold. Whether Abraham knew it or not, it was to him the completion of that promise which had been made to his early years, and it is in that light alone that posterity can regard it. It may be that in the mind of the patriarch there had often risen the desire to know the manner in which his dream would be fulfilled; it may be that from his heart there had often ascended the prayer that he might be permitted to see the form of this great day of blessing. If ever that desire was gratified, if ever that prayer was answered, it must have been in that trial of his later years, when the command was laid upon his soul to sacrifice the object of his deepest love.

That in the seed of Abraham all the families of the earth have been blessed is a matter of history, and it is not less a matter of history that the mode of blessing has been the sacrifice of a divinely human will. If Abraham saw that day and was glad, it must have been through an experience of sacrifice felt in his own heart; and where could he more appropriately find it than in the silence of that stern hour of mental conflict when he was called to make his choice between the hope of his human will and his trust in the will of God. G. M.

IV. Abraham's Death. Gen. xxv. 8. "*Then Abraham gave up the ghost, and died in a good old age, an old man, and full of years; and was gathered to his people.*"

WHAT is the meaning of those phrases, and how may they be true about you and me?

First, I want you to look with me at that lovely expression for the tranquil and completed close of a satisfied life. "He died," says the words, "in a good old age, an old man, and full of years." This supplement seems a perfectly correct one—"full of years." Now that last phrase is the one I want to fix upon. It does not seem to me to be a mere synonym for longevity; that would be an intolerable tautology if it were said three times over: "an old man," "in a good old age," "full of years."

There must be some other and some deeper meaning in the phrase, as I take it, than that. And if you notice, still further, that the expression is by no means a usual one, that it is only applied to one or two of the Old Testament characters, and those selected ones, I think you will see, still further, that there must be some other signification in it than merely to point to length of days.

It is employed, for instance, in reference to the patriarch Abraham, to the patriarch Isaac, when there are almost the same words, verbatim, repeated. Then we find that the stormy and adventurous career of the great king David, with its wonderful viscissitudes and alternations, both of moral character and fortune, is represented as being closed at last with the tranquil and crowning glory: "He died full of years, riches, and honour."

And then we read about the great high priest Jehoiada, whose life also was full of large vicissitudes, strange parallels, strenuous strife, vigorous effort of reformation—we read of him, that with all the storms behind him, he died at last "full of days."

And the only other instance is in reference to the character of Job, the very type of the glad man who has passed through a great many of the ups and downs of fortune; and to him there is given the great compensation at the end, and the lovely picture with which that book closes of returning prosperity, the morning sunshine breaking in upon the seclusion and the storm of the night; the lovely picture of returning prosperity and repeated domestic joys is crowned at last with this, which is intended to be the very summit and climax of the peace that is breathed evidently over the whole concluding narrative was: "Job died, full of years."

The words then, as I take it, mean something a great

deal more than the mere dull fact that the man had completed the ordinary tale and term of human existence. I think we shall get to understand them better if we make a very slight and entirely warranted change, and instead of reading "full of years," read "satisfied with life;" having exhausted its possibilities, having drunk a full draught, having had as much as he wanted, having nothing more left to wish for, having the stormy desires all quietly passed behind him, satisfied, and so willing to go.

Now, there are just three things that I want to say about this first thought. I want you to notice, for the guidance of all of us, that it is possible for each to make his life of such a sort as that wherever it stops, whether it runs on to the apparent maturity of old age, or whether it has in it a very limited period, the man shall go away from life feeling that it has satisfied his desires, met his anticipations, and been all very good. Possibly, that is not the way in which a great many of us look at life; that is not the way in which a great many of us seem to think that it is a part of Christian and religious character to look at life; but it is the way in which the highest type of devotion and the truest goodness will always look at it. There are people, old and young, who, whenever they look back, whether it be over a long tract of years or over a shorter one, have nothing to say about it, except, "Vanity of vanities, all is vanity!"

There are some of my audience listening to me, I have no doubt, who stand, as a man may do, with his back to the sunshine, and all in front is flooded with light; and when he turns about, all behind is dark and dreary. Plenty of us, whose memories contradict our hopes at every point, and at every moment, and who can only expect blessedness and felicity in the future by giving the lie to, and forgetting the whole history of, our life. Plenty of us to whom the future lies like the Garden of Eden, and behind us there is a blasted country like what Abraham saw when he looked down from the mountain-top on the plain of Sodom, and saw slime pits, and smoke, and sulphur, and stench.

Because your past has been a godless past; because your past has been a past in which passion, inclination, whim, anything but conscience and Christ, have given their commandment of what you ought to be, and of what you ought to do. And so you live in a fool's paradise of expectation about the future; and all the while the bitter words of the *blasé* voluptuary, who is represented as writing the Book of Ecclesiastes, are the only words that express what is your mode of life, " vanity of vanities, windy strife, and vexation of spirit."

Put by the side of that this calm picture of the old man going down into his grave and looking back. Ah! what at? *What at?* Field for his memory he had since those long, long ago days, when he came away from his father's house an exile. How all the hot anxieties of youth, the desires and occupations, have quieted themselves down. How far away now seem the warlike days of his life when he fought the barbarian kings. How far away the pangs of heart when he journeyed to Mount Moriah with his boy, the cord, the wood, the knife! His love has all been buried in Sarah's grave, a lonely man for many years. And yet he looks back, and as God looked over His creative work, he looks back and says: "It was all for the best, and the great process of my life has been ordered from the beginning to the end by the hand that shapes beauty everywhere, and has made all things blessed and sweet. I have drunk full draughts, I have had enough. I bless the Giver of the feast, and push my chair back, and get up and go away." He died an old man, satisfied,—satisfied,—with his life.

Ay! and what a contrast that makes to another set of people. There is nothing more miserable than to see men, as their years go on, gripping harder and tighter at this poor, fleeting, mendicant world that is getting away from them; nothing sadder than to see how, as the opportunities and the capacities and the time for the possession of it dwindle and dwindle and dwindle, the almost ferocity of the desire with which some of us seek to make it our own increases. Why, you can see on the face of many an old man and woman a hungry, eager, dissatisfied look that has not come from the mere corrugating of the skin, nor the wrinkles of anxiety, nor the physical changes. A selfish passion of acquisitiveness looking out of the dim old eyes; tragical and awful to see a man, as the world goes from him, grasp at its skirts as a beggar does at the retreating person that refuses to bestow an alms upon him. And there are plenty of us who feel that that is our desire; that the less we have before us of life here on earth, the more eagerly we grasp at the little that still remains, trying to get some drops out of the broken cisterns that we know can hold no water. How different this blessed acquiescence in the flitting away of the fleeting, and this contented satisfaction with the portion that has been given. But all that does not mean any diminution of interest in even the smallest trifles of the world that lies round about us; because there is another kind of misuse of life which is very common, which looks like satisfaction, but is not satisfaction. There is a satiety, a disgust, a weariness, a saying : " Man delights me not, nor woman either! I am tired of it all, and there is nothing new under the sun." This man had a wholesome enjoyment of life till the last moment of it, and a wholesome detachment from it even in the enjoyment of it. And I come to you, and I say to you it is possible for you all to wring the last drop of sweetness and blessedness out of all the circumstances of life, to make even its disappointments into satisfactions, and to make of the whole of it the very thing that you want, that you feel you need ; to look back upon it all, and feel that it has been blessed and good. And yet not to cleave to it, but to be willing to let it go. And I beseech you to ask yourselves, whether the course of your life is such as that. If at this moment God's great knife was to come down and chop it in two, you would be able to say: " Well, I have had enough, and now contentedly I go!"

Well now, there is another thing of the same sort, and yet a little different, which I want to say a word about. I want you to look at the possibilities of your making your life what this man made his—a complete, rounded, perfect whole, because he had accomplished the great end for which life was given. Scaffoldings are for buildings, and the days and years and moments of our earthly lives are the scaffoldings. What are you building inside, brother? What kind of a building is it that is going to be there when the scaffolding is knocked away, and the walls stand there and remain ? The river rolls down, bringing tons of mud and alluvial deposit; the moments, the thoughts, the words, the deeds,—are there any grains of gold brought down with it? If your life and mine has done one thing, or rather two things which are one thing, for us, then, long or short, it is a complete life. If it has not, long or short, it is a wretched fragment and a miserable abortion. Man's chief end is to glorify God and to enjoy Him for ever. Has your life helped you to do that? If it has, though you be but a child, you are full of years. If it has not, though your hair be whitened with the snows of the nineties, you are yet incomplete and immature. The great end of life is to make us like Christ and pleasing to Christ. If life has done that for us, we have got the best out of it, and the life is complete; never mind about the number of the days. Quality, not quantity, is the thing that determines the perfectness of life; and like as in northern lands, where there is only a week or two from the melting of the snow to the cutting of the hay, there may be in a very brief space of time, and a very short portion of a little life, there may be a work which makes life complete. Has it been done in your life?

There is a suggestion, further, in this verse of the possibility for us all, not only of looking back and feeling that all has been for good,—not only of making our lives complete, be they longer or shorter, because they have contributed to the formation of a Christlike character and led us to know God,—but also the possibility of our being willing to go or willing to abide, because we are satisfied with life.

Ah! most of us grasp at the continuance of our earthly existence as a man whirled down the stream would do at any straw that has toppled from the bank. Physically, of course, there will always be the desire you will never get away from, that men will always want to live the bodily life as long as they have bodies to live it with. That is a mere physical fact; but we may master that and come to this position, which good old Richard Baxter has put in words whose very simplicity makes them eloquent and memorable:

> "Lord! it belongs not to my care,
> Whether I die or live."

* * * *

> "If life be long, I will be glad,
>   That I may long obey;
> If short, yet why should I be sad
>   To soar to endless day?"

So this man here in our text was full of years, not wanting to go, not merely tired of life, willing to abide, willing to depart, satisfied.

Or, as I said, like a man sitting at a table, who has had his meal, and is quite content to sit on there, restful and cheerful, but is not unwilling to put back his chair to get up and go away, thanking the Giver for what he has received.

Ah! that is the way to die; and how is it to be done? Why, the secret of it lies in the commandment which Abraham received and obeyed: "I am the Almighty God; walk before Me, and be thou perfect." That is to say, a life of simple communion with God; the realizing His presence and feeling that He is near, will sweeten disappointments, will extract all the good out of life, will make us victorious over its pains and its sorrows, will turn all that comes to us into a joy and a blessing, will make it all contribute to the satisfaction of our desires, and will bring us to feel at the last that we are ready for life and ready for death; that this world and the next are but two of the mansions of our Father's house; and Death, the dark narrow corridor that connects the one to the other. And so we shall be ready and say: "Whether we live, we live in the Lord, or whether we die, we die in the Lord. Living or dying we are God's." And so it does not matter, so much as people think, whether we die or live.

And now I have a thing or two which I want to say about the last words of this text. "He died in a good old age, an old man, and full of years; and was gathered to his people."

Well, that too is remarkable—a symbol very seldom employed in Scripture. It is only found in the very early books of the Old Testament, and there only in reference to a very few persons.

But if you will observe the language, I think you will see that there is in it a dim intimation of something beyond this present life—a life beyond. He "was gathered to his people" is not the same thing as to say, "he died." That is disposed of in the earlier portion of the verse in two phrases, one of which is remarkable: "Abraham gave up the ghost, and died." Being "gathered to his people" is not the same thing as being buried. That is disposed of in words that come after: "He was gathered to his people, and his sons Isaac and Ishmael buried him in the cave of Machpelah." It is neither the equivalent of death nor of burial; it conveys, dimly and veiledly, that somehow or other though Abraham was buried that was not all. He was buried; yes, "he was gathered to his people." Why, his own people were buried away in Mesopotamia, and his grave was never near them. What is the meaning of the expression? Who were the people that he was gathered to in death? "The dust shall return to the earth as it was, and the spirit shall return to God that gave it." Dimly, vaguely, veiledly, but unmistakably as it seems to me, here we have expressed a premonition and feeling after the thought of an immortal self that was not in the Abraham that his sons Isaac and Ishmael laid in the grave at Machpelah, but was somewhere else, and for ever.

That is the first thing, the dim hint of a future. Anything more? Yes! "He was gathered to his people." Now remember, Abraham was a wanderer all his life. His life was shaped by that commandment: "Get thee out from thy father's house, and from thy kindred, and from thy country."

He never dwelt with his kindred all his days. He was a pilgrim and a sojourner, a stranger in a strange land; and though he was living in the midst of a civilization—great cities whose walls ran up to heaven—he pitched his tent beneath the terebinth tree at Mamre, and will have nothing to do with all that civilization; an exotic, a waif, an outcast in the midst of Canaan all his life. Why? Because "he looked for a city which hath foundations, whose Builder and Maker is God." And now he has gone to it, and he is "gathered to his people;" the life of isolation is over.

He is no longer separated from those around him, or flung amongst those that are uncongenial to him. He is gathered to his people, he dwells with his own tribe, he is at home, he is in the city.

And so, dear brethren, life for every true man must be an isolated life, a lonely life, after all its communion. He dwells upon islands with his fellows, all separate dwellings, dotted over a great archipelago, each upon his little rock, with the sea dashing between them. But a time comes when, if our hearts are set upon that great Lord whose presence is communion, we shall be brought together, and enter into the city. The future is the perfection of society; and amongst the people, Abraham found those that had gone before him; and reunion is sweet to the wanderer. So you and I may find—

"That with the morn those angel faces smile
Which we have loved long since, and lost awhile."

"He was gathered to his people." Ay! and there is another thought here, and that is association. According to affinity and character each is "gathered to his people;"— to the folk that he is like, and that are like him; the people with whom he had sympathy; the people whose lives were shaped after the fashion of his own. That is possible. Men will be sorted there. Gravitation will come into play undisturbed, and the pebbles will be ranged according to their weights on the great ocean-coast where the sea has cast them up; all the big ones together, and sized off to the smaller ones, regularly and steadily laid out. "Like draws to like."

Spiritual affinities, religious character, the moral character, will settle where we are, and who are our companions when we get yonder. And some of us would not altogether like to live with people that are like ourselves, and some of us would not find it very tolerable.

The men in the Dantesque circles were made more miserable because the men around them were of the same sort as themselves, and some of them worse.

And an ordered hell, with nobody for the liars but liars, and nobody for the thieves but thieves, nobody for impure men but the impure, and nobody for the godless but the godless, would be hell indeed!

"He was gathered to his people," and you and I will be gathered likewise. Judas went to his own place— the place he was fit for, the place which he had earned, the country to which he belonged! So shall we, so shall we!

Let us see to it that we take Christ for our Saviour, and give our hearts to be shaped and purified by Him; and our country will be where He is, and His people will be our people, the people with whom His love abides; and the tribe to which we belong will be the tribe of which He is the Chieftain and the Prince. And so shall we ever be with the Lord.

V. Isaac. HEB. xi. 20. *"By faith Isaac blessed Jacob and Esau concerning things to come."*

THAT story of the blessing, which Jacob got by craft from his father Isaac, presents very many singular features which we cannot enter upon now. But it is a miserable story all round. What with the doting fondness of the old man, the craft of the mother, the selfish lying of Jacob, and the savagery of Esau, it is an ugly picture, every bit of it.

And yet there was one little point of light in it, one redeeming thing about it that the writer of the Epistle to the Hebrews here puts his finger upon with certainty. He says—"Yes! it is a wretched story! There is nobody comes out of it very clean; but that man that spoke, he spoke, however imperfectly apprehended, the truth. He had in him the little germ of all that was good and noble in human nature, because the blessing that he gave he gave *by faith.*" And whatever else was bad, that was good. And whatever else was of the devil—and there was a great deal of his in the story—that was of God.

And so that helps to redeem the whole story, and to lift it up into another region altogether. "By faith Isaac" foolish, fond, doting, blind, blundering, weak as he was, "by faith Isaac blessed Jacob and Esau concerning things to come." I need not enter upon the question, although it is one that would afford very fruitful consideration as to how these came to lie, side by side, in the patriarch's experience, all these manifold faults and imperfections, and yet some kind of prophetic power which made his blessing a prophecy, and therefore a reality that could not be altered when once it was spoken.

That would take us too far away; but what I would rather fix upon for our consideration is that one thought of the faith that the writer here signalizes as being predominant in the character,—at least, more than distinctly there.

And the next thing that I would suggest is, that we get here the faith of this man and of all of us in its substance. Isaac's faith, what was it? A firm reliance, rising sometimes to absolute certainty, of things far beyond the ken of mortals, his faith at first sight grasped material blessings, but they were unseen ones, and that is the point that this writer could dwell upon first.

But that does not go to the bottom of it, although a great many people seem to think, and we hear them speak as if faith was concerned only with the unseen. Not necessarily. Faith at bottom has not to do with things, but with persons; and Isaac's faith—like that of all those other heroes, sages, warriors, and patriarchs in this grand roll-call in the Epistle to the Hebrews—whatever it was secondarily concerned with, was primarily concerned with God. God's word and character, what He had shown himself to be, was the object of these men's faith. And sometimes the object of their faith was a God that threatened, as in the case of Noah. Sometimes it was a God that commanded, as when the Israelites compassed the walls of Jericho; sometimes a God that promised, as in the case of Abraham, Isaac, and Jacob. Sometimes their faith laid hold of a past fact, sometimes upon a present fact, sometimes upon a future one; but wherever it led them, the materials of it was their confidence in God, and they believed His word utterly.

Or, to put it into other words, our faith may either go backward or forwards or upwards; it may either be concerned with the deep things of Divine revelation, or with the common things that lie round about us. We take them all because we trust in God, and faith is confidence in the Divine Lord of past, present, and future. And then, as this chapter says at the beginning, "Faith is the substance of things hoped for, the evidence of things not seen." What our faith has to grasp is God in Christ, and only through Him do we see the things that are unseen. First, we must "behold the King in His beauty," and then and thereby we shall "see the land that is very far off."

And so this old story shows us that the beginning of faith is confidence in God; and the field in which the faith that trusts Him moves and expatiates is the blessed region beyond, into which the eye cannot pass, but in which certain hope and desire may walk, blessed and calm as the angels of God.

Brethren! everything that lifts a man out of the mire of to-day helps to make him good and pure and strong. Even the poorest earthly anticipation, if only it has got about it the magic touch of being in the future and being unseen, is more noble than when it is possessed. That is why people say about this world's good, "The chase is better than the prey when caught," the run is more than the hare. Everything in the future is invested with a halo that disappears when you get near it. The mountains that ring our horizon in the country of the Alps look violet and roseate in soft glow, and when you get up there, they are cold cliffs and rocks and snow; barrenness and roughness and death.

The future, even when it is made of the same stuff as the present, is more ennobling in its effect upon a man than itself will be when he gets beside it. But if, instead of living on these lower levels, we lift our eyes up to those everlasting hills, and live by the power of that unseen reality, then all life is transfigured, ennobled, purified, and the man becomes greater because he lays hold of the things unseen, and he lays hold of them because he first lays hold of God.

And then another lesson that we get very strikingly in the story of Isaac's life is faith in its operation. How singularly the second of the great Jewish patriarchs differed from the first and the third. Not a hero like Abraham, not a man with a strong life like Jacob, Isaac had no need of the perfecting discipline so necessary for Jacob before he could become Israel: he never attained to anything like the greatness and nobleness of his father. A decent, plain, quiet man, living all his days with his flocks and herds in the south; no heroisms, no force of character, just a respectable, ordinary, quiet, pastoral chief. When the Philistines quarrelled with him about a well, he quietly went away and dug another; when they quarrelled about that, he dug a third; and so passed all his life in the desert. He seems to have had few causes of excitement—no great changes in his life, was never impelled by any desire to seek them. He had no Divine revelation, as his father and his son had in their lives. There he was, quiet in the land. " Blessed are the meek, for they shall inherit the earth."

And it is very beautiful, I think, to see in his life how the same principle that made the grand organ music of the enumeration of its effects in this chapter, the same principle that " subdued kingdoms, wrought righteousness, obtained promises, stopped the mouths of lions, quenched the violence of fire, waxed valiant in fight, turned to flight the armies of the aliens ;" and so on, dropped down to the low level of this very prosaic, commonplace life, he found a sufficient field in making that quiet mission peaceful and pure, and wrapped about with God through his earthly days. Let us take that lesson : there is no need for great events in our lives—great services, great sacrifices, great manifestations of the Divine favour. The life that runs smoothly may be as full of faith as the life that stormily surges amidst the rocks and comes down the cataract. There may be as much power in the still river among the pastures of the south of England, that flows gently and quietly in its course, as there is in the torrent that dashes among the mountains. The life of a quiet domestic character, with nothing conspicuous about it, may be as truly and as blessedly under the influence of the highest Christian principle as the noblest and the greatest of those recorded here. Not the outward form but the inward motive makes the greatness of the life, and the field of faith may be the fireside and the back of the counter and the home circle. Its trophies may be as great amongst those whom there were none to praise and very few to love as amongst those whose names are written highest and in most perennial characters on the grateful remembrance of the Church of God.

Isaac was as truly a son of faith as the hero Abraham, or as the far richer and more complex character of his son Jacob. And then I might point you to two things in Isaac's life which bear upon this question. There is very little recorded about him, as you will see if you will turn to the Book of Genesis; but there are two things told about him, one concerning his history and the other concerning his friendly relations with the people amongst whom his lot was cast. He dwelt a long time amongst the Philistines, and there, as I said, they quarrelled about the wells. He simply gave them up, and went and dug others. Well, take that lesson. One of the most marked effects of Christian faith ought to be that of making men gentle and forbearing; not holding on by their rights tooth and nail, fighting with everybody for a penny, so that nobody shall say they got the advantage of them. The effect of true Christian faith will always be to make a man yield rather than fight, suffer wrongly rather than shriek, and call heaven to earth, and take claws and teeth in order to contend for what is his.

That principle is as true to-day as it ever was, and our Lord Himself has told us, in words that it is very convenient for us to say are to be interpreted with much limitation: "He that compelleth thee to go a mile, go with him twain. If a man will take thy coat, let him have thy cloak also." Faith makes men gentle, ay! and more than that, the faith that makes men gentle tells its own story to the outsider. These same wrangling and dishonest Philistines, that stole the wells and then turned Isaac out of their territory, because he was getting too strong for them, and they began to be afraid of him,— what did they do next? He quietly went away, and as is always the case, he was scarcely gone when they sent for him to come back again; and they say to him: "Come back to us, for we know that the Lord is with thee."

That is to say, if your faith is worth the snap of a finger it will tell its own story to outsiders. They will be glad to have you beside them for more or less worthy motives; but the motives we have nothing to do with, the point is that it will be like the "ointment of the right hand that bewrayeth itself, and it cannot be hid." And bad as the world is, it is not so bad but that it knows a good man when it sees him; and bad as it is, it is not so bad but it has a kind of respect for him when it sees him. And in the long run, whatsoever persecution and wrong-doing there may be, "the meek-doing shall inherit the earth" in a real sense; and the meek man will get what a good many people would sell themselves to get—the good opinion of the men around him; just because he does not look for it, or care to try to get it, but simply lives righteously. For though the Philistines may steal the wells, they all the while respect the man from whom the robbery has been made.

And then let us take consolation from the other thought, that this man was a man of faith, though he was a man of a great many imperfections. I said at the beginning of these remarks, that the story of the blessing was an ugly story all round, and Isaac does not come out of it very clean either. And there are other points that come out of the narrative of his life, which show that he was by no means a faultless monster; and yet for all that he was a man of faith.

Now that is not a pillow for lazy people to lay their heads upon, and say: "There is no need for me to strive after the perfection of my faith, because it may co-exist with imperfection." Yes! it may. But did you ever hear that it could exist with imperfections that people knew about and did not try to mend? Is there anything in the Bible that says that a man's faith is consistent and upright up to a certain point, without his doing anything to remedy or prevent failure?

Faith may be consistent with failure; thank God we cannot say how much failure may co-exist with faith; but let us remember that all faith is necessarily effort, that the smallest sin that we do not fight against will be like a little grain of sand dropped into the works of a fine clock, it will spoil all the wheels and break the mainspring sooner or later, that is if you do not get it out.

And so whilst there is no reason for anything but humble penitent confidence even in the consciousness of imperfections, there is no reason for any reliance upon my faith which is not accompanied with honest, continual effort to fight against my thoughts and my sins. And, thank God! the quiet husbandman, whose life ran in one level all along, scarcely ever brightened by anything great or grand, as far as we know it, rose at last, though amidst many faults, into a flash of grand, vivid consciousness of a blessed future.

And that is what you and I have to hope for, by God's grace, if we keep near to Him, doing our common tasks in cheerful godliness; at the end even of a very prosaic, commonplace, low-lying life, there may come a gleam, as upon some winter day there comes a bit of red in the sky towards the west, there may come a gleam at the last that shall show us all the brightness to come, ay! and make us feel that it is a real thing.

And so, living by a quiet humble faith, we may die in the triumph and faith that grasps the things unseen, because it reaches out its hand to grasp the unseen and eternal.

VI. **Jacob at Bethel.** GENESIS xxxv. 1. *"And God said unto Jacob, Arise, go up to Bethel, and dwell there: and make there an altar unto God, that appeared unto thee when thou fleddest from the face of Esau thy brother."*

IT was somewhere about thirty years since Jacob had vowed that vow which, even when he made it, was not of a very high tone. He made his bargain very tight when he said: "If God will be with me, and will keep me in this way that I go, and will give me bread to eat, and raiment to put on, and see that I come again to my father's house in peace, then"—after he has done all that for me—"then shall the Lord be my God!"

Yes! I should think so! He was his God before He did all that for him. "And this stone which I have set for a pillar shall be God's house; and of all which Thou shalt give me I will give the tenth unto Thee."

Well, it was not much of a vow to begin with, but if we think of the exceedingly leisurely manner in which he set about keeping it, there is even a darker hue over the patriarch's character, even at its highest and its best. And a very little comparison of the events, as they may be deduced from the narrative, will show us that God had done all which Jacob had laid down as the conditions ten years ago; that Jacob had "come back to his place in peace," having prospered far beyond all hope and expectation. He had gone out a fugitive and come back a rich man; gone out lonely, come back with all his household and his wealth. And when he had thus come back, instead of going straight to Bethel to fulfil his vow, he settled himself quietly down at Shechem; and in that lovely valley, the fairest spot in the whole land of Palestine, he buys a bit of ground, makes himself exceedingly comfortable, and seems to have forgotten all about the vow that he had made. So that there needs this: "And God said unto Jacob, Arise, Go up to Bethel!" "Do you remember? *Go up to Bethel*, and dwell there; and make an altar there."

You might almost put these words into inverted commas; the Lord is quoting the vow: "Make there an altar unto God." And then comes a very sharp twinge: "That appeared unto thee when thou fleddest from the face of thy brother."

Ah! Is not that a picture of a great many more people besides Jacob? How many of us, for instance, think of our religion very much as if it was an umbrella or a cloak, a thing for stormy weather! How we pray when we want anything; how when God's hand is upon us, and sickness or perplexity or disaster or loss, or the rupture of family ties comes to us and opens for a moment a glimpse into the kingdoms beyond, how we can pray then and live decided then! And how, when the storm has passed, and the burden is lifted off our shoulders, how we do just like Jacob did, settle down at Shechem, and forget all the past when we lay there with our head on the stones, and the black night above us, and a dark dim, future before us. Ready to vow at the beginning of a questionable undertaking; very, very slow to pay at the successful end of it. Ready to say: "When I am commencing this task, the issue of which I do not know, the difficulties of which I may not be able to meet;" ready to say then: "If Thou wilt do so-and-so, then shall the Lord be my God." But when He has done so-and-so, not in such a hurry to pay the vow. How many of us have more prayers for the unknown future on the 1st January, than we have thanksgivings for the forgotten past on the 31st December! It is not Jacob only that was full of vows at Bethel, and in thirty years forgetting them just because God so completely remembered His part.

Well, and there is another way of looking at it, for I only want to take the plain practical lessons out of this little story now. A good many resolutions that most of us made in the early days of our Christian career, how many of them can we look back upon and say we have kept, and how many of them have gone to water? Jacob was not a young man really when he began his course at Bethel, but he may stand for us as a type of the buoyant, joyful, confident resolutions which we are so apt to make at the commencement of our career.

There is nothing sadder, I think, in the history of the Christian Church, and in the history of the individual souls that make it up, than the dreadful frequency—I was almost going to say uniformity—with which the beginning of the Christian career is always so much more bright than the reality of that same career when years have passed. Is there any reason why it should be, so frequently as it is amongst all of us Christian people, the experience that the beginning of the course promises far more fairly than the middle and the end of the course realizes? Why should the morning always be the sunniest part of the day? Why should it always cloud over; or, if not always, at least so often that it is little exaggeration to say always? Why should the average Church member and professing Christian, in all our communities, be obviously a man or woman whose religious growth has been stopped and stunted? Why should it be that most of us have in our memories a Bethel at the beginning, the vows made at which are unfruitful to this day? Is it so, my brother, or is it not, with us?

Well, let us go on with the story, and see what it was that kept this man from going there and building his altar and doing as he said. There are two things clearly that kept him, besides the fact that in the years that passed, the impression of his early days had been forgotten, and that the very continuance of the Divine mercy had made him less conscious of it than he was at the beginning, when it was all problematical.

One of the Fathers says somewhere, that "God by assiduity loses admiration;" and that is one reason why these vows were not rendered, viz. that the gifts had been so continuous that the continuity had destroyed the impression of its greatness and had deadened the sense of admiration. If there had been breaks in it, parentheses, no man would have felt it more. No man enjoys health so well as the man who has good health now and then broken up by a great many bad days.

But besides that one operative cause there are plenty in

the narrative. What did Jacob do as soon as he got this commandment? That will answer the question what it was that kept him from doing it before. "Arise! Go to Bethel, and build an altar." "Then said Jacob unto his household and all that were with him, Put away the strange gods that are among you, and be clean, and change your garments." "And they gave unto Jacob all the strange gods which were in their hand, and all their earrings, and Jacob hid them under the oak which was by Shechem." And when they had got rid of them "they journeyed" and came back to Bethel.

Well, put that into other words, and it comes to this: The man settled himself down at Shechem. There was a great valley, and more grass for his cattle there than there was at Bethel; it was a better place to pitch. "Business prospects were more promising" at Shechem, and of course we know that that is the first thing that any man ought to consider in all his ways. And so of course it would answer better to stop at Shechem than to go to Bethel. The plainest dictates of duty said: "Stop at Shechem! Never mind the vow!" And he stopped there; and he was very nearly getting into the same position that his relative Lot got into, when he and Abraham stood on the hill-top here, and looked over all the plain of Jordan; and Abraham had said: "You choose first the bit of land you like." And Lot saw the cities of the plain; he saw the plains were fertile, and he knew the cities were sinful, but he answered: "I will go down among the godless ones. There is plenty of pasture there." And we know what it led him to; only God's mercy stopped him before he got to the end. And Jacob did not go to Bethel, because the pastures where he was were good.

That is to say, the thing that tugs us back is this poor sinful, miserable world; the thing that keeps us from fulfilling these resolutions is because the world is always plucking at our skirts and keeping us from rising. The thing that ties us down to the past, which we know is an unworthy past, is, in nine cases out of ten, the mere incapability of getting rid of the temptation of earthly treasures and earthly conveniences and comforts.

And we must do as Jacob did—huddle them all together and bury them under the oak-tree, and leave them behind us, before we can go onwards to build the altar of God at Bethel. And another thing that I must just touch upon. There must have been something very wrong in Jacob's household before there could have been idols and emblems of idolatry amongst them sufficient to make it necessary to get rid of them. How came that about, that Jacob's wives and sons and daughters were people of that sort. Such a household, so wild a set, with a wife that was an idolater, with sons that were murderers, with daughters that were light of heart and light of conduct—such a household as that did not say much for the patriarch's wisdom and holiness. And it was because of the domestic associations being against him, and keeping him from going to Bethel, no doubt, that he delayed so long before he went.

Which being translated is just this :—Let us take care that a man's foes shall not be they of his own household; and that those that are dear to us shall not be hindrances in the way of a consistent and unworldly Christian profession. And you fathers and mothers, do you see to it that you do not set up or permit ways of living, occupations, amusements, associations, companionships, in your household, which war against your best interest, as well as against that of those who are more immediately concerned in it. And remember, the one way by which we can fulfil our early resolutions and keep the mid-day and the evening of our Christian life up to the level of the early hopes of the bright morning, is the old way of sacrifice and surrender, and the offering up of everything that is a hindrance to our communion with the God of Bethel.

The first step towards the building of the altar was the bundling together of all the strange gods that had tempted these people, and the digging of a hole there below the tree, and putting them all in, and covering them well over with the sods, and leaving them there for anybody that liked to find them.

And then let me remind you how this sacrifice is rewarded by the rapt vision and the renewed and enlarged promise from the God of Bethel. He goes to the place : I wonder what he thought when he got there, and saw the old stone that he had stuck up there forty years

E

before, and remembered how, when he had stood by it, his heart had been heavy within him until he saw that vision at the top of the ladder, and tried to recover for a moment those early thoughts with which he had set out on his journey. I wonder if he said to himself: "What a poor ungrateful creature I have been! I will try to make it better for the time to come, at all events."

"And the Lord came unto him again, and blessed him," and confirmed to him his mighty name of Israel, and the promise of the land. And then Jacob raised his pillar, and poured out a drink-offering; and, with a double meaning, called the name of the place once more "Bethel," the house of God.

That is to say: the old man's vision may be a deeper and a more glorious edition of the young man's dream. The one in the night, the other in the day; the one a narrow promise, the other a wider word; the one limited almost to an earthly blessing, the other expanding to immortal hopes and celestial glories. And thus the fathers that knew Him that was from the beginning may know Him with a deeper knowledge, and hope in Him with a grander hope, than the young men that start on their careers with the knowledge of the future.

But remember, the surrender of the idols is the only way to see God; and they who, for dear love's sake of the Christ that died, come with their broken vows and lay them at His feet, shall find pardon, and shall receive a nobler vision than even that with which He blessed the beginning of their Christian course.

VII. **Jacob's Death.** HEB. xi. 21. "*By faith Jacob, when he was a dying, blessed both the sons of Joseph; and worshipped, leaning upon the top of his staff.*"

THERE were surely plenty of pieces of Jacob's life that might have served the writer's purpose better as illustrations of faith than these two comparatively neglected events at the close of it, and surprise has often been expressed, that, with the whole field of the recorded biography of the patriarch to choose from, the writer should have chosen just these two little things,—the dying benediction and the dying adoration. And yet perhaps we may, without being fanciful, find a reason in the very comparative insignificance of the act. The smaller the thing done the more perhaps is it an evidence of the all-pervading power of faith in the man's life. It is perhaps more to say about people—they did the little things of life by faith, than to say—they did the big ones. Anybody can come to the height of a great action, but to have my faith so close to my hand that it naturally influences the trivialities of my days, that is a demonstration of its power in me. And so I think there need be no stumbling-block in the minuteness of the event that is chosen as the illustration from the life of Jacob. There is another remark, viz.: that there are two very distinct incidents recorded here in inverted order to that of their occurrence. The one—the benediction upon the sons of Jacob; and the other the event that preceded that, which is recorded by the side of it in the Book of Genesis, when the patriarch, dying, sent for his son and exacted from him an oath that he would not leave his bones there in the land of Egypt, but would bury him in the land in which he had no inheritance; and when the promise was given, fell back, as our Bible has it—in adoration; or rather turned himself on the bed in adoration, and in quiet triumphant contemplation of the God in whom he trusted. The explanation of the diversity of expression in my text to that of the alternative in the Book of Genesis—"worshipped on the top of his staff"—the explanation of that variety is very simple and natural. The Hebrew which means *bed*, means also *staff* according as you supply one or another set of vowels—you know there were no vowels in the Hebrew language—which leaves some expressions a little doubtful at times. The translator of the Book of Genesis has adopted the one reading, and the translator of the Septuagint,—which for the most part the Epistle to the Hebrews follows,—has adopted the other. But there is nothing at all incongruous, the dragging in the mention of staff, but it is natural that the bed should appear when a man is dying, and the picture is of the old patriarch turning himself upon his bed in an attitude of adoration and contemplation, and, thinking of God, and thankful that his bones should not be laid in the alien soil of Egypt, but carried to the land of his forefathers. And so I think out of these two incidents there come two or three important lessons. The first of them is—looking at this far-off glimpse into a life lived under such diverse conditions and regulations to ours, that the man's faith works in such a different fashion to what it works with us. Looking away into this far-away, strange, and unfamiliar mode of life, we learn first of all to understand what is the *real* throbbing, living heart of that thing we call religion. Here is this man—the writer of this book says—exercising the special *Christian* virtue of faith. And look how he explains it. At the beginning of this chapter he tells us that " faith is the substance of things hoped for, the evidence of things not seen," as if he was explaining it as having mainly reference to the invisible, to the future world. But notice that that is not the definition of faith, and that the writer of this letter does not give it as a definition. He gives it as the two cases of the operation of faith, not of its essence, that it enables a man to lay hold—as of a living substance—on the things which are unseen. That is the consequence and the effect of faith, it is not faith. For how was it that these old patriarchs were able to look forward through all the dim ages, and to call the things which were not as though they were, and to believe that that land was to be theirs? It was because their faith was kept—not with the things unseen and hoped for—but with Him that had promised the things; and deep down beneath the things that they expected, lay the confidence that they cherished in the promising God. And so I call you to notice that wheresoever the eye and hand of faith may be turned, the essence and the heart of it is the grasp of the living God. And secondly a reliance on Him and on His word. On the surface, this old chapter seems to deal with faith as the substantiating and bringing near to me all the things that are all unseen and anticipated; beneath, it emerges as the confidence of the soul in the promise; and beneath that, it appears as the confidence of the soul in Him that promised. Let me take a bold illustration. Suppose a man said to you, there is £1,000 to your credit in a bank. Well, you might say that the £1,000 was the object of your faith, but that would only be a very loose and incomplete way of putting it. Or you might say that his word was the object of your faith, and I don't quarrel with your way of putting it. But below the reliance on the *word*, there is the reliance on the *speaker* of the word, and that in the last analysis, it is neither the gift promised, nor the promise of the gift, but the promiser who gives the gift, with which a man's faith is to be conversant. And so you will take this chapter, this grand deed-roll of heroes of the faith; though at first sight it seems as if the word was employed in a different shade of significance from that which it usually occupies in the Old Testament, a little more looking lets us see that it is the same idea throughout; and that the language on which your salvation and mine is suspended, is simple affiance and trust of our whole spirits in the manifested God who "spoke unto the fathers by the prophets," and in these last days hath spoken unto us by His Son. He Himself is the living object, the only adequate object of a man's confidence and trust. And so from this,—if only we will rightly understand it,—there comes forth this plain thought, that however bright and blessed our inheritance beyond, that with whatsoever fair and substantial forms faith may legitimately people the else unknown and solitary future, howsoever bright and glorious—yet far less bright and glorious than the realities which they shadow—may be the visions which it conjures beyond the worst darkness beyond the grave, not *this*, but the *word* of Him who brought life and immortality to light; and not even that word, but *Him*—the Speaker—in the fulness of His own infinite verity, is the object of our faith. "I am the way, and the truth, and the life," and we obtain an inheritance amongst them that are sanctified through the faith that is in Christ. And so still further. I would have you look at a thought closely connected with this one thought I have been dealing with, and yet different from it, and take that unfamiliar picture of a type of devoutness and Godly living, so far removed by circumstances, and race, and character, from our modern notion of what a good man is; take it—that type of the dying Jacob—as an illustration of the fact of the substantial oneness and identity of,—call it religion, or call it faith,—in all ages, and at all stages of knowledge and culture. Jacob's faith was yours and mine. Jacob's creed was not. The progress of God's self-manifestation and infinitude of wisdom, and truth, and love, and knowledge, lay all dark and unknown to him, which has been revealed to and manifested to us; but yet, with all the variety in the language that the faith grasped, the faith that grasped it was the same. And whether it was the God revealed partially, and yet adequately, in vision and sign; or whether it is the God revealed, not completely, and yet so far as human possibilities are concerned, perfectly, in Jesus Christ, the hand that it leaned upon is the same. And we look across the ages away into the dim distances where life was so different to what it is to-day, where laws of right and wrong were so much modified, in regard to what they are now. We look back to the fierce militant exclusive religion of those early days, and beneath that we see the very same thing that binds men to God to-day, and will do beyond the end of time; for the faith of earth is the faith of heaven, and although at one end of the line stands the world's grey fathers, with their early, contracted creed; and at the other end may stand the saints perfected in knowledge, as in purity and in love, all these are in one line, and are united to God by one and the same faith. And Jacob with his faults and sins and limitations, and you and I, on whom the ends of the earth are come, journey on the same path to the same Father. I do not need to dwell upon the possible applications of a thought like this, in regard to our own times and circumstances, and the plea that may be built upon it for a far wider construction of the limits of God's house and Christ's kingdom than we are so ready to impose upon the one and the other. The measure of the temple and the walls of the New Jerusalem is the rod which comes from heaven, and *our* measuring rods are not adequate to that task. Only, let us remember, no false and spurious liberality under the guise of recognising an identity of faith under all varieties of manifestation. You can take the position of these Old Testament saints, and, seeing you live at a time when so much more has been taught us than they possessed, the faith that laid hold of a creed like theirs to-day would not be their faith. The faith that knits a man to God is a faith that accepts whatsoever God the Lord hath revealed; and so says, "Speak, Lord; for Thy servant heareth." Then notice how this same story, or these two stories, which are smelted into one illustration and instance here, give us also the thought of the ennobling and refining influence of this confidence in God, and occupation therefore with the unseen future. There is no more significant lesson in the whole Bible I think than the difference between the character of this man Jacob at the beginning and at the end of his career. At first, a low, shifty, crafty, scheming Jew; with material objects and all manner of quirks and meannesses ever near him; and at the end, all that beaten out of him, and dignity, and simplicity, and contentedness, and lofty elevation, characterizing the whole life. And how did that serene and noble figure of a green old age with fulfilled desires, and immortal hopes; how did that emerge from the utterances we read about in the early chapters? Sorrow? Yes and no. Discipline of circumstances? Yes and no. Growth, the natural growth of character in changing years? Perhaps. But I think deeper than all this, that promise that God had given to him among His people had sunk in his mind, and that his thoughts and desires were more and more drawn outward and onward to an unseen future; and so by degrees the earthliness and the cunning, and the vulpine nature of the man dropped away, and was changed to the dignity, and grandeur, and statuesque simplicity, and beauty, the outcome and influence of a life conversant with unseen hopes and with the God that promised them elevating the nature out of all its lowness, and sinfulness, and selfishness, and setting it there on a pedestal. We all admit theoretically,—whether we do it practically or not,—that, given two men, a man who has purposes, and hopes, and anticipations for himself, or for some great cause for his fellows, running on into the future, a remote future, is, *pro tanto*, so far as that goes a bigger man, a better man, a wiser man, a stronger and a holier man, than the other man that is living from hand to mouth, and has no purpose beyond the end of next week, and no hopes that go stretching out away into the far distant. And we all admit that of two men, the man that lives, not only for immediate things, but for gross, palpable, material things, is a lower man than he that lives for the unseen, though far-off earthly unseen. That the student, the thinker, and the artist, and all men that have their delight in the region of the invisible, are nobler men by far than the contracted and animalised spirits that grovel on,—I was going to say,—like dogs hunting for truffles, grubbing along with their noses to the ground, only sniffing up the delights that may be there. Take the two men, the man that lives for to-day is a poor creature always by the side of the man that lives for to-morrow. And the man that lives for anything that he can put into his pocket, or look at, or stow away in his senses, is a poor creature compared to the man that lives for anything that is unseen, even though it be one of the things that are unseen and temporal. And so high above that elevation, and greater far than the influence upon any life of narrowness and weaknesses and trickiness, is the great hope that drives a man onward to the great unseen ideal that dwells only before that inward eye. And therefore, you and I, whose work is cast in toiling for our daily bread; working among the transitory things of life, have,—to speak roughly,—no other means of getting the counterpoise to the brutalising influence of the present and the seen, except faith in God, that makes us denizens of another world, and citizens of another country. I believe, of course, that the unseen and future objects which Christian faith brings near a man are infinitely mightier in than all the abstractions, or all the great objects of human pursuit the realization of which lies millenniums in advance. But for the most of men, you have next to nothing else to choose between; and the alternative lies here for most of us,—live for the gross vulgar present, or live for the majestic future, guaranteed to us by the living Christ, and the unseen realities that are there. And let us notice in this story how the life of faith was a life of growing nobleness and beauty; and so take the lesson to ourselves.

The last thing I shall refer to, is that this same incident may set before us the *power* of this confidence or faith, in the end of life. I do not mean to say as some people are disposed sometimes to preach, that the only way by which a man can die calmly is to die a Christian. God hath ordained that the physical act of dying is generally a calm and easy act. So I am not going to build upon that; but here is this man, who has been putting his heart on hopes that are still unaccomplished, hopes that have been the nourishment and sustenance of his soul for many and many a day; and he is dying, and there does not seem the slightest sign of them being nearer; and if anybody might have laid down to die and said, "Well, my life has all been a failure, and a blunder, and here am I the victim of unfulfilled expectations," it was that man. But instead of that, he lays himself down and says, "I die, and God shall be with you; carry my bones up with you," and he puts his hands upon the heads of the boys and says: "They shall be great in the land which God shall give you for a possession." And so his confidence has rounded off, to his own apprehension, the loose, fragmentary, and broken life, into completeness and beauty; and he felt that for all the past—and that comes out most lovelily in his words—that for all the past, that had seemed so strange, so perplexing, so sad while it was passing, there was a living reason. He looks at his son, and says, "And I did not think I should ever see your face again, yet God hath let me see your boys," and then he pats their heads and says, "Looking back here, I see God that was my Shepherd all my life long, the angel that redeemed me from all evil,—bless the lads." The past is beautiful, beginning to be intelligible, shaping itself into symmetry and meaning, into significance and mercy, the unaccomplished hopes are still true hopes, his dear ones he leaves to God; and so he says, "My hope is strong, dying as it was living; I know in whom I have believed, I know His faithful promise, I know I shall share in that." Let us set our confidence on the living love of the Divine Christ, and then when we come to die, if the life may have been failure, and sorrow, and disappointment, and many sins, we may be able to look forward and say, like that old patriarch prophet—"God's promise shall be fulfilled, I shall enter into the rest." By the side of that noble passing away of the Old Testament hero, set the triumphant one in the new. By the side of Jacob the patriarch put Paul the apostle: "I have fought the fight, I have finished my course, I have kept the faith; henceforth there is laid up for me a crown of righteousness." These lived and died in faith. In that faith may you and I live and die.

VIII. The waters of Marah.   EXOD. XV. 23-25.

"*And when they came to Marah, they could not drink of the waters of Marah, for they were bitter: therefore the name of it was called Marah. And the people murmured against Moses, saying, What shall we drink? And he cried unto the Lord; and the Lord showed him a tree, which when he had cast into the waters, the waters were made sweet: there he made for them a statute and an ordinance, and there he proved them.*"

THERE is no more dismal bit of country, perhaps, in the world than that strip of desert sea-coast which goes by the name of the wilderness of Shur, through which the Israelites were called upon to march immediately after passing the Red Sea. Sand and gravel, and limestone rock, all beaten upon with the pitiless glare of the sun, full in the eyes of this caravan of fugitives, as they marched due south for three days. They had no means of refreshing their needs, and one can understand how as the third day came to an end, and the long weary march was drawing to an end too, and the evening quietness came; how when they saw away on the horizon the feathered tips of the palm-trees that told of water, their drooping spirits would revive, men would stagger along a little less apathetically. And when they came to the spring there was an iridescent scum on the surface, and as travellers tell us the very worst water in all the peninsula; and one man tries and spits out the first mouthful, and another man tries but cannot manage it,—although he is half-dead with thirst it won't go down, and they cannot drink the water; and they call the name of it, with breaking hearts, "Marah!" And there were the little children that had never been accustomed to anything but ease in Egypt, and the burdened women with their kneading troughs on their shoulders, and the despairing fathers, a crowd of fugitives, and they all turn upon Moses, and cry against him, and Moses does the right thing. " He cried unto the Lord, and the Lord showed him a tree," or a bit of wood, for the word does not necessarily mean a living tree; and Moses puts it into the water, and the water becomes sweet; and, says the narrative, summing it all up, "there he made a statute and an ordinance," that thing, the bitter water, and the sweetening and the thirst, that is the statute for you, and an ordinance; "and there he proved them." Well, now the first thing I want you to notice, for these last words vindicate us in taking this story to mean something more than itself, as being the embodiment of a perpetual principle that applies all round and all ways, or in the old-fashioned language of the text, "is a statute and an ordinance." The first thing I want you to notice is this—Where is Marah? Close by the Red Sea. That is to say, cheek-by-jowl with the triumph, the first stage in the wilderness. As soon as the men got across and began their march, there is a couple of days or so at the first halting place to shake themselves together, and get themselves into order; and then the next stage is into this wilderness, this desert, and the next halting-place is out on that waterless plain. Like a steamer going out of Dover harbour, the one minute safe behind the stones, the next minute as soon as she gets outside the pier the whole surge of the waves upon her. Not going sailing down along some white ridge, like a ship going down the Thames a long time before it gets into broken water, but out into it at once, one plunge and there you are. Yesterday, they were crossing the Red Sea, with signs and wonders, to-day journeying through the waterless and dreary plain of sand. That is to say, God's road is generally very near its beginning a bit of ugly country, that will try a man's strength and his patience. Good old John Bunyan saw that the Slough of Despond was very near the wicket gate; and that is an old-fashioned way of putting an everlasting truth, that all good things worth doing, all Christlike life, and all high life of every sort, is hard at the beginning. Grammar is always drudgery, the rudiments are always difficult to learn, the apprenticeship is the worst bit of it. We may be quite certain that we are not on God's road if everything goes smoothly; and as a rule, His paths are rough and tangled at the beginning, and only afterwards do they broaden out, and open wide to us. The world does the opposite way; claps a bait upon the hook, entices men into wrong paths by giving them sweetness at the beginning and the bitter afterwards.

"Young gamblers always win, the devil takes care of that!" says the old proverb. So the man at the feast said, "when men have well drunk, then that which is worse, but thou hast kept the good wine until now." So in religious experience, when a man gets converted and brought near Jesus Christ, and finds out the depth of his own sin, and the height of God's love and mercy, very commonly there comes surging over his heart not very long afterwards a great regurgitation, as it were, of the evil that he thought he had got rid of; and a season of sadness and bitterness, measured often by the depth of his former joy and rapture. The crossing of the Red Sea yesterday, Marah and its bitterness to-morrow; and even if it is not so always, there is at any rate the big rule which is usually fulfilled in our experience, although upward and onward, yet God's paths have a trying bit very near the beginning, and even for the husbandman who laboureth first and is afterwards partaker of the fruit.

But that is not all. Marah, as I said, was next door to the Red Sea; but Elim was next door to Marah. Hear how the story goes on after that bit which I have been reading to you. "And they came to Elim, where were twelve wells of water," one for each tribe; "and three-score and ten palm-trees," one for each elder, "and they encamped there by the waters." How sweet the water, how grateful the shade, how blessed the change from yesterday with the bitter saline filth standing in the puddle there. Who can tell what made the Elim waters sweet? Yesterday's experience! What made the shade of the palm-trees so precious? The unsheltered blaze of yesterday's sunshine.

And so, never fear! Our lives will be carried out of the one into the other in God's own good time; and as sure as any of us may to-day be in Marah, to-morrow we shall be in Elim, for there is no human life but is passed, by a loving wise hand, through the alternations of bright and dark, summer and winter, both co-operate to the blessed harvest. So if any of you are camping by the side of the bitter waters, do not let your sorrows cause you to forget yesterday's triumph, nor your hopes fail before you grasp to-morrow's rest and peace. That is where Marah was.

Now, the next thing I want you to notice is, the right and the wrong way of dealing with the bitterness. They "murmured," and "Moses cried unto the Lord." Two ways of using your tongues about your troubles; one is to grumble and the other is to pray. Two ways of speech and thought. One is to set our backs up against what we have to carry, and the other is to go to God and say—"Help us, O Thou who hast laid this upon us!"

"They murmured against God." What! have you forgotten all His past dealings with you this last week already? "They murmured against God!" Why it is only two or three days since you were slaves in the land of Goshen there! You came out jubilant. Where is all your jubilation gone? Is a little thing like this going to turn your thankfulness into murmuring, and embitter your life? There are some people that have got a wonderful habit; if there is one little bit of cloud in their sky no bigger than a man's hand they go talking about it as if it were a great black thunder cloud that covered the whole zenith and threatened to drown them.

You may always make your life a pattern of brightness inlaid upon darkness, or of darkness inlaid upon brightness just as you like to view God's path. It is like a man lying in bed, half asleep, he gazes through his closing eyes and amuses himself with making figures out of the paper, sometimes taking one of the colours for a background, and sometimes another; and the whole aspect changes when he changes a different colour for his background.

And so with your lives. You may either grumble or pray about them, one or the other you will certainly do. It is the alternative for every one of us. We have thorns enough in our pillow, and burdens enough to carry. Let us never bend our backs till we know the burden is laid on them. We have miles enough to travel. Never let us start until we are quite certain that we have got hold of God's hand to keep us steady, patient, and cheerful, or we shall certainly be amongst the grumblers and the murmurers. So it seems to me to be a choice; either we shall be murmurers against some poor brother Moses or other, or else look up above the pigmies, the creatures, and the things, look right away up to Him and all our murmurings will die, and we shall go about with prayers and not with grumbling when once we have got hold of Him.

Well now, the next thing that is here is the secret of turning the bitter waters into sweet. It is a very remarkable form which the miracle takes here. God concealing Himself behind Moses; hiding Himself, so to speak, behind a material vehicle for His miraculous power,—something in the same fashion in which our Lord fell Himself, of complying with different customs and methods of doing wonders; to send one man to bathe in the pool of Siloam, to another using saliva in order to heal him, a touch of the finger to a third. And so God here does not do the thing straight away, but He puts in, between Himself the cause and the healing of the waters the result, two links—Moses and a bit of wood. The reason I do not know that we can find out, nor whether it would do us much good if we could. But at any rate there is a great similarity between this His first miracle of education which He wrought for these Israelites in the wilderness, and the first miracle of judgment wrought upon the Egyptians. This is making bitter water sweet; that was making sweet water—the Nile—bitter. Then, as to the object, a bit of wood. This sweetening of the waters was done with a bit of wood, the tree, or whatever it was that was cast into the water; the Nile was embittered by a bit of wood—the rod of Moses.

There may be a parallel, I do not know whether there is or not, but at any rate it is worth noticing. But putting that aside, what is the means by which we can turn all the bitterness into sweetness? Well, one can scarcely help noticing this, and thinking of the tree as shadowing another Tree, the Tree of Life, the Cross, which being put into any bitterness turns it into sweetness. That is to say according to the great words: "Consider Him that endured such contradiction of sinners against Himself, lest ye be wearied and faint in your minds." Consider Him, and the word used there is a very special one, it means "consider," in the light of comparison, compare your sufferings with Christ's. "Ye have not yet resisted unto blood, striving against sin." Compare His sorrows, His patience, His innocence; think of these things. "And did my Lord suffer," as good John Newton put it:—

"And did my Lord suffer,
And shall I repine?"

Put that Tree of Life into the bitterest fountain that we have to drink, and it becomes sweet.

But there is another side of the same thought, the secret of making all bitterness sweet is the recognition of, and the acquiescence in, God's perfect loving will as manifested in the trial. I do not believe there is any consolation for a great many of the troubles that we all have to bear sooner or later except that. A man stands beside his dead, and people go and pester him with the threadbare commonplaces of conventional Christian consolation; and he is ready sometimes to turn upon them with—" Miserable comforters are ye all!"

Oh! there is only one thing that will give ease to a man, the loving will of a loving Father. Get that into my heart and then the fieriest showers will fall soft like snowflakes, cooling and refreshing upon my heart, and I shall be able to bear it all. And there is nothing else, nothing in all the universe, that will arm you and me against "the slings and arrows of outrageous fortune," and the wild sea of troubles that comes storming upon every man some time or other, except only that one thing: "It is the Lord, let Him do as seemeth Him good;" which being cast into the waters, the waters are healed.

And they change their places. Marah becomes Elim, and the twelve wells open in the wilderness, and there are streams in the desert.

IX. Balaam. NUM. XXIV. II. *"Therefore now flee thou to thy place: I thought to promote thee unto great honour; but, lo, the Lord hath kept thee back from honour."*

BALAAM lived in circumstances sufficiently unlike our own. But human nature does not change with the change of civilisations, and the human conscience face to face with truth and with duty repeats its experiences, its efforts, its failures, its triumphs in the most distant climes and ages. Let us endeavour to study this history, however briefly, in a practical temper, and with a view to our own improvement.

I. Balaam, it need hardly be said, was a very eminent, he was even an extraordinary man. He lived largely among the wild race of the Midianites; but he had gifts and powers which, so far as we know, were entirely unshared by those among whom he dwelt.

He was, first of all, an observer, a careful observer of contemporary events. He was a man of trained political sagacity. In his last recorded prophecy we see how much interest he felt in the future of the neighbouring peoples, of the wild Kenite tribes, of the kingdom of Amalek, of the great monarchies of Central Asia, of the navies which had already begun to connect Palestine with the Western world. He was one of those men who generally look on at public life rather than take part in it, but whose judgment is valued by men of action as being the product of more reflection and experience than their own. Balaam thus corresponds to a writer on history or on politics among ourselves, who does not go into Parliament, but whose deliberate opinions have more weight than those of many Parliamentary speakers. He was consulted, he was allowed for, he was obeyed by energetic people on all sides of him, who felt at least that he saw farther than they did, and who were glad to lean on his advice and his directions.

And next, Balaam was in possession of a truth which, quite apart from its awful and intrinsic value, gives purpose and meaning to a human life; he believed in one God. He lived, we know not for how long, in the Mesopotamian city of Pethor; and here he might very well have fallen in with the descendants of those relatives of Abraham who, like Nahor, did not accompany Abraham in his migration to Canaan; and from these he may have learnt the knowledge of the one true God. This great truth was at the basis of Balaam's thought all through, although he held it in an inconsistent combination with Pagan practices of soothsaying and divination. He would seem to have fallen to a certain extent under the influence of the degraded public opinion around him, and so to have endeavoured to combine his purer faith with the popular heathen sorcery; just as we see people nowadays unite a serious profession of the Christian faith with proceedings and opinions which it really condemns. However, Balaam's knowledge of religious truth, so far as it went, gave him great power among his countrymen, and it led him, as was natural, to take a deep interest in the fortunes of the people of Israel. From his recorded prophecies it is plain that he had heard of the promises made to the Jewish patriarchs, that he knew something of the text of the Jewish records. He uses the

Holy Name itself, which was revealed to the Jews. He must have heard of the remarkable circumstances attending the deliverance of the Israelites from Egypt. Those circumstances had produced a profound impression on all the peoples of the south-eastern seaboard of the Mediterranean and the adjoining tribes. And while the fear and the dread of Israel fell on all the Amorite races, and while in particular Moab was sore afraid of the people because they were many, and Moab was distressed because of the children of Israel, Balaam would have been able to study the secret of Israel's deliverance from Egypt, and of Israel's successful advance across the desert, through his possession of the key of religious sympathy. The heathen around him saw in Israel's history the triumph of physical force, the triumph of good fortune, the triumph, at the best, of certain imaginary divinities like their own. Balaam knew enough to know that the explanation lay far deeper; and this knowledge, at any rate for a time, would have given clearness and decision to his judgment, and force and consistency to his action.

But, besides this, it is clear that Balaam was endowed in a high degree with the gift of supernatural prophecy. Not only could he anticipate the future more rapidly and accurately than ordinary men by the trained use of his natural faculties, but he had also the gift of prophetic insight into a future too remote, too unlike the actual present, to be anticipated at all by the unaided faculties of man. Of this gift his closing words to Balak afford one remarkable specimen. His prediction of the Star and Sceptre that were to arise out of Jacob is not fully satisfied by the conquests of David, of Omri, of Hyrcanus, but points to the spiritual empire of Jesus Christ.

And here we may pause for a moment to take note of the fact that a stranger to Israel, living among a heathen people, himself practising heathen arts, should have been thus distinguished by the possession of a great religious and supernatural gift. Israel alone was the people of Revelation in the ancient world, and yet here an accredited organ of revelation is found far beyond the frontiers of Israel, and his utterances are actually honoured with a high place in the sacred books of Israel. Now, this is in keeping with what we find in the whole course of God's dealings with man. God makes governments ; He creates and authorises sacred institutions ; He bestows the certificate of His presence and His approval here, and He withholds it there. And yet he is not so bound by His own rules that they confine His action besides compelling it. He shows ever and anon that His illimitable and exuberant life has outlets which lie beyond the bounds of consecrated system. Balaam was in one age what Melchisedec had been in another, what Job was in a third—an organ of truth beyond the frontiers of the kingdom of truth. And when, in our day, we see beyond the limits of the Church, beyond the limits of Christianity, conspicuous gifts, if not quite religious, or beautiful and even saintly characters that throw into the shade much that we find nearer home, within the enclosure of the sacred garden of the soul, this does not prove that God has done away with the ordinary rules and bounds of His dispensations of grace and truth ; it only proves this, that those rules do not always confine His action. Balaam, though not of Israel, was still a great prophet ; and this supernatural gift of prophecy enriched the political and religious knowledge which he had acquired naturally, enriched it with a new element of power.

Now, with gifts like these, Balaam was naturally a person of great public consideration. Among the Midianites he took rank even with the princes. His fame spread far and wide among the neighbouring peoples, especially among the Moabites.

Balak, the king of Moab, was in all probability himself a Midianite, who had taken the place of a native dynasty when Moab had been weakened by the Amorite victories ; and Balak would therefore have had opportunities of knowing what was thought of Balaam elsewhere. But men with no knowledge or interest in religions of their own are apt to make very odd guesses about those who are in any way connected with them. Balak seems himself to have looked upon Balaam chiefly as a very powerful wizard. Balaam's higher gifts would be scarcely intelligible to Balak ; or, at any rate, they were not what Balak wanted in the existing circumstances of Moab. Moab and its king were seriously alarmed at the steady, the persistent advance of the host of Israel towards their destined home in Canaan. Israel had now passed the desert, and was encamped in the plain of Moab, the low, flat district along the Jordan and the Dead Sea, which is fertilised by the brooks that run westward from the Pirathon Hills. And from these, their neighbouring heights, the Moabites could look over the camp of Israel. There was Israel encamped in his numbers, which were probably exaggerated by the terrors of the invaded Moabites; and Balak longed to strike a swift and decisive blow. He thought that if a great soothsayer like Balaam could be induced to devote the Israelites to destruction by a solemnly pronounced and public curse, then there would be no doubt about the issue of the impending, the inevitable struggle with Israel. "I wot," he said to Balaam, "that he whom thou blessest is blessed, and he whom thou cursest is cursed." In Balak's eyes, you see, Balaam was simply a weapon of offensive warfare. He had only to be brought into position where he might bear upon the enemy in order to produce results of decisive importance.

Balak's view of Balaam illustrates the way in which in all ages statesmen who are statesman and nothing else are apt to look upon religion and its representatives. They see in it only one of the great forces which modify and control human life; and they desire, by whatever means, to enlist it on the side of the policy or the Government which they for the moment represent. They do not take the trouble to understand what it is in itself. They do not see that it has obligations, laws, principles, which cannot be trifled with, if it is not to forfeit its essential character. They look at it, not from within, but from without; they measure it, not by its inspiring motives, but only by its social and popular results; and, as a consequence, they often make very great miscalculations about it, especially in cases where the absence of insight into the results of a religious creed upon human action, which comes from their lack of faith in that creed, is not compensated for by the sympathetic imagination which enables a man to put himself readily into the mental and moral circumstances of those who differ from him.

Now, this was Balaam's case. It was quite clear that Balaam's gift would be placed at his disposal unreservedly so he thought, if he only paid a sufficient price for it. If a first bid did not succeed, then he would make a second and a larger bid. He did not regard Balaam as having a God or a conscience to consult. Balaam was in his eyes simply a merchant of preternatural wares with a particular useful commodity to dispose of; and the only question was to ascertain his price.

This mistake as to the availableness of religion for any political purpose that may be immediately in view has been made in all ages of the world's history. Saul made it when, in his off-hand way, he offered sacrifice without waiting for Samuel; Jeroboam made it, when he tried to set up a new religion at Dan and at Beersheba, which was to supersede the old duties of the tribes towards their temple and their priesthood at Jerusalem; the princes of Judah made it, when in the last days of the monarchy of Judah they endeavoured to force Jeremiah to advocate what they thought the patriotic policy of reliance on Egypt against Babylon.

History is studded with examples of this mistake, which underlies, for instance, Hume's well-known advocacy of an established Church. Hume advocates what is oddly called the establishment of religion by the State; because, he says, this enables the State to take the religious principle well in hand, and so to repress its tendency to become a fanaticism, and to enlist it on the side of measures which the State may deem expedient.

Without discussing how far this theory is borne out by experience, we may observe that perhaps the most singular illustration of the error in question was afforded by the first Napoleon. When that extraordinary man had conducted the campaign of Austerlitz to a brilliant conclusion, he addressed himself, and with his usual energy, to religious questions. If at this time he had any creed at all, it was the creed of a half-convinced Deist. But for Napoleon religion was always chiefly a political instrument. He professed warm devotion to Mahometanism during the campaign of Egypt; he wrote to Pius VII. as a devoted son of the Roman Church, as a second Charlemagne. Napoleon then, in 1806, thought that his dynasty would be safer if the duty of devotion to himself and his dynasty could be introduced into a catechism which should be used in all the dioceses of France; and accordingly, under the head of the Fifth Commandment, a little political treatise—for such in effect it was—was framed in the shape of question and answer, in which children were told that they must obey the General who had recently suppressed the Republic by force, who had recently murdered the poor Bourbon prince that had fallen into his hands, and this under pain of eternal condemnation. Christianity owes all the support that she can give to existing Governments; but this general principle may be pressed to untenable lengths in particular cases. Napoleon's catechism was criticised, it was protested against, it was slightly modified, but as a whole it was received, it was taught in all the French dioceses for eight years, that is, until the peace. But acceptance of such a document as this cost the French clergy their moral influence; and Napoleon lived too entirely outside the sphere of conscience to understand that, by carrying his point against them, he had done his best to destroy that very power whose support he was anxious to secure.

To return. Balak set himself to work to enlist Balaam's gifts and powers on the side of Moab against Israel. First, a deputation carrying the rewards of divination, the price which was to be paid for the public curse which Balaam was to pronounce, went to him and failed. It was followed by a second deputation composed of much more influential people, and promising Balaam very great honour if he would comply with Balak's request. In the end this deputation succeeded so far as to induce Balaam to go back with it to Balak.

II. Here we are face to face with a difficult question—the real character of Balaam.

This subject was much discussed in the ancient Christian Church, and there were two very different opinions about it. On the one hand, Balaam was regarded by St. Augustine and others as a thoroughly bad man, as a devil's prophet, who was compelled by God, against his will, like the demoniac in the Gospel, to utter truths for which he had no heart. On the other hand, St. Jerome and others considered Balaam a good man in the main and a prophet of God, who fell through yielding to the temptations of avarice and ambition.

The truth probably lies somewhere between the two

opinions. Balaam was a mixed character, and the real problem that has to be dealt with, as we read his history with a practical object, is to discover, if we can, the ingredients of the proportions of the mixture.

On the one hand, Balaam was a man with a clear idea of duty based on a certain knowledge of God. He knew enough about God to feel that when there was no mistake about God's will it must be obeyed, if only for reasons of prudence. He knew enough of God's dealings with Israel to fear to trifle with God's plain commands.

When he was asked by Balak to curse Israel, he did not answer the question without first asking God for guidance; and when he was told by God that he must not accept the invitation, he at once declined. "The Lord refuseth me leave to go with you." When the invitation was renewed, he was equally decided. "If Balak would give me his house full of silver and gold, I cannot go beyond the word of the Lord my God, to do less or more." He only went at last when he had, as he thought, satisfied himself that God permitted him to do so.

And Balaam's sense of duty is not less observable when he had joined Balak. Balak naturally thought that if Balaam once came, there would be no further difficulty. But Balaam was careful to explain at once that he was not at all free to say just what he or Balak might wish. "Lo, I am come unto thee. Have I now any power at all to say anything? The word that God putteth in my mouth, that shall I speak." And so it happened. First there was a sacrifice at the royal residence of Kirjath-huzoth; and then the next day Balaam was solemnly taken to Hamath-Baal, a high hill connected with the Baal-worship, and commanding a full view over the camp of Israel, and there God met him, apparently condescending to manifest His will even through the pagan auguries which Balaam consulted, "and Balaam blessed Israel altogether." And then, when Balak remonstrated, Balaam asked, "Must I not take heed to speak that which the Lord hath put in my mouth?" and Balak probably thought that there was some sinister influence at work in the spot or in the air, or that Balaam had been unduly impressed with the imposing spectacle of the entire camp and host of Israel; and so they moved to another point nearer the encampment of

Israel, but commanding a much less complete view of it, as it would have been apparently shut out from view by a projecting spur of Mount Pisgah. And here again the altars are built, and the sacrifices offered, and the auguries consulted; and Balaam prophesied, and again he celebrated the strength and the assured victory of Israel under the Divine protection. There was, he said, no enchantment against Jacob; there was no divination against Israel "Behold, I have received a commandment to bless, and I cannot reverse it." And Balak was in despair—just as a man might be who has set a machine in motion whose working he is totally unable to guide or to control; he begged the prophet neither to curse Israel at all nor to bless it at all; silence would be better than these unlooked for blessings; but Balaam is still true to his text: "Told I not thee saying, All that the Lord sayeth, that must I do?"

One more trial, Balak thought, might yet be made. Balaam was taken by Balak to a spot celebrated then, celebrated afterwards, further north,—Baal-Peor, which looked over the waste valley below, and in which the Moabite king fondly hoped that the prophet might at last feel himself able to curse Israel; and the altars are built, and the sacrifices offered, but, instead of again consulting the auguries, Balaam looked out over the camp of Israel, which was still, though in the distance, within his view; and the Spirit of the Lord came upon him; and this time the blessing was more explicit than ever before: all the pictures which are most welcome to the inhabitants of the burning desert—the well-watered valley, the fertile garden, the spice-bearing aloe, the noble cedar—are summoned in his poetry to describe the assured prosperity of Israel. Israel's monarch was to be higher than the powerful chief of the Amalekites, higher than Agag; to bless Israel was to be certainly blessing; to curse Israel was to be certainly cursing. And here Balak's dismay gave way to indignation. "Therefore now," he said, "flee thou to thy place; I thought to promote thee unto great honour; but, lo, the Lord hath kept thee back from honour." And again Balaam reminded Balak that he had warned him of what might happen; and then he proceeded to utter a closing prophecy, which foretold the conquest of Moab itself by Israel, and the history of the other neighbouring peoples, and above all, the appearance of the Star of Jacob, under Whom Israel was to advance to the spiritual dominion of the world.

Throughout these circumstances Balaam apparently speaks and acts as a man who has a law of duty clearly before him, and who courageously obeys it. Balak was right in saying that the Lord had kept him back from honour. Whatever earthly wealth or consideration was in store for him at the court of Moab, this he forfeited altogether by his persevering obedience to the voice of God. Self-sacrifice is always respectable, and Balaam had his share in it. For the moment he might almost seem to rank with prophets and with apostles, and in that distant age, and according to his measure, to anticipate the reward of those great promises of the Gospel, " Whosoever hath left father, or mother, or lands, or wife, or children for My sake, shall receive an hundredfold, and shall inherit everlasting life."

But, on the other hand, this devotion to duty was clearly accompanied by another characteristic which explains why Balaam was really an object of God's displeasure, and why he came to a bad end. Balaam, you remember, when he was first asked by Balak to come and curse Israel, referred the question to God in prayer, learned that he ought not to go, and accordingly refused to go. This ought to have been enough for his guidance afterwards. But when Balak made a second application, Balaam, after first of all declining it, allowed himself to treat the question as still open, and he consulted God again. And then God answered him again, but answered him according to the desire of his heart, and bade him go. He did go, and God's anger was kindled because he went, and as he went on his journey he saw the angel of the Lord standing in the way, and his sword drawn in his hand.

How are we to explain this apparent inconsistency between the Divine command to go and the Divine anger at Balaam's obedience? Surely, by saying that the second answer of God to Balaam's inquiry was a reflection, not of God's will, but of Balaam's secret wish. There is such a thing—let us take note of it—as the creation of a false conscience. We may wish that a particular line of conduct might be our duty, until we persuade ourselves that it is really our duty, that it is really what God would have us to do. If instead of acting upon right when we know it to be right, we pray for further knowledge of duty, we may pray ourselves into belief that wrong itself is right. How easily this may be done, how unobserved and secret the process of doing it may be, is only too apparent to any man who keeps his eyes about him in our daily life. Some of the worst things that have been done in human history have been done by persons who have acted on what was at the time to them a sense of duty. But then the sense of duty has been a perverted sense; and the perversion has not seldom arisen from the secret disposition to read human and personal wishes into Divine laws and rules.

When we are once clear about a particular portion of God's will we ought not to reconsider it unless some entirely new facts come to light, which plainly make a real difference in the case before us. In Balaam's case, the problem of duty was exactly the same on the occasion of the second application that was made to him on the occasion of the first. The persons who urged it were more important, the bribe that was offered was higher; but this did not for a moment affect the hard question of duty. To reopen that question was to play a trick with conscience; and one such trick deliberately played with conscience may easily be fatal. Balaam's sense of duty did not give way all at once. We have seen how once, twice, and again he held out against the inducements and the importunities of Balak, and uttered the unwelcome truth which God put in his mouth. But, for all that, his moral constitution was sapped by a fatal wound; his notion of duty was clearly not what he could discover to be God's will, but only what God would not allow him to ignore. It was, as we say, a minimising rule of duty; and, wherever this is the case with a man, a moral catastrophe on a great scale is always possible. Balaam, the author of some of the most lofty and inspiring sayings, of the most majestic prophecies in the Old Testament Scriptures, ended by suggesting that a hideous temptation to iniquity should be placed in the way of the people whose moral superiority he had himself acknowledged; and he died fighting against the cause whose victory he had, at the cost of great personal sacrifice, proclaimed as certain.

III. There are three considerations which the history suggests.

The ministry of grace and truth to others may be quite independent of the personal character of the minister. Truth and grace are God's gifts, not man's. Man is at best an organ of the Divine utterances, the channel through which the Divine influence flows. God does not put Himself in the hands of His human instruments to such an extent as to make His purpose of mercy or of illumination depend on the personal consistency of His ministers with the commission they bear. The profession of a prophet, or a priest, or a clergyman, is one thing; his vocation is another. The first is conferred in the Church of Christ by a valid ordination; it is independent of the character of the recipient. The second is the antecedent and inward work of the Holy Spirit in the recesses of the character, and it alone brings the character into harmony with the work and the powers that fall upon the outward benediction of Christ in His Church.

Balaam is a very ancient and awful instance of the profession of a prophet wielded by a man who had no true inward vocation to prophecy. And Church history records many an example of men who have taught or worked with conspicuous success, yet have failed in the elements of personal devotion to Him whose livery they wear. As to their future our Lord has in merciful severity warned us: "Many will say to Me in that day, Lord, Lord, have we not prophesied in Thy name, and in Thy name cast out devils, and in Thy name done many wonderful works? and then will I say to them, I never knew you."

Another consideration is, how possible it is to know a great deal about the truth, to make sacrifices for it, to be kept back from honour out of deference to its high requirements, and yet to be at heart disloyal to it. When Balaam returned to Midian, he probably reflected, as men speak, with just pride on the manner in which he had conducted himself. He had been exposed to a sharp trial; he had stood it well; he had resisted flattery, bribery, force; he had been as good as his word; what had he not resigned at the call of duty? What had he not achieved for the cause of truth? And yet below all this there was the question, the fundamental question, as to the rectitude of his secret will. The surface obedience might cover, it did cover, an inward rebellion. There are in every generation lives like his. We seem to be gazing on the rosebud, perfect in its form and in its colour, but a worm is eating away the petals, and they will presently wither and fall.

Lastly, the true safeguard against such a fate as Balaam's is the love of God. Love is the salt which alone in this poor human nature of ours saves the sense of duty from decomposition. Had Balaam loved God besides knowing Him, he would not have asked for guidance a second time. One intimation of the will of those whom we love is enough, always enough, for a sincere affection. Love rejoices to obey, not because obedience is welcome to self, but because obedience is agreeable to him who is the object we love. Love rejoices in opportunities of resisting self; for love in its very essence is the renunciation and the gift of self, for the sake of another, to another, whether God or man.

Let us pray God that this great gift may be poured into our hearts by His Holy Spirit, that loving Him above all things we may obtain His promises, which indeed throw into the shade all earthly objects, which exceed all that we can desire.

H. P. L.

X. Joshua. DEUT. xxxiv. 9. "*And Joshua the son of Nun was full of the spirit of wisdom; for Moses had laid his hands upon him: and the children of Israel hearkened unto him, and did as the Lord commanded Moses.*"

JOSHUA was selected to finish the work of Moses; and it was of the first importance that the ideas, even in this remote era, of Moses should be continued, and that the whole spirit of his work should be promulgated. We may be sure that part of the endeavour of Moses' life was to secure this. "Joshua the son of Nun was full of the spirit of wisdom; for Moses had laid his hands upon him." He had received instruction from Moses. It was not done in a hurry, but through forty years, and, therefore, it lasted. It will not do to teach a man or nation hurriedly. We are disappointed sometimes because our thoughts, clear to ourselves, are not clear to others, or if our children do not understand the thought we have been giving them. Do not trouble yourselves about that; go on, if you believe what you are saying, and after forty years you will perhaps make men who will continue your work. They will be worth the making. The excitable ones who rush into excitement about you, will, when the time of difficulties comes, fall away. They are not rooted, and when the sun of opposition shines they wither away. Moses made a firm, fixed man of his follower, because he worked on him for many years.

Mark, Joshua was not a man like Moses; on the contrary, Joshua's nature was one entirely different from his own— a man whose genius was for war and not for law. Looking at himself through Joshua he saw his own faults in a different manner. That was wise; and in truth the one thing Moses cared for was the thought, not the form, the eternal thought which came from God. This course was wise, it was prophetic. The thoughts Moses gave to the people were to be continued under different circumstances. They were to be continued during almost incessant war, and next in the national sentiment; and he took care they should be cultivated and impelled in the mind of a warrior.

And the results? Some things are kept like one by their unlikeness to each other; respect and wonder and loving curiosity kindling respect and wonder and loving curiosity, and thus kindling themselves together. That was the friendship of these two men; and it was the foundation of Joshua's education for his work. The sketch I have given you is full of lessons for us, lessons I can only indicate. If any one wants, and you have anything to give them, do not neglect them because they are of a different nature to you. Dissimilarity of nature may be the one thing needed in order to carry on your thoughts afterwards in dissimilar circumstances from those which surround you. It pleases a man's vanity to be reflected by his fellows; but you will be foolish if you accept it. Your work given back to you by reflection will be spoilt. It would stagnate first and then be utterly spoilt. Seek for those to take your thoughts who have life in themselves, who will work their thoughts into yours, and who will give them new clothes in their own minds. For the one thing to be cared for and to secure, in truth, is the idea, and not its clothes. Of course you make the clothing, but the tendency is to dwell too much upon the clothing and to forget the truth itself. Do not be betrayed through vanity or the applause of men into that deadly error. Desire that the thought you possess or the truth you tell has new clothing put upon it through every change of circumstance; but if you keep old clothes upon it, the thought gets useless because of the clothing, and by-and-by your thought that you prized so is thrown on the dust-heap until some one comes by and finds it, and the old clothing is stripped off; and when the old garments, all rotted, are taken off, then the thought is a beautiful thing, and the finder reclothes it again for mankind. Thus take care, like Moses, that you have some one to give the truth to who will put a different clothing upon it; like Christ, who gave His ideas to twelve men, all different in mind, so that there might be diversities of opinion, differences of opinion, but the same truth in all.

So far for the stating of the friendship and the education between Joshua and Moses. How does Joshua first appear before us? As a warrior. He keeps that place till near the end. He stands forth as the very spirit of war from the time when he stands on the mountain side and cries, "There is the noise of war in the camp." The very war cry stirred him, and gave birth to that terror-giving shout with which Israel always rushed to battle. He recalls the memory of one of the Greek heroes. We see him in ambush and then turning like a lion upon the foe to destroy. We see him spear in hand calling upon the sun to stay and upon the moon to hold, while the pursuing host avenged their enemies—a splendid image of wild war, and he is its centre and inspiration. The career of battle, of which this was the last, began almost immediately after the exodus; more than forty years before this time the battle with Anak took place. Then began Joshua's training. No one can help seeing that Joshua's temptation was to feel that it was through his genius Israel won. It was not without reason, then, that the story makes Moses take him up the mountain, and while he looked into the darkness to leave Joshua on the outskirts. That was enough to take out of the man everything but his own sense of littleness. What overwhelming awe was his, those of us who have been alone upon the mountain or upon the sea when a mighty storm was raging, may conjecture. Then are we impressed with a deep conviction of God's presence. So also was the lesson of humility learned by Joshua when upon the mountain. It was a lesson for life. No man thereafter could more undividedly carry out the idea that all the success was God's alone.

The next step in his training was to learn how to obey, wherefore he became the servant, the daily attendant of Moses. He learnt the duties which should belong to him as a leader, through being the personal assistant of the leader. And we see why. He did this, not because it gave him a name, but because he needed out of his simple heart to express his love for his master in delighted service. That is the very best in the world that can happen to a man who has in after life to rule and manage others, who had such work as Joshua had to do. It teaches him how to rule, the things that must be done if rule is to be successful. It teaches that the truest service is that done through love, that the ruler's life must be such as to win love and conquer human affection, and that this is the true power of the governor. It was a lesson easily learned by Joshua.

It seems that this teaching of him to obey and to be humble went even still further, and that he was taken away from being a war leader. We do not see him mentioned in the succeeding wars; he stops behind with Moses. This is curious. It makes us think of the wonderful ways of God for him. He was not only to be a warrior, but was to guide the organization of the new national sentiment; the founding of a government. He was to stay with Moses and learn how it was to be done, to make friends with the other leaders, with the other advisers of himself afterwards. Therefore he was now to lay aside his special type of work for the time.

Again, had he alone led the host he might have been jealous of any one afterwards coming near his glory. He was therefore kept in the background for a time. That was an excellent lesson ; he knew the stuff of the men he had to command, and he lost all envy and jealousy of others. He was willing to give others their due, and to consider himself one hero among many. We read in Numbers that he had been jealous with regard to two prophets, and had exhibited the spirit of a martinet. This would have been fatal to his success. As it was, Joshua got rid of all his jealousy and martinet spirit. Not one of the complaints such as we find against Moses seems to have been made against him.

What a lesson is this not to be exclusive to those objects for which you have not a special genius; to retire from those things you do, or think you do, so well, in order to learn the other side of things a little ; to balance and steady your powers, and to do that because you have met some one, like Moses, whose qualities you think higher than your own. This will do wonders for your character, will check the evil and balance the good of your character ; enable you to see others do well the very things you think you do well, and help you to see this without jealousy or opposition. It delights you now to find men excelling in your own special business, for you care now not for your own fame in the thing for which you have a genius, but for the beauty of the thing itself. Self has been wrought out of you. "Would to God," you say, "all men were musicians and poets," because it is music and poetry you care for, and not your own reputation. That is a beautiful temper; it is the highest temper to which an artist can arrive. Though Joshua was removed from generalship for a time, he was learning an invaluable lesson.

He was sent out with eleven others to survey the land in preparation for invasion. With the sending him into the land was linked his future work as conqueror of the land. Moses changed his name. The new name enshrined his destiny,—a prince, a saviour. It was a kind of baptism of the man. Henceforth he knew what he had to do. It was a wonderful thing to have this new tenant in his heart ; and the change of name was but a faint symbol of the marvellous change within him. Just imagine as he went into Canaan, the intensity of his life. He was to conquer the land for the sake of the people, and the thought must have impressed him and given a new life to every act of his character. And it is delightful to picture to oneself the feelings that must have filled him as he went on day by day with the rest of the spies over the fields and villages and cities of the land he was to win, and where his fathers long ago had lived and suffered and died, and which he was permitted by God to conquer again.

Full of enthusiasm he came back, one faithful companion with him sharing in his excitement and courage. Now what happened? Now at the very height of his eagerness all his dreams, all that he had suffered through these forty days, were suddenly dashed and shattered like a Venetian glass. When the people heard of the report of the spies they were fearful. "Would God," said they, "that we had died in the land of Egypt! or would God we had died in the wilderness. And wherefore hath the Lord brought us unto this land, to fall by the sword, that our wives and children should be a prey? Were it not better for us to return into Egypt." That was Joshua's first trial, and truly it was sharp enough. Everything he loved and aspired to were shattered to pieces, and in the bitterness of his disappointment he might have been tempted to give way to their outcry, or to be untrue to the great object of his life. How did the man come out of this? In those times when a man is so tested, we see the real stuff of which he is made. "And they (Joshua and Caleb) spoke unto all the company of the children of Israel, saying, The land which we passed through to reach it is an exceeding good land. If the Lord delight in us, then He will bring us into this land and give it us; a land which floweth with milk and honey." What vigour, what practical faith in God there is in all these words. Now listen to these courageous words: "Only rebel not ye against the Lord, neither fear ye the people of the land, for they are bread for us; their defence is departed from them, and the Lord is with us; fear them not." But the people stoned them.

So the dream was shattered. It was a sorry thing for Joshua. He had to put quietly by his splendid anticipations for many years. But he took two things with him— great courage, which we find in his speech, and great faith in God.

I close with one or two remarks drawn from this. If we

are to do anything in our lives the time comes sooner or later. It came to Joshua, this time, when Moses re-named him and gave him his life work ; it came to David, when he was called to be king over Israel ; and it came to Christ, when he was baptized by John and went into the wilderness ; it came to Wordsworth on that dreary morning among the hills which he saw full of God, and when he was filled with thoughts of God ; it comes to all of us the day we feel, "This is my work, I will do it, God helping me." Our name is, as it were, changed ; we are baptized and consecrated by God. Some among you may be at that moment now. Have you, my brother, counted the cost, lest having taken up the work you leave it incomplete. See what lies before you ; search out the land you are going to conquer, going through it step by step, even as Gideon and the other scouts, finding out the difficulties ; and may the courage and faith you have be such that you shall see "This is prepared for *me*," for I shall be faithful and accomplish my destiny.

Some of you may have begun. How have you done it? Well and bravely, or lazily and fearingly? Having seen the difficulties, have you said in your heart, "Would God that I could get back to Egypt." Take this history as a warning—you will not get back to Egypt. You will wander and die in the wilderness, and as you look back you will know you have been untrue to your inspiration. It may not be so yet, there may be time to save your soul. The call is to-day, when you are baptized into your work, when the dew of its inspiration fills your soul like a summer's garden in the morning, when you hear its voice to you, "This is the way ; walk ye in it," or only if you recall enough to gain an impulse to go forward, thinking of how Joshua conquered, and of how Jesus the great Master rose from the dead with you. Have faith in God as your father, and in the courage of Joshua begin again. Be strong and very courageous, and all the powers of evil will fall before the faith and courage which you will receive from God Himself.

S. B.

XI. The Captain of the Lord's Host. JOSH. v. 13–15.

"*And it came to pass, when Joshua was by Jericho, that he lifted up his eyes and looked, and, behold, there stood a man over against him with his sword drawn in his hand: and Joshua went unto him, and said unto him, Art thou for us, or for our adversaries? And he said, Nay; but as captain of the host of the Lord am I now come. And Joshua fell on his face to the earth, and did worship, and said unto him, What saith my lord unto his servant? And the captain of the Lord's host said unto Joshua, Loose thy shoe from off thy foot; for the place whereon thou standest is holy. And Joshua did so.*"

GOD'S revelations of Himself are always to be shaped by the momentary necessities of the people at the time they are made. They take the form and the pressure of the instant's need, and vary according to the moment's wants. And so here the army of Israel was just beginning a hard struggle, under an untried leader,—Moses had been left behind at Pisgah,—and now they had the Jordan behind them, and in front of them the strong, fortified, and seemingly impregnable city of Jericho, embosomed in the palm trees there; and beyond it, the steep passes and the mountain land they wanted to win. So the soldiers of this army had no doubt their own cares and anxieties, and their leaders would feel the heavy responsibility of the occasion resting upon them; and so their commander seems to have gone away by himself, and to have been brooding, as he had been brooding many a time before, how he was to get into that fortified city up there which barred his progress, and was a menace of defeat and overthrow. And lifting up eyes, as a meditative man will do, not expecting anything, having no prevision of a supernatural visitation, and "lo," as our story has it, he was startled by the appearance of an armed man, standing statuesque and picturesque in close proximity. As I have said, he had no notion of a supernatural vision; mundane affairs were filling his mind, he has no preparation for anything of the sort, but with true soldier-like courage and promptitude, he strides up to him with the quick challenge; "Who do you belong to; are you one of us, or do you belong to them from the city there?" And then the hitherto silent lips uttered the answer, "I do not belong to you, you belong to me ; as Captain of the host of the Lord am I come up." And then down upon his knees Joshua bends before him and recognises that he himself is only second in command, and that this is the true Captain and Leader of the people. "What does my Lord say to thy servant?" "Put off thy shoes from off thy feet, and then listen and I will tell thee how this Jericho shall be taken." Without wasting your time with talk about this being legend or hallucination, or anything of that sort, and taking the story as we find it, with many large and valuable truths in it, I select one or two thoughts from it, and first of all I want to bring out more distinctly the profound significance of the person and the office of this Captain of the host of the Lord.

Notice that in this story, for whatsoever reason, there is a strange blending together of the two elements, humanity and divinity, the apparent humanity,—distinct and separate from divinity,—and yet claiming the Divine attribute. The speaker as the Captain of the host of the Lord, does not distinctly say that the host is his, and yet he is the Captain of the host that obeys the injunction of Jehovah himself. And then you find him in the subsequent portion of the narrative, speaking as endowed with the full power of Jehovah, and recognised by the obedience of the Leader of Israel as being thus invested, and his word identified with the word of the Lord, and his commandment with the commandment of God Himself. And you find still further that in the very page there come these words—"The Captain of the Lord's host said unto Joshua, Loose thy shoe from off thy foot; for the place whereon thou standest is holy ground."

Holy, because he was there. Another thing. "Loose thy shoes" are a quotation. When the angel of the Lord appeared in the burning bush in the wilderness, these were the words that were spoken—"Loose thy shoes from off thy feet." So far the story carries these points. A singular apparent identification with divinity, and a singular apparent separation from it. But the quotation from the story of the appearance to Moses carries us a step further. We are to recognise in this same human figure, armed and commanding, that figure which appeared to Moses in the flame of fire out of the bush. If you will turn to that story, you will find that in it the speaker is called the angel of the Lord, and that this angel of the Lord is spoken of with an elevation of tone, and an unhesitating application to him of Divine prerogative and functions, which separate him altogether from the hosts of created existences which stand before His throne who "maketh His angels spirits, and His ministers a flame of fire." And then that opens out the great wide door as to that old, difficult, and remarkable subject, as to the meaning and dignity and personality of the figure that appears glancing all through the Old Testament from Genesis to Malachi, the angel of the Lord. Let us glance at one or two brief quotations. I should ask you, then, to think of this first, the words of the dying patriarch when "he blessed Joseph, and said, God, before whom my fathers Abraham and Isaac did walk, the God which fed me all my life long unto this day, the *Angel which redeemed* me from all evil, bless the lads." In one benediction and invocation "the God which fed me all my life long," and "the angel which redeemed me from all evil," are incorporated. Then there is that to which I have already referred,—the appearance in the burning bush to Moses. And then there is another one: "The angel of the Lord encampeth round about them that fear Him, and delivereth them." There is a strange blending of the reverence for divinity, and the protection of some mysterious person,—the angel of the Lord. And then hear the commentary which one of the later prophets makes upon this strange story about Jacob wrestling with the man concerning whom he said, "I have seen God, and my life is preserved." Hosea said he had power over the angel and prevailed; he found him in Bethel, "and there he spoke to us, even the Lord God of hosts." And then the last of all the prophets of the old covenant, who gathers up into one so many of the threads that run through the whole series, seems to put upon it the top stone when he says, "Behold, I will send my messenger, and he shall prepare the way before me: and the Lord, whom ye seek, shall suddenly come to His temple, even the messenger of the covenant, whom ye delight in," etc.

And now put that altogether,—and there is a great deal more than that,—and it seems to me that the answer to the question, Who is this mysterious creature that from the beginning to the end of the earlier revelation,—parted from, and yet united with, the Divine name and nature,—whom the prophet Isaiah calls " the angel of the face " ; that the answer to the question, Who is he ? the answer is that it is *The Eternal Word* that from the beginning was the agent of all Divine revelation, and who from the first manifested the Father's glory. And in these mysterious, evanescent, merely apparent assumptions of the human form and human speech, was giving, as it were, a kind of preludings, and far-off preparations of that great, full, and perfect revelation of His, when " the Word became flesh and dwelt amongst us." And so I think the answer to the question,—who is the Angel of the Covenant? is, He who in the fulness of time,—made of a woman, made under the law,—came to redeem them that were under the law.

There is another point before I come to the more practical teaching of this story, and that is, what I call the office and functions of this Captain of the Lord's host. Whether you accept the idea that this is a Divine personal activity, or whether you believe that it is simply some created person or servant of the uncreated Divine power; it remains the same—the Captain of the hosts of the Lord. And what are these hosts ? That little camp of the Israelites amongst the palm trees there ? Surely not. Is it the other camp which one of the patriarchs saw in his vision; as the narrative says, in its archaic simplicity, " The angels of the Lord met him, and he called the place Mahanaim "—that is, " two camps ; " my little camp down here ? that great one up in the heavens ? There is included these personal existences dimly revealed which seem to gather round about us, but there is gathered in it all the forces of the universe, which is not chaos,— as the old Hebrews had found out long before natural science and philosophy had found it out,—but all obeying the Divine impulse and finger of the will that had created them ; thus, the stars in their courses, the seasons in their succession and order, the stormy winds, the dragons in the great deeps, every creature in the whole universe except those who by rebellious wills have run away from the fair order. These are the hosts, of whom this is the Captain.

It seems to me, that none else or other than He, of whom

in later days it was said, "All things were made by Him, and without Him was not anything made that was made," was fit to rule with his Commander's truncheon the mighty forces and embattled hosts of the universe, viz. Christ as the King, the King of kings, the Lord of lords, the Lord of nature, the Lord of angels, for they must be included, the Lord and Ruler of all that are, and they serve His purposes as Captain of the Lord's hosts! And then if this be anything like the true—howsoever inadequate—interpretation of the words before us I need not more than prompt you of how these thoughts are in immediate anticipation of great New Testament thoughts; Christ is the Prince of Peace. Yes, but Christ said, "I came not to bring peace upon earth, but a sword;" and His peace is first of all righteousness, and not until the righteousness is secured is the peace proclaimed. His name, which is Jesus, is the same as the Captain and Leader in our story,—Joshua who led the people through many a hard fought field to victory; and the Captain of the New Testament salvation shall lead men through many a struggle and difficulty and wavering hesitation and critical conjuncture, safe over the beleaguered cities that stand in opposing strength thickly round our path, right through to the Heavenly Jerusalem beyond. His warfare is the exhibition of His love, His gentleness, His forgiveness, and His healing, in the face of all the powers of evil that set themselves against Him. And so Christ is the warlike Christ, warring a merciful warfare that knows no peace because it is righteousness. And so with this interpretation of the significance of the person and function that is set before us in this vision.

And now I will try to put as simply as I can one or two broad lessons that come for all time out of this incident. Its significance in that petty incident in the history of the world has long since been exhausted; and if it were only for the sake of this people this incident happened it would not be worth my while to consider it, but we must disengage these principles from the mere transitory things of which they are the revelation. So notice how this attitude of the mysterious person, of the angel of the Lord, carries with it great and everlasting truths upon which you and I may lean our whole weight. There are two different ways in which I look upon this incident: one of them, the great warfare that is always going on in this world between God and the devil; and the other, the narrower one, the battle-ground of which is my own heart, and the combatants are Christ and my own worldly lusts. And so with regard to the first thing, that He Himself, Jesus Christ, in no metaphor, in no exaggerated figure, in no mere influence of His patient action; but by present helpfulness and present work takes part in the perennial fight that is going on in this world between good and evil, and strikes on the side of good. You remember that grand vision with which the gospel stories end, of the Lord lifted up in heaven; and how one of the evangelists puts it in its most picturesque form when he says, "He was lifted up and put on the right hand of God." What a strange contrast this! Is this Captain gone to some safe distance, and watching the fight down in the valley below, while the men are struggling with grim death—Himself with no smell of gunpowder on Him. Is that the kind of leader? God forbid. They went forth and preached everywhere, the Lord working with them and confirming the word with signs following. Them down here, Him up yonder, breathing His influence over the field everywhere. The old legend that many a one has been strengthened with, of the two pale horsemen who had charged at the head of the soldiers on the plain of Marathon, all of these are but adumbrations of the truth that wherever a man for Christ's sake strikes out against any kind of evil or abomination, he may be sure that he has Christ at his side. And how much soever we may feel that the work is nothing, and that all the talents that guide a wise and benevolent man are counteracted by the tendencies of human nature, do not let us be downhearted and disappointed; it is only the false appearance of things. The kingdoms *will* become the kingdoms of our God and His Christ; and His help is not in vain and it is said truly of this, as is untruly said about another kind of conflict, that this battle, "though baffled oft is ever won." Christ clashes His sword down into the scale; that outweighs everything else. And you, weak man or woman, if you stand by yourself and the world against you, if you can say "Jesus Christ and I," you and He would be in the majority, and your labour is not in vain in the Lord. So Christian man and woman, and all of you that in any way are helping on that great cause, be of good cheer, and do not only look at these high battlements of that Jericho there, but lift up your eyes and behold the Captain of the hosts of the Lord. Take up your weapons and He will bring you victory. And so the same thoughts, with a brief and slight modification, apply to the other department in which that same metaphor is placed. Jesus Christ has fought all that fight that you and I have got to fight. No man can front a temptation which does not appeal to the experience and the memory of Him who began His career by facing the wilderness and the devil, and ended His career on the cross, which was an intense superlative of all temptations. And so when we come into the fight with the cavillings of our own hearts, when we try to get the mastery of our own passions, and to resist the temptations that beset us round about; and when we begin to discover, after being beaten so often, how little strength we have of ourselves, let us think of Him who served in the ranks before He became commander, and who knows all about the battle, and do not go into the fight at your own charge. Do not fancy that your own firm resolution will enable you to repel temptation; do not think that your own strength, or motives drawn from your own person, will be ever adequate to make you a conqueror in the fight with lust, and passion, and sense, and self, and earth, and the devil. You have not done it in the past—you will not do it in the future. Jericho will stand untouched as far as you are concerned unless you put yourself into His ranks, the ranks of the Captain of the hosts of the Lord. Be Christ's soldiers and servants, and do not attempt a campaign in your own strength, or there is nothing before you except shame and defeat; but rather as this Joshua here, "What saith my Lord unto His servant?" And you will get all the reply you want, and as you want it, and in the shape and at the time you need it, until at last you will be able to say, "Now unto Him that has made us more than conquerors, unto Him be praise and honour and glory for ever." And He will fulfil the promise that He has made to us all, "To him that overcometh will I grant to sit with Me in My throne, even as I, the Captain and Leader, overcame, and am set down with My Father in His throne." Amen.

XII. **Barak's Faith.** JUD. iv. 9. *"And she said, I will surely go with thee: notwithstanding the journey that thou takest shall not be for thine honour; for the Lord shall sell Sisera into the hand of a woman."*

BARAK, to whom these words are spoken, is mentioned by name in the epistle to the Hebrews amongst the heroes of faith. It is not quite easy at first sight to see the reason for this selection. Who and what was Barak, as the Old Testament paints him, that he should have a place given him in the other half of the Bible, that half of the Bible which tells of life and immortality brought to light by the gospel? To answer this question we must look below the surface of the story, and then we shall see that in the personal insignificance of Barak lies the very reason of his everlasting renown. It is very interesting to fasten, in reading the books of the Old Testament, upon those shadows cast before by coming events and future revelations, which show the one Hand and the one Mind in the composition of the book. Although revelation is always progressive in its disclosures, and although as the Epistle to the Hebrews says, God spake in old times to the fathers in many parts and portions, rather than in full completeness, and although this method was essential to the education and intention of all God's dealings, with the race as well as with the man, still it pleased Him to give here and there glimmerings and glimpses from the very beginning of the meridian Gospel-day; enough, at least, to attest the continuity of the revelation and the divinity of the Revealer. Instances of this are very common. We have an example of it in the two chapters before us. And it is the more seasonable, perhaps, to notice it, because infidelity, sometimes clever, but always superficial and ignorant in its treatment of Scripture, has fixed upon the story of Sisera, and notably upon the panegyric of Sisera in the Song of Deborah, as one of the most assailable points in the Bible; and therefore it is particularly desirable to call attention, as far as it can be done with truth, to beautiful points and traits in the actions and characters here set before us. It ought to be sufficient, so far as the taunt to which I have referred is concerned, to remind ourselves that there is no assertion whatever in the Bible of the inspiration of the song of Deborah: "Blessed above women shall Jael the wife of Heber the Kenite be, blessed shall she be above women." The chant may have been nothing more than the pæan of a patriot over the deed which had set her country free; it may, for anything told us in the Bible, have been no more prophetic utterance than the counsel of Balak which taught Balaam to cast a snare and deadly seduction before the children of Israel; for anything contrary to good morals in that burst of eloquent song, the Bible, and the God of the Bible, is no more responsible than for those terrible lapses of the Royal Psalmist, of which this is the solemn closing estimate, on the part of the Bible and its Author—"But the thing which David had done displeased the Lord."

There is probably a deeper principle of interpretation involved in the question, namely, that in the field of morals itself, the revelation of God and the inspiration of God have not been precipitate, but gradual.

Two revelations, certainly, avowedly waited for Christ Himself. The one was the revelation of immortality, and the other was the revelation of charity. Of both these, shadows were cast before. Saints walking closely with God had in them the instinct of immortality; saints walking mostly in God had in them the struggling, flickering light of charity. David could say, "I will behold Thy face in righteousness, and when I awake up in Thy likeness I shall be satisfied." And David could say, in the far-off retrospect of his chequered and past youth, "Is there not any of the house of Saul, that I may show the kindness of God unto him?" These were rays and voices from the excellent glory, showing that above and beyond the clouds of human passion and ignorance, there was already and always a bright light in heaven. But these glimpses were by their nature exceptional and intermittent. As a rule, courage was then a higher virtue than patience, devotion than forgiveness, patriotism than charity. Let us, brethren, who have received the Christian revelation concerning these things, look to it that we lose not the stronger and sturdier virtues in the easy flatteries and the plausible compromises of a loose and flexible Christianity.

The spirit of Deborah, in its very heartiness, may still teach us something—something which shall nerve the arm for what Scripture calls "the resistance unto blood" in striving against sin, while it may lend its energy to that most excellent grace, charity, out of which whosoever liveth is dead before his time; it can never be superfluous to take off the edge of a moral difficulty in the paths of Divine revelation. The parade of such difficulties before minds unused to thoughtful inquiry, keeps thousands and tens of thousands of our countrymen from the very porch and vestibule of God's Word. Probably no argument, certainly no reproaches, will avail much for the reinstatement in faith and worship of men who have once admitted, willingly or unwillingly, the cruel objection, the more cruel sneer, the most cruel jest of an ingenious and industrious infidelity. These we must, by any or by all means, in duty and in mercy, endeavour to rescue; and while here and there, by the grace of God, our efforts will be crowned with success, yet that success will rather be in the providential dealings of the Invisible with the lives and hearts of men, which they will then know must bow before a power and a love which cannot always be evaded or trifled with, and which will make them in the end confess in secret in their found-out soul—"Yes, there are mysteries in religion which I cannot fathom, but the mystery of mysteries is my own being. Yes, there are difficulties, moral difficulties, if you will call them so; contradictions, discrepancies, if you will call them so; but the difficulty of difficulties is how to be good and how to be happy, and the contradiction of contradictions is the conflict between inclination and duty, between the life which must die and the life which cannot die. And, under the stress of this divided and distracted condition, I must and will put it to the proof, the personal proof. Perhaps there is for me a Father in heaven; a Father whom to know is to solve a problem; a Father who will perhaps explain Himself one day, but whom, if He never explains Himself, I shall seek and I shall serve and I shall love still. We come back to the text, and to a few brief lessons for ourselves from the actions of the characters before us. In an age and season of perpetual unrest, how refreshing to our spirits to have before us some example, albeit in the remote past, of a judge who could dwell under the palm tree between Ramah and Bethel, and to whom the children of Israel could go up for judgment. Were it only a picture in contrast and contrariety to a possible present, I would not tantalize you by exhibiting it. Who does not yearn and pant for rest—for a pause at least—an interlude of quietness? Who does not complain, whose countenance does not bear the mark either of excitement or else of fatigue? The age in which our lot is cast has determined not to waive its activities; the man who can crowd the greatest number of engagements into one day is, with us, the diligent and industrious man. Every office, every dignity up to the very highest, is measured and judged by the scale of hours given to business, by the multitude and the multifariousness of its separate things done. Brethren, it is an unfair and unrighteous judgment. Nothing is easier than to live a life all in sight and all in evidence. The difficult thing is to live any other: to have no solitude and no privacy suits that spiritual indolence, at all events, which is in all of us by nature. If, in addition to incurring no blame, we can often get praise for a life lived all in sight of the sun, this redeems the conscience from its sense of one relation, the highest and holiest of all, being left unfulfilled and unrealized, adding that pleasantest sensation of all, the being compassioned for neglect of duty, till at last the man loses the very power of repose, of so much as the enjoying a holiday, and the whole being becomes that external, that superficial, thing which has no yesterday and no to-morrow, certainly no remembrance of any Divine Rock from which it was hewn or any Divine source to which it must eventually return. You may say indeed that the life lived under the palm tree between Bethel and Ramah must have been fearfully monotonous, utterly without incident, mentally as well as physically stagnant, also that it is idle to draw lessons from a state of things quite impossible now. What would a judge or a bishop be thought of in these days who should try to act on that principle? Few men, it may be urged, are capable of profiting by leisure, even if they could find it. The practical life is at all events useful; it lays the axe at the root of many kinds of sin. Let us admit all this, yet let us bewail for a moment the accompanying ease. If the right kind of men, and but a few of them, could be set free to think, to advise, to originate, to counsel, what a gain would this be to a people laden with care, full of intellectual and spiritual perplexities, and feeling themselves terribly alone in a difficult and embarrassing way! For lack of this many lives go utterly astray and many minds are wrecked on the shoals and sand-banks of doubt. It might be said that the two influences of action and thought are commonly kept distinct in the present state of things, and those that want counsel have no lack of help from an innumerable crowd of helpers. Unhappily the thinkers are too much isolated from action, so that they run into vain and profitless speculation, having no help for this life nor hope for that which is to come. The moral of it all is: Busy men, snatch moments of reflection. Even if these are rare moments, if well used, they will fertilize, will tranquillize, will consecrate the long hours of toil. When you die your life will not vanish like the lives of those who neither feared God nor regarded man; they will have left a sweet memory behind them, and they themselves will pass naturally into the heavenly rest which remaineth.

The second thought is the true place and dignity of woman. We see it here in the positive and in the negative. Deborah was a prophetess: God spake to her; she saw within and beneath the appearance of things. That is a prophet. She did not allow the visible to crush out the invisible. She was not appalled by the nine hundred chariots of iron: she did not feel that King Jabin and his great general were invincible because for twenty years they mightily oppressed the children of Israel. She saw through these, and knew still that there was a God in Israel who rules in the kingdom of man, and who, though He tarries long and sometimes sets up over nations the basest of rulers, can yet be called on by prayer, and in the long run will make it to be well with the righteous. Deborah was a prophetess, and the spirit which I have tried to describe is the spirit of prophecy. Having it, she was, as a matter of course, an influence in her generation. Men who sought her for judgment doubtless went away the better for having seen her. In a great emergency she obtained that influence. She called Barak to her, set him his task, assured him of his commission, and even consented at his request to accompany him on his march. This was heroic, but it was also feminine: Deborah did not assume the command of the army; she was the influence, she was the inspiration, but she left the leadership and the generalship to another. Not for nothing have we the record of another woman on the same page with that of Deborah. We shrink instinctively from the false dealing and the bloodstained hand of Jael; she has overstepped the line between the feminine and masculine—nay, between the enthusiast and the fanatic. That impassioned cry, "Blessed above women," has never found an echo, and never could have found an echo, in any evangelical heart; that cry has given care and pain and trouble to many champions of revelation. We cannot receive it as the voice of God's Spirit, except in some modified and softened sense in which it hails, and justly hails, the victory, however soiled and damaged, of the alone moral theistic nation as a victory in the long run, and in a large view, of the cause of progress, the cause of development and therefore, in some sense, the cause of mankind and of the world. But the chapter teaches us that woman is to be content with that honour and dignity which God has made hers. Influence is hers, inspiration may be hers, alike to the sword of Barak and the nail and the hammer of Jael. God rarely puts into one hand both influence and power; those who grasp at the latter usually lose the former. Influence in one sense indeed, is power, but it means the moral, social, spiritual power only.

One last thought occurs, and it might seem on first hearing to conflict with the foregoing, but it is not so. Deborah says to Barak, "Hath not the Lord God of Israel commanded?" and he replies to her, "If thou wilt go with me then I will go; but if thou wilt not go with me, then I will not go." She rejoins yet again, "I will surely go with thee; notwithstanding the journey that thou takest shall not be for thine honour, for the Lord shall sell Sisera into the hand of a woman." We are not concerned with the last phrase, "The Lord shall *sell* Sisera into the hands of a woman." The Scripture writers see the hand of God everywhere. They go so far as to say, "Shall there be evil in a city, and the Lord hath not done it?" That distinction, important in its place, which we make so commonly between the ruling and overruling, was merged for Scripture writers in the one thought of the Divine empire and omnipotence. "What!" they ask, or seem to ask, as a pregnant question, "Can God do anything certainly, except He do all things really?" Thus, if the hostile general bows and falls at the feet of a Jewish assassin, they say, "The Lord delivered Sisera; the Lord sold Sisera into her hand." The overruling is for them an agency. They are not afraid of any cavilling; for them it is so.

But the thought before us is different. What was the character, the differentia of the faith of Barak, that the epistle to the Hebrews should single him out for mention? And we find it here in the self-forgetfulness of Barak in doing God's work. What if one woman set him on it, and another woman is to finish it? What if the journey he took was not to be for his own honour—should that stop him? What will the troops say if they see a woman marching by his side; if they see him consulting her for his tactics; if they hear him confess that she is his monitress and superior? Shall that not deter? No. It is God's cause; God's honour, not his, is the thing to be aimed at. Here is faith forgetting itself in the cause of God. Brethren, it is a grand heroism; for lack of it much good work is spoiled, and much more is left undone. It may be a matter of controversy whether a Wilberforce or a Clarkson was earlier in the field against the slave-trade. The workmen of God do not fight about these things. There is a phrase which is often used of God's agents; they are called "humble instruments." Yet this same modest disclaimer asserts the instrumentality. Propose to omit the name from the subscription list, from the list of patrons, where will the humble instrument be then? "The journey which thou takest shall not be for thine honour;" no, for one woman suggested it, and another woman was to complete it. What then? Faith is willing to have it so, for faith is the sight of the invisible, and rests on an invisible power. He that speaketh of himself seeketh his own glory, but he that seeketh His glory that sent him is true, and no unrighteousness is in him. What shall I more say? The time would fail to tell of the faith of Barak, who took a journey not for his own honour; who obeyed the call of a woman saying, "Hath not God commanded?" and left to another woman the last stroke of victory.

Brethren, let us do the prescribed portion; small and poor if it be, it is better for the like of us; let us do the little portion set us of the world-wide and age-long work of God, and then fall asleep in the spirit of one who wrote these last words in his diary the night before he was suddenly called home to be no more seen: "There are works which by God's permission I would do before the night cometh, but, above all, let me mind my own personal work, keep myself pure and zealous and believing, labour to do God's will, yet not anxious that it should be done by me rather than by others, if God disapproves of my doing it." Be this our spirit in life and in death, and toil itself shall be rest ere the long rest comes!

C. J. V.

XIII. Ruth and Boaz. RUTH i. 22. *"And they came to Bethlehem in the beginning of barley harvest."*

YOU will not expect a meagre abbreviation of the beautiful story of Ruth. It seems to me that a preacher who would attempt anything of the kind would act like one who, standing on the outskirts of a forest, and had seen the glory of the wintry sunset gleaming through the branches, should then take a few dry sticks from the trees as a specimen of the glories he had witnessed. I assume that you know the beautiful story of the Book of Ruth, and I shall only attempt to draw some of the chief moral and spiritual lessons which appear to me to pervade it.

I. In the first place it seems to me that the Book of Ruth exhibits to us an eternal law of God's kingdom. I mean that, in the worst and darkest times of the Church, God has had His own people. We are led directly to this law by the objection which has been made to the story of the Book of Ruth, that such sweet and genuine piety is utterly inconceivable in the dark and stormy times of the Judges. But if you bear in mind the truth that the very purpose of the Book of Judges is to trace out the law of retaliation, and to show how national sin is connected with national punishment, you will see why such narratives of exceptional piety like that of Ruth should be excluded. But there is a more satisfactory answer in the fact that ever since God had a Church on earth true spiritual religion has never been utterly extinguished. Faith can always say with the Apostle that there is "a remnant according to the election of grace." When God's holy dove is driven from cities and the abodes of men, that bird of sweetest note can be heard singing in remote places, even in dens and in the clefts of the rocks.

And consider for one moment how this law has been exhibited from time to time in our own Church of England. It seems to me to be a great mistake to suppose that spiritual religion totally disappeared 150 years ago, until it was as if accidentally discovered by some excellent men in the suburbs of London about seventy years since. Just take two instances in the history of the Church of England. Take the reign and court of Charles II. There are many who will remember that wonderful picture of the last Sunday in the Church, when the gallery was filled with boys, singing lewd songs, and the king was to be seen playing with a group of dissipated companions. Yet even here the life of Mary Godolphin was hidden with Christ in God. She walked through the fire, and there was not so much as the smell of it upon her raiment. Even here she lived according to rules simple and direct, and which many would find as useful in a London suburb as they were to her.

Or, again, when we come to the Georgian era, and light upon certain histories written as if in vitriolic acid. No doubt there is enough darkness about them, and we light upon clerical slanders rather than upon the souls of men being cared for, and of dioceses being superintended. Yet even at this darkest period there was one on whose face men saw a glow. Bishop Butler was sent to preside over the see of Durham, while in remote places of England there were men of the stamp of the Wesleys. The soil may be ever so rank, the spiritual atmosphere ever so unwholsome, but still the Apostle's words remain, " His seed abideth "— abideth in him that is in God. Never has the Church been so dead but that the voice may be heard which said of Sardis, " Thou hast a few names even in Sardis which have not defiled their garments ; and they shall walk before Me in white : for they are worthy."

Now of this great law, the survival of holiness, we

have a beautiful instance in the Book of Ruth. You will observe that the Bible in this respect differs from all our preconceived notions. History, it is sometimes said, is a pall covering dead men's bones; but at least it covers them gracefully. The king shows off gracefully in the hands of some great master of the art, so does the statesman who claims for himself a sort of Divine right of always acting with the majority. As we frame history it is all perfect and sublime. It should be a passing on of saints and martyrs with a cross on their shoulders, and a crown on their brow, to the throne of glory. But as God has framed history, how different it is! Its every page is stained and blistered—stained with blood and blistered with tears. And of this feature in Old Testament history, the Book of Judges is an example. The Divine narrative closes with a sigh. "In those days there was no king in Israel; every man did that which was right in his own eyes."

Now, over against all this stands the Book of Ruth, in which the characters are drawn in simple life. An air of truthfulness and reality pervades the book. In support of this I need only remind you of the beautiful language of Naomi with regard to Ruth herself. I find a German critic saying that "Ruth is not a marked character." But is that a real objection? What is the true and high ideal of woman? Is she simply a thing of nerves and bones? Is it for her to wash the wounds of pain, or to minister in old age, and in daily sickness? We entwine the memory of a woman dear to us with sickness and suffering relieved.

Ruth embraces the true religion with her whole heart. Boaz sees that she has come to put her trust under the wings of the Lord God of Israel, not a young proselyte caught by those who wish to entrap her. She comes with her whole heart, and that heart a broken one. She is the type of the Gentile Church, she is the firstfruits of that great multitude of all nations, and kindreds, and tribes, who have been drawn to the Cross. Then you notice another thing after Naomi has addressed her daughters-in-law; "Orpah kissed her mother-in-law, but Ruth clave unto her." We all know how much these little gushing tokens of affection mean in sweet-mannered women. Truth, propriety, affection, these are the old combined virtues that formed the character of Ruth.

Then we have Boaz. There have been times when the young have needed encouragement, and it is well to encourage those even who are growing old. The voice of a philosopher reminds us that the work of the world is done by the young, that the golden decade is between thirty and forty, that men as they grow older become lost to enthusiasm and to faith. Now the words of Boaz have a Bible tinge, and his memory is haunted by Bible echoes. "And, behold, Boaz came from Bethlehem, and said unto the reapers, The Lord be with you. And they answered him, The Lord bless thee." Think of that beautiful service in the harvest field! It is no exaggeration to say that some one might come into Westminster Abbey, and when the last light of day is stealing in through the clerestory, when the priest says, " The Lord be with you," and the choir responds, "And with Thy Spirit," you may catch the echo of words once spoken during the barley harvest of Bethlehem."

II. We may learn a lesson on the law of social life. There is throughout the book a constant reference to the Levitical law. There is the "goel," the redeeming kinsman. But I wish you specially to observe the beneficence of the law. I wish that some who speak of the barbarous character of the old law would take their Bibles and read the 18th chapter of Leviticus. You will there see that God ordained that a portion should be reserved for the poor and the stranger. The law gave a measure of wealth to the indigent. It solved in this way one of the most terrible problems of our modern society. While it did this there was an ample margin left for the exercise of private charity. The corner of the field was defined to mean a portion that in modern language would have been a poor-rate of fourpence in the pound. It was not a system of outdoor relief, for the Book of Ruth shows us that there was great delicacy to be observed in giving. There is a difference between the alms you fling and the present you give. And thus there is a moral even in children's presents. But I think it should be observed in favour of the old Levitical law that this England never found out till the reign of Queen Elizabeth the difference between the pauper and the vagabond, the difference between misfortune and crime. Depend upon it, as the spirit of the Old Testament works, the bitter taunt will become less and less true that England is a paradise for the rich and a purgatory for the poor.

III. There is an Evangelical law connecting this book of the Old Testament with Christ Jesus our Lord. Perhaps, in modern times, we have heard too much of Ruth as an idyll, and too little of it as a sacred book of the inspired canon. We have been called on to see her as she appeared to the poet Keats, too little as she appeared to St. Matthew linked in the genealogy of Jesus Christ. We cannot dispense with the genealogies of the New Testament. They do not consist simply of long lists of difficult names, but contain something far beyond. Over and over again, in some layer of the soil, the naturalist finds traces of animals now extinct; yet give him one vertebra, and he will form the entire structure. So these names, which may at first appear only cold petrifactions, only want an interpreter to start them into a new life. I need not remind you that Bethlehem is connected with history and prophecy again and again. In Psalm xxxii. 6, 7, we seem to hear echoes from the old Church, singing "Venite adoremus." Then there is that old strain again in the beginning of the Book of Micah, and you will remember it in connection with the histories of Saul and the death of Rachel. Yes, and in Bethlehem was the birth of Him who made it the most celebrated place of all except Calvary. As we hear of Bethlehem what do we think of? Of the mystery of the Virgin's womb, of that true humanity which was born there like unto us in form and feature, like us in all but sin, and by the mystery of that Holy Incarnation each one may find pardon and peace.

IV. Lastly, we learn the law which pervades the life of every true believer. The Book of Ruth may be an idyll, but it is an idyll seen in a Divine light. Those two boys that had been taken from the widowed mother early—have we never seen one in middle life like Naomi, with her hair flecked with grey, and who, when she speaks, can but say, "Call me not Naomi; call me Mara, for the Almighty hath dealt very bitterly with me"? No doubt the history is given us because it is a specimen of the Divine guidance of the believer's life. We may learn that our lives are not random things, and that there is no such thing as chance about the Christian's life. This story of Ruth, like every story of the highest sort, would lead us to perfect trust in Him who wants His own dear children to lift up their hands to Him when in darkness. They must wrestle in the darkness before they can face the sunrise. God seems to keep silence when we pray. We ask, and God seems not to give us the things for which we pray. Ah! but He gives us far better. There are some who may pray for their Mahlon and Chilion. They may have asked for the life of their children, and God answered the prayer by giving them a long life—even life for ever and ever. And some Ruth here has prayed for one dearer than life, and he has gone down in youth and beauty, and now the grass waves over him, for God has taken him. And then, as time has gone by, she has found a refuge under the eternal wings, a home that shall not pass away. Amidst all weariness she can sing,—

> "Be the day weary or be the day long,
> It ringeth at last to even-song."

W. A.

XIV. David. 2 Sam. xii 7. "*Thou art the man.*"

EACH of us has but one life in this world, a life of infinite possibilities, alike for blessedness and for ruin. The stake at issue is so tremendous, that every human life, in its struggle against destiny, has in it the elements of the grandest tragedy.

> "Lo, 'tis a gala night! Amidst
>   The lonesome later years,
> An angel throng, bewinged, bedight
>   With robes, and bathed in tears,
> Sit in a theatre to see
>   A play of hopes and fears,
> While the orchestra plays fitfully
>   The music of the spheres."

Out of the pages of Scripture, with the exception of two poets, Dante and Shakespeare, it has rarely been given to any mortal man to indicate anything like the elements of awfulness and pathos, of beauty or of deadliness, which may lie in the story of any man. That story is scarcely ever truly told. There are but two autobiographies in the world—the Confessions of St. Augustine and the Confessions of Rousseau—which the world has taken as the genuine efforts of any man to exhibit himself as he really was. Biographies written by others are rarely more than a record of mere external events. It has happened to us, I dare say, sometimes to read the biography of a man whom we knew very well in life, and in doing so we may generally see that the deepest elements of the man's life, as we knew them, have been untouched. There has been no attempt to explain the outward manifestations; the keynote of all the discords and all the harmonies has after all been never struck. The fact that in the Scriptures, we have the lives of men written truthfully, and in their essence, however briefly, gives to the Bible no little of its strange power. It holds up the mirror to nature, and shows us human souls as they really were, with none of the falsities, none of the suppressions, none of the exaggerated eulogy and the tedious triviality of modern biographies. It goes to the heart of human life. It pronounces with sovereign finality the one decision: "He did that which was good," or "he did that which was evil, in the sight of the Lord."

We may mention three men in particular, of whom full and detailed records are given to us. Each of them marked a great epoch: each of them was a representative man: they were Moses, David, and St. Paul. We may be sure that there were deep reasons why these men should have been set apart, to occupy, with their story and with their writings, so large a space in the Holy Book. We will glance at some of the facts in the life of one of them,—David. Perhaps it may throw light on some truths respecting sin, and penitence, and pardon.

We see the son of Jesse, first, a beautiful, innocent, noble boy, with boundless capabilities for a holy and happy life. A thousand such have been born into the world, with bodies of perfect health and symmetry, with minds of quick intelligence, with spirits capable of being attuned to the sweetest melodies of heaven. Thousands of boys have been born into this world, for whom the design of God—until they themselves, aided by the fraud and subtlety of the devil, or man, have fatally marred it—was, that they should grow in wisdom, and stature, and in favour with God and man; that they should prove a blessing to themselves, and to the world into which they have been born; that their path should be as the path of the just, as a shining light that shineth more and more unto the perfect day. Moses, the goodly child drawn from the reeds of the river, was such a boy. Joseph, pure in the furnace of trial, was such a boy. Samuel, called in the night-watches, before the light of the Temple had yet gone out, was such a boy. Daniel, simple, temperate, holy, in the midst of a cruel and corrupt court, was such a boy. John the Baptist, the stern, strong prophet of the wilderness, was such a boy. St. Benedict, and St. Francis, and St. Bernard were such boys. And these, and many others, have grown up into brave and godly men, in city or in wilderness, in prison or on the throne; through evil report or good report, they have held fast, even to the end, the purity and the glory of the human life which God had given them. We ask of one who has shown such early promise,—

> "And has that early hope been crowned with truth?
> Has he fulfilled the promise of his youth?
> And borne untainted, through the world's wide field,
> Virtue's white wreath, and Honour's stainless shield?"

Yes, sometimes he has. None of these, indeed,—not Moses, or Joseph, or David, or St. Bernard, or St. Benedict, or any one of them,—was perfect: the world has seen but one sinless boy, and one sinless man—the Lord Jesus Christ. And so far is sinlessness from ensuring that earthly prosperity, of which most men think most of all, and for which they spend their strength, and even sell their souls, in vain, that the one life of perfect holiness which alone the world has seen, ended amid taunts, and gibes, and howls of execration, from priest, and Pharisee, and mob, upon the bitter cross. Men usually fix upon the outer facts of life as being of its essence. Ah! let us learn the value of this estimate.

> "'Tis not the whole of life to live,
> Nor all of death to die."

Every life, the good as well as the bad, has its necessary martyrdom: the only important thing is, *how* the martyrdom was caused. There are God's martyrs, content in the very fire, to whom the heavens open amid all their toil and anguish from a sinful and unregenerate world. There are the devil's martyrs, who, swallowing his gilded bait, are rent by his lacerating hook, and whom he lays contemptuously on the ground to gasp and die. There are those who die by their self-inflicted martyrdom, the souls who sell themselves, the multitudes who commit moral suicide by the edge or the poison of the passions, which, instead of mastering, they encourage. There are the martyrdoms of healing retribution, those whom God makes sick with smiting, but only that they may repent, and who, even in the drowning waters, seize hold of His saving hand.

It is to this last class that David belongs. He fell grievously, and he was chastised, because he was a son. He sinned, and he suffered. He was saved, indeed, but it was so as by fire. We see him, first, a happy boy amid his sheep-folds, in the glow of health, the dew on his gracious golden hair, the fresh wind of the wilderness in his ruddy cheek, as he faithfully performs his narrow duties, and, with the dauntlessness of a pure heart, slays the lion and the bear. And as he thus fed his flock like a shepherd, afar from cities, their strife, their squalor, their temptations, desiring nothing but the yellow dates from the palm-tree and the water from the brook, he felt and sang: "The Lord is my Shepherd; I shall not want. He maketh me to lie down in green pastures; He leadeth me beside the still waters. He restoreth my soul; He leadeth me in the paths of righteousness for His name's sake." Happy, perhaps, for David, had he never changed that way of life in those blessed and simple years! In those days his thoughts were pleasant as roses, and pure as the dew upon their leaves.

> " Love had he found in huts where poor men lie,
>   His daily teachers had been woods and rills,
> The silence that is in the starry sky,
>   The sleep that is among the lonely hills."

But man does not choose his own destiny. The small, sweet idyll ended. One day the boy is summoned from his sheep in the wilderness to his father's house. There he finds that the grey-haired prophet of his race has come to the family sacrifice. All his stalwart brothers pass before the seer, but, bold as they are, and like the children of a king, Samuel, who is no longer to be deceived by tallness of stature, feels that the Lord has not chosen these, and pours the fragrant oil of consecration on the head of the boy who was despised by his brethren. Another day he is summoned to the tent where the mighty Saul is sitting in moody madness, troubled by an evil spirit from the Lord, and nothing but the sweet notes of the boy's harp can dispel that agonizing gloom. Another day makes him spring into the hero and the darling of his nation. He visits his brethren in the camp; and, strong in the strength of the Lord,—because his heart is pure alone of the house of Israel,—with no other weapon but his sling and the smooth stones of the brook, he slays the giant champion, and puts to flight the armies of the Philistines. From that day forth, the innocent shepherd-life is over. He is a warrior; he bears the armour of the king; he is sent on perilous enterprises; he sits at the king's table; he marries the king's daughter; the king's son loves him as his own soul, with a love passing the love of women; the maidens of Israel, with timbrels and dances, extol his fame and his prowess, even above that of the warrior Saul. But, while the youths of Israel, doubtless, envied his glory, he found, even thus early, how rare it is in life that there is a line of light in the life of any man, without many a line of darkness to intercept and close it in. Saul eyes him with a deep smouldering malice, which bursts every now and then into fits of murderous fury. At last he is forced to flee from this hated and imperilled life. Then he becomes an outlaw, the head of a band of men, who, but for his strong influence, might have been lawless freebooters. He is mixed up of necessity with war and raids and forays. His hand is stained with blood; but, in spite of all, he still holds fast to the law of his God. He controls his followers; he restrains his passions; he bears his trials with heroic cheerfulness; he works for honourable ends; he takes no revenge. Loyal to the last, he spares again and again the life of his unrelenting foe. Gallant and chivalrous, in the robber's den as in the king's palace, he still does not forget the God of his youth, nor forsake the covenant of his God· And so, at last, he too becomes a king. God says to him: "Thou shalt be the shepherd of My people Israel." From the sheepfold, from following the ewes great with young ones, God took him that he might feed Jacob, His people, and Israel, His inheritance. And here, too, he is not at first found wanting. He shows himself a brave, a faithful, a magnanimous king. He still shows, in his lofty place, the wisdom which adversity had bred. What our Alfred was, as a civilizer and a law-giver, what Edward III. was, as a statesman and a soldier, what gallant Henry V. was, as a favourite of the people after the glory of Agincourt, that David became to the united tribes of Israel and Judah in the zenith of their glory. Here, then he stood at last on the summit of human wishes. The despised youngest-born of his family, the rude shepherd-boy of Bethlehem, has become a hero, and a hero-king. And the king conquers all his enemies round about, and builds his palace, and brings the Ark to Mount Zion, and raises as his capital the city of Jerusalem, to be famous thenceforth for ever.

There is no need to dwell on the story of David's shameful fall. You all know it. He was sitting on his palace roof. That cool place of retirement had often been hallowed by the melodies of his better thoughts. From thence, as he watched the birds streaming towards the sunset, with their golden feathers and silver wings, he had sung: "Oh, that I had the wings of a dove, for then would I flee away, and be at rest!" There, as he gazed on the starry midnight, he had broken forth in the immortal Psalm: "The heavens declare the glory of God, and the firmament showeth His handiwork." Far different was his mood in this evil hour. He was secure and full-fed; and his thoughts were base, and sensual, and vile. Doubtless, the prayers which might have saved him had been forgotten, or but carelessly uttered. Doubtless, his service in the house of God had become but one of dead orthodoxy and self-satisfied form, no better than the hawk's shriek, or the lake's murmur in the summer eve. But that was why evil thoughts and impure desires had entered into the temple of his heart. Satan wakes, though man sleeps, and, seizing the opportunity given him by the undefended soul, Satan flung upon it a fiery arrow, which should rankle and agonize until the end. The sin of David; the root of it in unguarded passions and careless hours; the awful warning which it involves; the necessity of the girded loins and the burning lantern; the illustration of the way in which one sin paves the road for a multitude of other sins which are worse than the first; the glimpse that it gives us into the bottomless abyss which the sinful soul cleaves before its own wandering feet: all this is full of instruction, but it is not our subject. We have now to glance for a moment rather at the consequences of the sin, at the remorse which followed, at the pardon by which it was at last healed.

It is, as you know, the awful property of a great sin to open the eyes. The man who has never before suspected the depths of his own vileness, sees, as under the lurid glare of a lightning flash, what he is, what he has been, how low he has sunk, to what awful, inevitable retribution he has laid himself bare; but this does not always happen at once. David's eyes were not opened by his guilt and treachery. Rather, they were sealed in penal blindness. He did not feel those stains of infamy which ought to have burned into his conscience like flakes of fire. Consequences waited, the punishment was delayed, the doom was pronounced, but the execution was deferred. Bathsheba was in his house; Uriah lay dead under the walls of Rabbah, basely deserted, treacherously murdered, by the king for whom his brave sword had been drawn. David, the man whom God had chosen, was a murderer and an adulterer, a vulgar Eastern despot stained with lust and blood; yet his guilty soul did not awake from this strange, drugged sleep. Everything was going on as before. No lightning flashed, no thunder rolled, no earthquake rocked the ground at Jerusalem. All men still bowed before the king, and as he stood in the Temple service, among the white-robed Levites, and amid the sounding of the silver trumpets, he did not remember that he had forfeited the clean heart and the free spirit; that he was no longer what he had been; that he was worthy no longer of standing among God's chosen ones, and that he, the king of the chosen people, was a vile and guilty man. Not only did awakenment not come to David instantly; it did not even come gradually. God left him to see if conscience would awaken, and it did not awaken; and it was only when the king was living on in contented crime, guilty and impenitent, that God sent Nathan to him, to tell him that parable of the ewe lamb. It kindled in David a flash of his old nobleness; and, when he had indignantly condemned, out of his own mouth, his own far more heinous iniquity, then, with a terrible voice of most just judgment, with stern face and pointed finger, the seer broke out with his passionate message: "Thou art the man!"

Then, indeed, David saw it all. The scales dropped from his eyes. He saw what he was, and what he had done. God had convicted him. He made no excuses. He stood abashed and confounded before men, before God, before his own conscience, an ashamed, self-condemned, and miserable man. Deep, earnest, sincere, intense, agonizing was his repentance. You read the records of it in his seven penitential psalms; you hear it most of all in the sobbing of the broken heart in the 51st Psalm. And because he repented from his heart, abhorred himself, abhorred his sin, amended his ways, therefore God forgave him. He gave him back the clean heart and the free spirit. He took not wholly His Holy Spirit from him. Yes; but remark that, at the same time, God taught him, and through him taught us, and taught the world, that remission of sins is no condonation of sin's earthly consequences. "It is against the ordinances of Providence, it is against the interests of men," said a well-known statesman, "that immediate reparation should be possible when long evils have been at work; and one of the greatest safeguards against misdoing would be removed, if at any moment the consequences of misdoing could be repaired." If David had given occasion to the enemies of God to blaspheme, he has also given occasion to take awful warning, for God did not spare him. It availed him nothing that he was a poet, a warrior, a king of the chosen nation, the builder of Jerusalem. It availed him nothing that he had been the innocent shepherd-boy, the gallant chief, the national deliverer; nothing, that the maidens of Israel had sung his praises, and the priests of Israel chanted his holy songs. God suffered the consequences of his sin to uprush over his head in deluge. The freight of his bark of life, his peace, his fortune, his crown, and his happiness, went by the board with one deadly crash, amidst a chaos of waves and storms. From that day the sword never departed from his house. From that hour dark spirits haunted his pillow, and unclean wings flapped about his roof. His sons, beautiful and bad, had not seen him restrain his passions, and they did not restrain theirs. He had wounded others in their tenderest affections, and he was wounded in his own. He had humiliated a woman, and his own daughter was humiliated. He had taken the wife of another in secret, and *his* wives were taken from him openly, and in the sun. As he sinned, in like manner he suffered. There was a frightful likeness between the iniquity and its consequences. He had slain Uriah by treachery, and by treachery his own son was murdered. He had lifted his heel against his friend, and his own friend lifted the heel against him. He had brutally invaded the sanctities of a home, and the sanctities of his own home were brutally laid waste. He was in the power of the rough general who knew his guilty secret. Shimei openly cursed him, and flung dust at him. His favourite—his darling Absalom—revolted against him, and drove him away, weeping all day long, up the slopes of Olivet. And from the heart thus sorely wounded, from the affections thus terribly devastated, from the dignity thus vilely trampled into the dust, at last, when the rebel, and the darling of his soul, was slain, in defiance of his orders, in contempt of his agonized entreaties, there was wrung at last from him the exceeding great and bitter cry, as he went up to his chamber over the gate, and wept, and as he went he cried, "O my son Absalom! My son, my son Absalom! would God I had died for thee. O Absalom, my son, my son!"

So did the sun of David's house set into obscure darkness; and so, while it was yet day, it sank slowly down into seas of blood. Surely his life and fate may teach us at least these, among many lessons: one is, that, though we repent, we must not expect the physical, the natural, the earthly consequences of God's broken laws to be done away. Even for David it was not so. His sun never shone again. No more peace; no more victories; no more glory; no more maidens' songs; no more sweet, peaceful home for him; "no poppy, nor mandragora, nor all the drowsy syrups of the world," could bring him back the sweet sleep which he had owned before. Henceforth the poet, the hero, the king, is a broken man. Another of his sons, his much-loved Adonijah, revolts from him; and then the miserable scene ends in the resignation of his throne, and the chilling of his blood. Old and unregretted, he shivers miserably into his grave, and with scarce so much as the cry, "The king is dead!" rises the glad shout for another, "Long live the king!"

But it is yet a sadder thing to see that neither do the moral, the spiritual consequences of a great sin end with itself. A man may rise after his fall, but he rises as a cripple. Henceforth we read of David scarcely anything but dubious acts. There is the strange treatment of Mephibosheth, the son of Jonathan, who had loved him with such heroic love. There is the vindictive behest to Solomon about his general Joab. There is the shockingly mean command to bring to the grave the hoar hairs of Shimei, whom he so ostentatiously pardoned. There is the horrid story of the sacrifice of seven of Saul's sons, and among them the youths, over whom Rizpah, the daughter of Aiah, watched, as they lay dead in the dim and lion-haunted ways. One would think it was some mean Arab sheik bequeathing his blood-feuds to an avenger, and not the sweet Psalmist of Israel. Morally, as well as in all other things, David, though repentant, though forgiven, yet shaken and weakened by his fall, became the wreck of his former self.

Then, lastly, notice the falling of all beauty into darkness, and of all glory into dust. Notice that all human beauty, valour, wit, genius, success, glory, are vanity of vanities; that man is nothing, and that God is all. Great David died as the fool dieth. So died the glorious young Greek Alexander, who conquered the world. So died the wise Henry II., cursing his rebellious sons. So died our gallant Plantagenet, the hero of Creçy and Poictiers, "mighty victor, mighty lord." Low on his funeral couch he lies—no pitying hand, no tear to grace his obsequies. So died the last great conqueror of modern days, Napoleon, on a petty island, squabbling with a poor English sailor about etiquette and about champagne. Man is as great as he is in God's sight, and he is no greater.

Have, then, these truths no lessons for us? If David reaped as he had sown, shall not you reap as you have sown? Shall not you, young men and young women, reap the whirlwind, if you sow the wind? Shall you not reap misery, and anguish, and moral deterioration of heart, and deadness of spirit, and sin, springing up as dragons' teeth in Protean forms of grief and punishment, if you sow to the world and to the flesh? Yes; and yet all this, and more than this, you are able to bear if you can feel, as, after all, David did feel, that in the midst of all, and in spite of all, though he walked even on earth amid the purging flames, and felt their scorching agony, he could feel, as we may feel, that, for the sake of David's Son and David's Lord, who died for us, he still had the blessedness of him whose iniquity is forgiven, and whose sin is covered; that through whatever shames, and agonies, and moral failures, God would deliver his soul from hell, His darling from the power of the dog; and that He who is Life, who rose from the dead, would not leave his soul in hell, neither would He suffer His holy one to see corruption.

F. W. F.

XV. The Failure of Elijah's Faith. 1 KINGS xix. 13. *"And, behold, there came a voice unto him, and said, What doest thou here, Elijah?"*

IT has been more than once observed that some of the men who, as we say, most distinctly leave a mark upon their age are liable to great changes of spirits, alternating between buoyant enthusiasm and something like despair. At first sight it seems as if the resources of human nature are after all very limited: that which is expended in one quarter must be withdrawn from another. The waves which raise their crests so proudly above the accustomed level of the ocean imply, as we know, each one of them, a corresponding interval of depression. As the Psalmist says in his bold hyperbole, "as high as the heavens, and down to the valleys beneath," of the rude experience of his countrymen in the Phœnician waters, so it is often with the life of men, and especially of public men. The great effort which rivets the attention, which perhaps gives an impression of extraordinary strength or capacity, is often dearly purchased by succeeding hours of depression and weakness.

Something of this kind was the case with the late Bishop Wilberforce. The buoyant spirits, the generous enthusiasm, which made him what he was in the pulpit, in the senate, at the public meeting, was dearly paid for by periods of great despondency, when all things seemed dark, when nothing seemed possible, when he was perhaps less equal to the demands of duty than very inferior men.

I. From this characteristic of enthusiastic natures the mighty prophet who is before us was not by any means exempt.

So great was Elijah's power both over men and over nature that in after ages his countrymen came to regard him as an altogether preterhuman personage, whose conduct was not a precedent for, or a sample of, that of ordinary men. In later times this idea of Elijah was enhanced by Malachi's prophecy about his expected coming before " the great and terrible day of the Lord."

So that when John the Baptist appeared it was a common opinion in Palestine that " this was Elias which was for to come." When, then, St. James quotes Elijah as an example of the efficacy of prayer, he prefaces his argument by what might seem to us before consideration a very obvious and trite remark, but a remark which was by no means unheeded by St. James's first readers. He says that " Elias was a man of like passions as we are ; " Elijah, he means, had his share of impulse and of weakness ; and therefore the power of his prayers is an encouragement for others than himself.

Now, that Elijah was what St. James thus said of him, is plain. At Carmel he was at the height of his moral ascendency, of his supernatural force. True, since his first message from God to Ahab he had been a fugitive, he had been fed by the ravens in the torrent brook of the Cherith ; he had been dependent on the charity of the devout widow in the heathen town of Zarephath. But no sooner does he return to the soil of Israel than he asserts his astonishing power over all who come in contact with him ; for he, too, in his measure, had a share in that promise to the King Messiah, " Be Thou Ruler in the midst, even among thine enemies." Obadiah, Ahab's trusted minister, falls awe-struck before him; Ahab himself, who has spared no pains to compass his death, acts as a man might act under a resistless spell, and submissively, though with evident reluctance, carries out his orders; at his bidding the eight hundred and fifty prophets of the newly imported nature-worship of the Phœnicians are marshalled upon Carmel, and he confronts them in his solitary weakness, in his solitary strength.

And then follows the appeal to the people to choose between Baal and the one true God, the challenge to the prophets of Baal, their long but fruitless pleadings prolonged from the early morning till the evening sacrifice that Baal would somehow own their offering,—pleadings accompanied by frantic self-mutilation, and redoubled as they listen to the prophet's terrible irony; and then, after their final failure, Elijah's measured preparations in accordance with the forgotten principles of the ancient ritual, his solemn invocation of the God of Israel, the fire from heaven, the adoring confession of the awe-struck people, "The Lord He is the God, the Lord He is the God," and the terrible extermination of the idolators.

Taken altogether, there is no other scene like it in the Bible. Elijah on Carmel represents a man's moral ascendency over his brother man in the name and for the glory of a religious truth carried to its very highest point of effective power.

And now the scene has changed. Elijah is not on Carmel, but on Horeb. The idolatrous priesthood was indeed exterminated; but Jezebel remained. She had her projects and her means of vengeance, and the prophet who had triumphed when confronted by the king, by the court, by the people, by the whole hierarchy of the false religion, must escape if he would save his life from the implacable fanaticism of the queen. He first fled to Beersheba, far away to the south, beyond the frontiers of Israel, a town indeed of Judah, but on the very confines of the wilderness beyond.

He left the boy who waited on him, in the town, veiling as we all of us do, his moments of extreme depression even from those who knew him best, and then he wandered out despairingly into the desert, and prayed that he might die.

And here he was braced for his journey by food which

I

was brought him by no human hands—a type, as it was always thought by the Christian Church of the early ages, of that strengthening and refreshing of the soul by the body and blood of Christ which enables the Christian pilgrim to cross life's long desert on his way to his true home.

Still in deep depression, after a journey of forty days, Elijah reached the sacred mountain, the scene, the very scene, of the great revelation to Moses. Its hallowed associations, its dreary and awful solitudes, were in keeping with the prophet's thoughts.

He entered into a cave, a grotto which was associated, it is likely, by the local tradition with the name and with the work of Moses; and he gave himself up to the thoughts which crowded so darkly on his mind. Why had he succeeded so well only that success should issue, as it seemed, after all in failure? Why had such strength as had been vouchsafed him been followed by such weakness? Was not everything forfeited for which he had struggled? Was not his ministry closing in discomfiture and in shame, while the insolent and idolatrous queen and her weak and wicked husband were completing the ruin of the religion of Israel? What was the use of attempting anything further? All was really lost; and those who, like himself, had given their all to the losing cause, had only to bury what might remain of life in sadness and obscurity. These, or such as these, were his thoughts, when solemnly, and once and again, the searching question came to him, "What doest thou here, Elijah?"

II. Observe here how God discovers himself to Elijah. "The Word of the Lord came to him, and He said unto him, What doest thou here, Elijah?" The Word of the Lord that Word which was lodged in Elijah, that Word of which he was the instrument, the organ, and which he had proclaimed so vividly, so terribly to others, now turned its voice, I had almost dared to say its eye, in upon himself. This Word or message which the prophet bears is, we thus see, not his servant, but his master. It is not a work of his own mind which he may control, or manipulate, or silence at pleasure. It is a truth which, if it be in him, is yet utterly independent of him, and to which he himself owes an obedience no less than does the very humblest of his hearers.

The prophet of old, the minister of Jesus Christ at the present day, is always the servant of the truth which he proclaims; and he carries it for his own "reproof, correction, instruction in righteousness," no less than for that of his people. To the question, "What doest thou here?" Elijah could not but reply. It was—so it seemed to the prophet—it was for his zeal for the cause of God; it was his tragic despair, it was his isolation, it was his sense, his crushing sense, of impotence and of failure which had brought him thus to Horeb. "I have been very jealous," he said, "for the Lord God of Hosts; for the children of Israel have forsaken Thy covenant, thrown down Thine altars, and slain Thy prophets with the sword; and I, even I only, am left; and they seek my life, to take it away." And this answer is neither accepted nor rejected. It is passed by most significantly without a word of reproval or of rebuke.

If the prophet would know more about God, about himself, he must come forth from the cave, he must stand face to face on the mountain side with the Infinite. And then, as centuries before, on this very spot with Moses, "the Lord passed by."

The Author of nature, who is also the Lord of conscience, often speaks to conscience through the changing aspects of nature; and thus nature is a book written in characters which those who live in communion with God know how to read. For them the wind, the earthquake, the lightning, are not merely physical phenomena, forces or effects of which they can or cannot, as the case may be, furnish themselves with an adequate scientific account, they are outward signs of invisible realities that belong to the human and to the moral world.

Nature is a robe of beauty, distinct, indeed, from the Creator Himself, since it is the work of His hands, but luminous with the revelations of His mind and of His will. What was "the great and strong wind that rent the mountains, and brake in pieces the rocks before the Lord" but a natural figure of the tempestuous impulse which had carried the prophet onward ever since he left in his early youth his native hills of Gilead? What was the earthquake with its deep warning mutterings, with its violent shocks of upheaval and of ruin crashing through the wild valleys around him, but an image of convulsions of which Elijah's own soul, and many another soul around, had been the scene? What was the lightning playing incessantly around the prophet on the mountain side but a reflection of the heaven-sent burning zeal which had been from the first the spirit of his work and of his life?

And yet as the wind, and the earthquake, and the fire succeeded each other, the prophet felt that they no longer meant for him what they would have meant as he stood of old on Carmel. They were signs of states of mind which once seemed instinct with the life of God, but which now, for the first time, he knew to be without it. "The Lord was not in the wind." Strong religious impulse may be more than half physical, a matter of temperament, a matter of constitution. Earthly passions in some natures may take this precise form; the language, the intended, the professed objects may be of heaven, the spirit of earth. Even though mountains of opposition are rent by it, even though rocks of prejudice are broken in pieces by it, and changes brought about which fill the thoughts of men, and which live in the pages of history, yet it may be that the agency which effects all this is in itself destitute of anything that is properly Divine, that "the Lord is not in the wind."

"And the Lord was not in the earthquake." Spasmodic terror may be only terror; the thought, or sight, or immediate apprehension of death may convulse, does convulse to its very depths the human soul. But mere mental agitation may be only desperate. "The fear of the Lord," as distinct from the fear of anything else, "is the beginning of wisdom." Whether the Lord is or is not in these great earthquakes of the soul depends, generally speaking, upon the soul's previous relations with Him.

"And the Lord was not in the fire." He had been in the burning bush; He was, in after ages, in the fiery tongues at Pentecost. He was not in the fire which played around Elijah on Horeb. Religious passion carried to the highest point of enthusiasm is a great agency in human life; but religious passion may easily be too inconsiderate, too truculent, too entirely wanting in tenderness and in charity to be in any sense Divine. Christendom has been the scene of the most Divine enthusiasm of which the soul of man has ever had experience in the whole course of its history. But Christendom has also been ablaze again and again with fires; and those fires are not extinct in our own day and country of which it may certainly be said that the Lord is not in them.

"And after the fire, a still small voice." In physical impulse, in convulsive terror, in the white heat of emotion, dealing with sacred things, we may seek for God in vain. But when conscience speaks clearly we may be sure of His presence. Conscience is His inward messenger, and in its quiet whisper we listen to an echo from the Infinite and the Unseen. We may, alas! play tricks with it; we may drug it, we may corrupt it in many ways, we may eventually silence it. But if we will let it alone, if we will reverence it, if we will listen to it, it places us surely in the presence of God.

"After the fire, a still small voice." Conscience then repeated the question, "What doest thou here, Elijah?" and the question implied beyond all doubt that Elijah had better have been elsewhere, and that the state of mind which had brought him to Horeb was not altogether right or healthy. Elijah was still in deep gloom; he had yielded to it, and now he heard within him the voice of reproach: "What doest thou here, Elijah?"

III. Now let us observe the character of Elijah's despondency. Its motive beyond all question was unselfish and noble. It is true that he does complain, "They seek my life, to take it away"; but he is here only thinking of himself as the representative of a great cause, and he is not speaking in his private or personal capacity. As a man he would, if it might be, gladly die: "Now, O Lord, take away my life; for I am not better than my fathers." So he had prayed in the wilderness of Beersheba. But as a prophet he desired to live—to live for the sake of the truth which he had at heart. He felt that the sword which would strike him was really aimed at that which for the moment he represented. The forsaken covenants, the ruined altars, the slaughtered prophets—these filled his mind and heart; these explained why it was that he was so far from the frontiers of Israel, and a fugitive in the mountain sanctuary of Horeb.

Such a despondency as this is surely a much better

thing than a jaunty light-heartedness, which is at the bottom based on a selfish indifference to all the greatest and most precious things in human life. It augurs ill for a State when its citizens are satisfied with their individual prosperity, and have no eye or care for the public weal. It augurs ill for a Church when its members talk of a personal religion, as if there was no thought, no care, no prayer, due to the great society of Christians united to our Lord and Saviour—to what St. Paul calls "the body of Christ."

Prophecy has a stern word for those who are "not grieved at the afflictions of Jacob"; and history condemns unsparingly the royal sybarite who calculated that the world would last his time, and who then added, "After me, the deluge." The motive of Elijah's despondency was noble; but, in itself, his despondency was wrong. He might have remembered that what passes for the moment on earth is no measure of what is determined in heaven; he might have reflected that, while duties are ours, events are in the hands of God; he might have associated himself with those lines, already ancient, of David, written, as we now know with little less than certainty, when the first mutterings of Absalom's rebellion were being heard, and when the faint-hearted men around him counselled flight from his difficulties: "In the Lord put I my trust: how say ye, then, to my soul, that she should flee as a bird unto the hill? For, lo, the ungodly bend their bow, and make ready arrows within the quiver, that they may privily shoot at him who is true of heart; for the foundations will be cast down, and what hath the righteous done? The Lord is in His holy temple, the Lord's seat is in heaven." Had this been in Elijah's mind he would still have been somewhere near Jezreel. As it was, he had failed for the moment, great prophet as he was, to set God's will so clearly before him as to keep close to the work that was given him to do. For the moment, even Elijah had done what we all are tempted from time to time to do. He had set aside the claim of duty in favour—mark this well—in favour of the indulgence of sentiment. And because this sentiment was strictly religious sentiment, gathering round a great and an ancient sanctuary, he had disguised from himself that he had erred and strayed so far from the ways of God; and therefore when the question flashed upon his conscience it was like the lightning on the path of some benighted wanderer among the precipices, "What doest thou here, Elijah?"

"What doest thou here?" Elijah, we have seen, had his own account to give of his being where he was. But behind his excuses, as they died away into space, behind them was the voice of duty. "And the Lord said unto him, Go, return on thy way to the wilderness of Damascus: and when thou comest, anoint Hazael to be king over Syria: and Jehu the son of Nimshi shalt thou anoint to be king over Israel: and Elisha the son of Shaphat of Abel-meholah shalt thou anoint to be prophet in thy room."

IV. Now these directions, whispered by "the still small voice" to the conscience of Elijah, involved two principles. First, Elijah was not to dwell on the abstract aspects of evil; he was to address himself to the practical duties that lay around his path. Evil in its vast, massive accumulations, evil in its widespread, its ancient empire, evil in the strong and subtle ascendency which from time to time it acquires among men, is indeed beyond us. We, in our separate weakness, cannot banish it from the world. We lose precious time if we try to weigh and to measure it. Our first wisdom is to pray to be delivered from it. There it is, a fact, a vast and terrible fact, permitted for reasons which we guess at rather than decipher.

If the children of Israel had broken the covenant, if they had destroyed the altars, if they had slain the Lord's prophets with the sword, this was indeed a passed fact, a permitted fact, and so far it was beyond the control of Elijah. We only weaken ourselves by dwelling upon mischiefs which we cannot hope to remedy. We have only a certain amount of thought, of feeling, of resolve, each one of us, to dispose of. And when this has been expended unavailingly on the abstract, on the untangible, it is expended; it is no longer ours, and we cannot employ it when and where we need it close at home.

And, secondly, Elijah was to begin his work with individuals; he was to deal with men one by one. "Anoint Hazael, the heathen monarch, who, yet heathen though he be, has a place in the Divine government of the world.

That duty lies furthest on the frontier of thy work. Anoint Jehu the son of Nimshi; he will execute the impending judgments on the apostate king of Israel. That piece of work lies closer to thy appointed sphere of labour. Above all provide for the continuance of thy ministry when thou shalt have gone hence. Make Elisha the son of Shaphat prophet in thy room. That shall be thy first stern, thy most sacred and imperative, duty."

One of the familiar fallacies of an age like ours is the notion that men can really be improved in the deepest sense of the word if they are dealt with in masses. General legislation, the vague influence of the press, or of oratory, social movements which deal with men in the block, which ignore the care and the needs of the separate soul; these are common enough. And this fallacy is the result partly of the characteristic opportunities of the modern world, partly of the inertness which shrinks from the hard and humble work of dealing with single characters. These general measures have, no doubt, their value, sometimes their very great value, as supplementary influences; but they are almost worthless when they are regarded as substitutes for that careful indispensable labour with single souls which alone secures real changes in hearts and characters.

A proclamation in general terms would have had little effect upon Israel. The anointing of Jehu, the appointment of Elisha, were, as we know, to be pregnant with consequences.

"What doest thou here?" To every human being in his most serious moments this question must be suggested: "Why am I where I am, doing what I do, thinking what I think, saying what I say? What is the motive which shapes, which guides my life, making me do this rather than that, making me take this turn in life rather than the other; choosing these friends, throwing myself into these interests, into these trains of thought, into those associations, into those enterprises?" Something, perhaps much, may be determined by antecedent circumstances; that is to say, by the hand of God acting through accomplished events, and so far suspending or limiting personal liberty.

But beyond this there is a margin in which we all are free. Even those who cannot in the least degree control their personal movements, since they are, for whatever reason, dependent upon others, can entirely determine where they will be, what they will be doing in the sphere of thought and of purpose. We are all of us masters, if we will, of that inner world which each man carries about within him; and that world has its Carmel as well as its Horeb no less than the outer world around us. And the serious question for every man is whether, so far as he can judge, he is, according to his measure of strength and opportunity, endeavouring to do that portion of the will of God to which the circumstances which surround him, to which the powers and opportunities which have been given him, clearly point as meant for him and for no other man to do. What it is exactly that engages each one of us matters little, comparatively little, if the motive to be doing God's will is actively recognised.

It may be the most important duties in Church or State; it may be the daily toil of the shopboy or the domestic servant, all is equally ennobled if the great motive be there; all is equally degraded if the great motive be absent. "What would you do," a very good man was once asked who was playing draughts with his little son, "if you knew that you would die in five minutes?" "I should finish this game of draughts," was the reply. Work and recreation are equally legitimate if each is treated as part of the will of God, if throughout life the awful significance of life as the great gift for which we must surely account to our Maker, which has been purchased back from ruin by the Incarnation and the death of our Divine Redeemer, be steadily kept in view. There may be very good reasons for spending portions of it on Horeb as well as upon Carmel. But the essential point is that we should be where we are, that we should be doing what we do, because, so far as we know, He who has given us the gift of life wills this, wills nothing else respecting us.

H. P. L.

XVI. Elijah's Flight. 1 Kings xix.

THIS event in the life of Elijah is one that took place a great while ago; and the circumstances in which it happened may seem very unlike our own; and Elijah himself, to whom it happened, was so different from ourselves, and so far above us that, all things considered, little instruction may be expected to be derivable from this or any other part of his history. The only feeling he is fitted to excite may seem to be wonder. When we come upon him in the pages of the Bible it is like coming upon a skeleton of superhuman size, or upon a gigantic suit of armour—we can only express astonishment at the greatness and the strength of men of former times. Well, if this were the only feeling which this history raised, it might not be amiss to entertain it for a time in our minds. The feeling of wonder at the greatness of others is a very wholesome feeling, and is closely connected with another, equally salutary,—the feeling of sadness at our own littleness. Yet the greatness of this prophet need not be any obstacle in the way of our deriving benefit from his history. Rather, it should be helpful to us. For, just as if we were examining the joints and mechanisms and the adaptations of the human body, the body of a giant would present them to us in their fullest and most visible form, so in a very great mind we shall be able to see most clearly the movements of mind, its strength and joy, as well as its weakness and despondency.

The only part of the prophet's history which can be touched upon is his flight to Sinai, and only a few of the more obvious points in that which have a practical bearing.

I. We may notice the circumstances of the time in which Elijah was placed. These circumstances were full of interest. So far as things then could resemble things now, the state of parties at that time was not unlike the state of parties at present. There had always been in Israel an idolatrous, disbelieving party. The history throughout its whole length shows a polluted stream of idolatrous worship running side by side with the true worship of Jehovah; and sometimes this idolatrous current became so broad that it gave its own colour to the whole stream of the people's religious life. They were idolaters in Ur of the Chaldees—"Your fathers dwelt on the other side of the flood in old times, even Terah, the father of Abraham: and they served other gods."

They were idolaters in Egypt. In the wilderness their

idolatry broke out when "they joined themselves unto Baal-Peor, and ate the sacrifices of the dead." They were idolaters in Canaan. Even David's wife, the daughter of Saul, possessed idols, with one of which she deceived the hired assassins of her father, and saved her husband's life. The idolatrous elements were numerous, and pervaded every class in the nation, and only awaited some hand skilful and strong enough to combine them, in order to acquire the command of the people's thoughts, and assume the place of the established faith. This was found in Jezebel, daughter of the king of Sidon, and her feeble husband Ahab. The latter appears to have been not so much vicious as weak—one who, like a spoilt child when refused his wishes, fell sick and would not eat. And thus he fell completely under the guidance of his unscrupulous wife. At her instigation he introduced the worship of Baal—" He reared up an altar for Baal in the house of Baal which he had built in Samaria. And Ahab made a grove; and Ahab did more to provoke Jehovah the God of Israel to anger than all the kings of Israel that were before him." He made Baal-worship a State religion. But he went further. He was not satisfied with toleration for himself, he sought to suppress all other worship. He issued orders for the murder of Jehovah's prophets, and the throwing down of His altars. And with a fatal fickleness and subserviency, the people gave in to the despotic will of the effeminate tyrant. Elijah pleaded this condition of things before the Lord in the wilderness—" The children of Israel have forsaken Thy covenant, and thrown down Thine altars, and slain Thy prophets; and I only am left, and they seek my life." The country was passing through a religious crisis, and there could be seen that sifting of men which goes on at such a time.

There were, as on all such occasions, three parties—the true worshippers of Jehovah, the strict idolaters, and the middlemen, who were neither. These last were, no doubt, the most numerous. Perhaps the body of the people belonged to this class—men, as Elijah described them, who halted or limped between two opinions; men not firm on their legs, but limping, being neither worshippers of Jehovah, nor good idolaters. Some belonged to this class because they thought it safest to side with the majority. Some because they could not go all the way with the extreme Jehovah-party; yet they resented the king's high-handed proceeding, thinking it a dangerous infringement of liberty. Some because the problem presented to them was too difficult for their solution, and they were unable to decide, being drawn sometimes to one side and sometimes to another.

And some belonged to this great middle party on principle, because it was a middle party. They disliked extremes. In every matter there was a great deal not essential, and men ruined their own cause by their offensive stickling for this. The worship of Jehovah was no doubt essentially the true religion, and its supporters might be excellent men; but they were certainly narrow. If they insisted less on names, and forms, and definitions, it would be well. If they were more tolerant, and accepted the good that was in all men—might it not even be said, in all things —and the deep, religious feeling that was in their hearts, even if the form in which it showed itself externally was not always to their liking, they would make much greater way and find their usefulness much enlarged. It must be admitted that the old forms of Jehovah-worship, which suited a rude people in the wilderness, might not be adapted to the feelings of an accomplished and educated nation that had enjoyed permanent empire for 600 years.

Religious teaching must be accommodated somewhat to the wants and relations of the age, and it was news to them to hear that all that was to be attained of truth and goodness amongst men had already been found, and was to be had embalmed in the practices of their own particular religion. It seemed certainly possible that some other portion of mankind, even Zidon, had found something good which they had missed, and this fanatical closing up of every inlet against the thought and the belief of every portion of the race besides themselves was surely a mistake.

Such was, perhaps, like the state of parties, and the feelings that existed at this time. It was a time of confusion and breaking up of old beliefs. Cross currents were running, and eddies, that caught men and whirled them about. The waves were so broken that the real direction of the current was not seen. Perhaps few discerned what was really at stake. One mind at least took in the whole meaning of the issue. He was not blinded by that way that men have of speaking of religion,—saying it is an inward thing, a kind of feeling, and if the feelings be right it matters little what the external object is that excites them. To him the external object was everything: "Choose ye this day whom ye will serve; if Jehovah be God, follow Him; but if Baal, then follow him." He knew that according to the external object, so very soon will be the feelings and the life of the worshipper. Elijah, whether of set purpose or under a sudden impulse, permitted himself on Carmel to use force. He met the king's violence with equal violence of his own. Perhaps no other course was left him; but more likely it was a mistake. But the temptation was very great—in the full tide of excitement and with the multitude at his back. But he should have remembered that the multitude would be at any one's back who would show them force, particularly of a rude kind, and though at his back to-day they might be at Jezebel's to-morrow. And so they were. And the crowd that under the influence of his great miracle confessed their faith on Carmel with such fervour, crying, "Jehovah, He is God; Jehovah, He is God," bowed submissive to Jezebel's threat to take the prophet's life in Samaria: "So let the gods do to me, and more also, if I make not thy life as the life of one of them by to-morrow about this time." And Elijah arose and went for his life.

II. Observe now the circumstances of his flight and his despondency. Elijah fled. That was necessary. He fled into the wilderness; not to Zidon as he had done before, not to any of the neighbouring peoples, nor beyond the Jordan, but to the wilderness. That is where you expect him to flee. In any moment of his life the waste was congenial to him. Its bleakness and isolation were but the counterparts of his own mind. His favourite abode was among the mountains, by the brook Cherith, with only the monotonous rush of waters in his ear among the silent hills. He preferred the ravens for company to men. He seemed alone among men. His greatness made him solitary. There are some men solitary for other reasons, just as there are some mountains. Some hills in our neighbourhood stand alone though they are not great. The forces of nature and time have carried away what surrounded and touched them, and left them solitary. And circumstances sometimes alienate or remove men's associates from them, and they stand apart, not possessing, whether they seek the confidence of others or no. But some mountains stand alone because of their grandeur. Giant hills crowd about the foot of Mount Blanc, yet in their midst he is alone. They cannot reach the same altitude as he, and go with him but a little way. Into those regions of cloud and sky into which he towers they cannot rise. And thus it is with the highest minds. In common things others can accompany them. They can be followed to a certain height, but there other men and they part company. In those lofty regions where only heaven is about—in dense clouds or Divine light—they stand solitary, and being alone, even in the midst of men, they naturally seek solitude.

But Elijah fled to the wilderness of Sinai. That also was characteristic. Sinai is the wilderness of wildernesses. On the back of natural terrors moral terrors are accumulated. There Jehovah, before whom Elijah stood, showed himself most clearly. That side of God which Elijah had most sympathy with was most fully manifested there. He was the prophet of law, of force, of terror; and he longed to realize the Lord more fully. He would penetrate into the very place of terrors. He would see the mountain where the Law was given, its rugged front, once veiled in awful smoke; its long fissures, which might have been ploughed by the very lightnings of that dreadful day—might it not be that Jehovah Himself might, as to Moses, appear to him?

My brethren, does not this flight of Elijah to Sinai exhibit a figure of ourselves? May we not say of it: "which thing is an allegory?" Do we never flee there, too? In our conflicts with laxness, and the licentious Baal-worship of our day, when the battle is going against us, do we not invoke the God of Sinai against our adversaries? At all events do we not find refuge in Sinai ourselves? I think men flee there often still—when they are wearied with the indifference and vexed with the laxness of those about them. There is an asperity in their frame of mind, a fierce earnestness, a longing, stimulated perhaps by opposition, for a sight of truth as it is; and that easy-going acceptance of it which satisfies most men will not be put up with by them. And it is the severer forms of truth that we desire —law, right, justice, a word of God pure and simple—and our toleration for men whose thinking tends to milder truth; to rub away the edges of sharp doctrines; to run every doctrine away into a region over which falls a mist of uncertainty, saying this is mystery, this ends in God, we do not know, we can only guess—our toleration for minds of this class is very little. Their hesitation or reserve seems to us but inconsequence or sluggishness, and our mind with its keen dogmatic edge will have no compromise, our cry is Sinai—law.

On his way towards Sinai, somewhere about the wilderness of Beersheba, in the south of Palestine, there fell upon Elijah that singular weariness of life and despair which we wonder so much at in him—which we wonder at, but gladly accept,—for it is the touch of nature that makes us and him kin. He came and sat down under a juniper-tree and requested for himself that he might die. "It is enough; now, O Lord, take away my life!" Some part of this despondency might be due to physical weakness, for he fled for his life. But it was almost altogether spiritual. This was the morrow of the day of his transcendant success on Carmel. The tide of spiritual power had never risen so high even in his soul as it had done on Carmel. God had never obeyed him so implicitly as then, and in the presence both of royalty and the masses of the nation. Never before had he felt so confident and wielded with such absolute mastery his sway over men's minds. Never perhaps before had such thoughts risen in his mind as rose then of a kingdom conquered for Jehovah, and a nation born in an hour, and a realm cleansed from all impurities, and every knee bowed to the Lord.

Victory for God was secure, and he was the conqueror. That was yesterday. And to-day spiritual reaction has set in in his own soul, and he is a fugitive, crouching under a bush in the wilderness, the facile crowd returned to its impure rites again, not one voice that dares to raise itself on the Lord's side—the kingdom which seemed the Lord's not thrown back as it seemed, but hopelessly Baal's—all his efforts lost. It is no wonder that complete prostration overtook him, and that he requested for himself that he might die. It is a hard moment in a man's life that, such as had now come upon Elijah ; when a man has given the energy of his life to one cherished purpose, and has hoped for it, patiently waiting till the years should roll past, when the promised prize should fall to him ; enduring many hardships, cheered by the prospects ever coming nearer of success, and refusing to let himself think of defeat, his mind always saying to itself that it could not be but that he would succeed. It is a hard moment when at last, through some perversity of will of one in whom he trusted, or some unworthiness of others, or some great error in calculation, defeat ensues when victory was judged secure, and when the once compact purpose of his life is broken into pieces like the fragments of a vanquished host which no commander can ever rally or re-unite. At such a time only this remains to him, that he judged it truth for which he struggled, and that the means he used seemed to him the best, or at least worthy ; and this, that at any rate God remains to him, to whom he can appeal to judge his cause, and, if he have fought in vain, to release him from the unavailing strife.

III. The last thing to notice is God's treatment of His desponding servant.

First, he gave him bodily food, for that was needful, and as we pray daily, "Give us this day our daily bread," and as He hears us ordinarily so to hear us is not beneath His greatness when we pray in circumstances extraordinary. Then in the strength given him He brought him to the Mount of God. He gratified his longings, He satisfied his spiritual aspirations. That which he so greatly desired to see He showed to him. He took him up to the very height, and down to the very deeps of that kind of realizing of Himself which he longed to attain to. God as he conceived Him, and as his heart delighted in, He showed him in perfection. Nay, for his sake He almost re-enacted the terrors of Sinai. "A great and strong wind rent the mountains, and brake in pieces the rocks before the Lord ; but the Lord was not in the wind : and after the wind an earthquake ; but the Lord was not in the earthquake : and after the earthquake a fire ; but the Lord was not in the fire." Sinai over again, and the Lord not in it at all. Was it for this that he had come so far—was this the fulfilling of the dream of his life, and the reward of his unexampled might and toil? "And after the fire a still small voice. And it was so, when Elijah heard it, that he wrapped his face in his mantle." This is the Divine method of teaching, the full meaning may be beyond us, but it pointed back to Elijah's past career, and it pointed onward to one who should use no force, who should not cry, nor lift up, nor let his voice be heard in the streets.

Elijah's methods were tried on himself—power, force, law, Sinai—and the efforts were naught. The Lord was not in the earthquake or the fire. Did the prophet never wonder at the obdurate king, at the besotted people, at the fickle crowd, at the mad vindictive queen? What had he been plying them with all his days? Miracle on miracle, a gloomy demeanour, heavens of brass; famine, thirst, death, law, force. Did he wonder now after his present experience, or was his wonder now not turned in upon himself? He had been enabled to sound the depths of that conception of God, which had all his life fascinated him—he had come to his place and he had found that God was something different from his idea of Him, and that His power was not of the kind that he imagined. Yet there must have been a parable to Elijah in the earthquake and fire which was powerless, followed by "the small voice," in which was God Himself—a parable of Sinai and Calvary. And might there not rise up before him, some such scene as he was yet to witness in the Mount of Transfiguration, and to share in when the thunders of Sinai should die down and become lower and lower through successive ages, till at last they were succeeded by the "still small voice" of one who "did not cry, nor lift up, nor cause his voice to be heard in the streets," but who was God with us "unto them which are called, both Jews and Gentile, Christ the power of God and the wisdom of God;" "for what the law could not do"—even though wielded by an Elijah—"God sending His own Son in the likeness of sinful flesh, and for sin, condemned sin in the flesh: that the righteousness of the law might be fulfilled in us, who walk not after the flesh, but after the Spirit."

This history suggests two lessons. One speaks to those of us who, like Elijah, are set over men in the Lord, and the other to the people.

(1) We may see how, though God deals most mercifully with His desponding servants, He yet gives them to understand that despondency is out of place somewhat— is not a state for men who have work to do. He dealt most mercifully with Elijah. He gave him bread to eat. He brought him to the place of His own awful manifestation. He allowed him to revel in those conceptions of Himself dearest to his soul, to sound them to their deeps. He instructed him, not by plain words, but by indirect displays from which he could not but gather where his mistake had lain. All this was the treatment of a wise and merciful Father. But in the midst of it all He kept saying to him, "What doest thou here, Elijah?" The scene of labour was elsewhere, and he was here. And as soon as it was possible to send him back to it the Lord said unto him, "Go, return; and when thou comest, anoint Hazael to be king over Syria: and Jehu the son of Nimshi shalt thou anoint to be king over Israel; and Elisha the son of Shaphat shalt thou anoint to be prophet in thy room." Arise and return to the world and life. His work was not done. In spite of weariness of the world he must face it, he must handle its forces as he finds them, and do his best to direct them. He must not recoil from meeting open foes like Hazael, superficial reformers like Jehu; there they are, and the servant of God must use them for the best. He must mix with them, study them, comprehend them, declare God's will to them, and use them for the Church's advancement. Action, not despondency, is demanded.

(2) For there is no reason to despair. We are often cast down with our small success, and ready to throw away the weapons of our warfare and acknowledge defeat. But Elijah's history shows that success is often much better than appearances would suggest.

"The kingdom of God cometh not with observation." No influences can be quite lost, only their result is not immediate—"As the rain cometh down and the snow from heaven, and returneth not thither again, but watereth the earth and maketh it bring forth and bud, so shall My word be that goeth forth out of My mouth." Perhaps all good servants do more work than they imagine. Elijah thought he had saved his own soul. God showed him 7,000 men who had not bowed the knee to Baal; and as God's servants do more than they think they are doing, so they will find God putting upon them at the last an unexpected honour—an exceeding weight of glory. This temporary darkness in Elijah's life was swallowed up in the light of the end, and the honour God put upon him in the latter days was unspeakable, when he stood beside the Son on the Mount of Transfiguration. So that it seems that wherein men fail is forgotten by God, and wherein they succeed is the measure of the glory that is bestowed on them.

But the influence of a true man of God is profound Elijah thought his influence fleeting and superficial, but it was deep and pervading. Two brief reigns passed over, one of two years and the other of twelve, when the harvest began to be reaped. The nation was full of the spirit of smiting against the bloody and idolatrous house of Ahab. And when the prophet went to anoint Jehu the son of Nimshi, so ripe was the time for a change that the army immediately hailed the new monarch, crying, "God save King Jehu." And the carnage which followed in Ahab's house was terrible and complete, and the religious as well as political revolution which followed was thorough.

It was Elijah's spirit working in men—in the army, among the citizens, in the prophets that came after him, in the Rechabites—the severe, pure, monotheistic spirit, the spirit of truth, the spirit which is omnipotent when it rises in the hearts of a people. Surely here is hope and encouragement for any one that is set over men to be their spiritual guide and to lead them into the way of God and of His Christ. Be assured, that any defeat we suffer is only apparent: victory at the last is certain. Tears may accompany your sowing. It is a hard soil, this human mind which you have to break up and deposit the precious seed in. Yet it is a deep and fertile soil after all. What harvests have been already reaped from it, of godliness and self-devotion, and of all those glorious ideal creations of the mind.

And you know how the growth of this good seed in it tends to make it deeper, and to cleanse it of its weeds, and what a rich harvest it may be made to yield at the last. Think of the reverence, and affection, and enthusiasm for knowledge and truth, and for a pure and broad human life, you may call out in the young—of the steady attachment to sound principle which you may create or confirm in those that are grown up—of the patience and resignation in sorrow and affliction which you may teach to those that have to suffer, and how you may bring the light of religion into the lonely cottage or the humble dwelling of the poor, which will brighten up every face and gild the straitened ways of life as a ray of sunshine will pass through the narrow windows and lighten up the furniture within. Ah, it is not in Parliament or on the battle-field that deeds are done that are great in God's sight: it is rather on that stage which to men's eyes seems narrow, but is the widest of all, where individual human souls are engaged in playing out the great drama of their own immortal destiny, rejecting or accepting, amidst the manifold struggles of mind, the truth which God by you is presenting to them. Think of the influence in a crisis of soul like this, and how a word or a look or a gesture may exert an influence even to eternity! Think of this, I say, and bring to bear upon your task every resource of your own mind, of circumstance, and of the word of God, strong in the Lord and in the power of His might.

But there is another lesson which this history teaches. The lesson is this: the necessity of standing by those set over you. Elijah's despair was due largely to his loneliness, to his having to fight the battle of the Lord single-handed. And Elijah was a giant such as men are not now, and yet the forces of the enemy were too strong for him. He had not the support of the people. There were many that agreed with him so far, a number who agreed with him out and out; there were many meek, mute souls throughout the land who wished him well; but they wanted courage. Their feelings and their sympathies were right but they were not the men that soldiers in God's army are made of, and of the most it had to be said that they wanted one essential thing—they were not firm in their principles. They halted between two opinions.

Hence their sympathy and enthusiasm rose to fever height one day and was cold as the dead the next. The lesson goes deep. To-day you may be enthusiastic, your sympathies are aglow, the tide of feeling rises high in your heart, and there is no bound to the extent to which you wish well to the cause which your spiritual leader represents. And you may feel that it is a great cause, as great because really the same as that which Elijah represented; the cause of the one true living God against all denials of Him or all substitutes for Him—the cause of a pure morality in the land inseparably connected with a pure worship—the cause of the independence of religion of the control and manipulation for State purposes by civil rulers, whether they be fools like Ahab, or harlots like Jezebel, or whatever they may be—the cause of the existence of true religion in every heart and home in the country. It is the same cause now as then; all this you may feel now, and you may believe that the feeling will remain.

So did the crowd on Carmel on the day of the gladness of Elijah's heart. But on the morrow they feared to lift a finger for him. My brethren, if those set over us are to be successful we must stand by them; and if so we must be at one with them in principle. I do not say in every opinion which we may hold or express, but in the great principles which move their own lives, and for which among you they have to contend. You must share with them in their love of the Lord that bought you. You must hold with them, one Lord, one faith, one baptism, one God and Father of all, who is over all, and through all, and in you all. Everything you do must have its root there; and then your sympathy with them in all their contendings for this will be keen and intelligent—without it your sympathy with them in their work will be languid and evanescent and go no deeper than a certain *esprit de corps* peculiar to a sectional Christianity,

It will arise merely out of opposition to others from enmity to the opposite camp, and having no root in itself, when a real conflict comes will wither away. Spiritual teachers in all ages, perhaps, have fallen into the error of Elijah. They have exaggerated, they have gone into extremes into which those whom they taught could not follow them. It is not necessary to follow them into their extremes; but these extremes are greatly due to their feeling of being isolated, and of the immovable insensibility of those whom they have to instruct. Cordial co-operation, cordial sympathy from you in the great general truths of the faith will remove these feelings and these exaggerations, and then Christian teaching shall become calm and simple and natural, and the stream of Christian truth and life, instead of being like a noisy brook, dashing itself against everything within its reach, will advance like a great placid broad river without a wave upon its surface, absorbing into itself on all sides every contribution of the thought and life of men, and moving on with a power that nothing can resist, and bearing on its bosom to a blessed end this human family which Christ loved and gave Himself for.

A. B. D.

XVII. The King Conquered. 2 KINGS vi.

THIS chapter is about one of the battles of the king of Syria against Israel. You remember about Naaman. Naaman was captain of the host of the king of Syria, yet he does not appear, at least by name, to take any part in this war. He may have been here, he may have been in the background, but I rather infer that, since he went back to Syria, not only with a new skin, but a new God, probably he fell into disfavour, or was in some way held to be disqualified for his former supreme military position. A very wonderful thing that. Naaman came to be healed of his leprosy, and he got more than he wanted. That is the perpetual history of all earnest men who come to the right quarter for help. No man can come to church, to the living God, with a right desire, without getting exceeding abundantly above that which he came for; no matter what he came for, if it was of the right quality, of the right nature, and within the compass of the gifts of God to men, within the limits and boundaries of time, then he got exceeding abundantly above that for which he expressly came. Naaman said, "Well, I will go to him, and I will see if this man can cure me of this leprosy;" and he not only got a new skin, so that his flesh came again as the flesh of a little child, but he got a new God, a new theological conception, a new standpoint from which to view the universe, and to estimate his own life; and that is what is always happening, and must occur to the end of time. You cannot come to God for any one bounty proper to be received at His hands, without receiving with it some additional blessing, if so be you are willingly opening your heart to receive whatever God in His Almighty power and beneficent grace may be pleased to give you. Naaman, then, has gone back again with a clean flesh, the leprosy all gone, and with the God of Israel as his God, and now Syria once more projects war against Israel. I want to study the projection of that war, and how things occur under combinations of circumstances to which you and I ought to be no strangers. Begin, if you please, at the eighth verse.

"Then the king of Syria took counsel with his servants, saying, In such and such a place shall be my camp." Was there anything amiss then? I think there was. Not on the bare reading; the verse reads well enough—it seems to have been a proper thing to do—and sometimes we do a proper thing improperly. Sometimes we tell the truth falsely. How is that? In the telling of truth itself, we may give a false impression—we may preach the gospel destructively: we have not only to announce the good news—the glad tidings—but to do it in the right tone, with gentleness and tenderness and persuasiveness and sympathy. And falling down before men, we have oft entreated them with vehemence and passion, that they may accept the testimony we bring. Well, but the king of Syria consulted his servants—was not that right? Possibly so—if he knew who his servants were. Is there any one man on earth you can really trust in a crisis? Are there not some points in life when the true consultation is divine and not human? Are there not some critical moments in your life when you must not speak to the nearest and dearest friend you have, when your life must culminate in a supreme agony, and all your communications must be upward, and not lateral, and never downward? Well, methinks that grand old Roman was right when he said: "If I thought the shirt on my back heard what I was saying to myself I would tear it off and burn it." That man will succeed, will do something in life. He knows that there are times to be familiar, conversational, communicative, when you may say to the public, "Now my heart is open, come in and see all you can see, and see it for nothing"—and this wins great reputation for geniality and communicativeness. People talk to him as a very familiar, condescending, kind, amicable, and communicative man altogether; but he knows exactly when to shut the door and to look dumb. Do you know what it is to look deaf? You cannot look deaf if you are hearing all the time unless you have the supreme mastery of yourself. A deaf person looks so different from you—I see that you are hearing, in your skin, in your eyes; the very hair on your head says, I am listening all the time; I am feigning deafness, but I hear all you are saying. You cannot be deaf unless you are supremely master of your own nature; but this great man, this great Roman, looked dumb, looked deaf, looked stone-like. There was no reading his face. Ben-hadad having got an idea, could not be trusted with it. He called in his servants, constituted them into a kind of Divine Consensus, and began to tell them what he was going to do—and there was an end of him.

How many people would succeed if they could be silent? —how many people would do well in life if they knew when to hold their tongues? They would do exceedingly well if they had not so many people in their confidence; but there are some people who chatter, chatter, chatter, always telling what they are going to do—what they are going to do to-morrow, what they are going to do the day after to-morrow,—and they never do it. How can they— talking so much about it beforehand? It is like running five miles before leaping over a wall—you are so tired with the running that when you come to the leap you cannot do it. Be quiet sometimes—keep your own counsel. "How is it, Commodore," said a man to old Mr. Vanderbilt, who is just now dead, "that you have succeeded so well in life?" "Well," said the old man, "first, by minding my own business, and secondly, by never telling anybody what I was going to do, but just doing it." Ben-hadad was no Commodore Vanderbilt in this respect. He called all the people together and said in effect, "I know now what I shall do," and he told them all about it, and thus split himself up in a dozen different directions. He lost that concentration, that consolidation, that cannon-ball-like compactness of perfect solitude which gives a man supreme power in supreme and definite crises in life.

Let us see then what happened after all this talk. "And the man of God sent unto the king of Israel, saying, Beware that thou pass not such a place; for thither the Syrians are come down. And the king of Israel sent to the place which the man of God told him and warned him of, and saved himself there, not once nor twice," but many a time. So the thing got abroad. Well, now, here is Elisha. Elisha is no soldier. No; Elisha, to use a modern phrase, never fired a gun in his life. No—he knew more about a plough than about firearms — excuse my modernizing the instance. What did he do? "There was a little city, and few men within it; and there came a great king against it, and besieged it, and built great bulwarks against it; now there was found in it a poor wise man, and he, by his wisdom, delivered the city." What did Elisha do? What you, dear little child, can do: what you, feeble woman, can do: what you, man of no public status or influence, can do. What was that? He warned —he gave warning, he gave caution, and suggested prudence. He pointed out the difficulty and how to avoid it. Just observe, then, how we serve one another in life. The Apostle Paul complains that if a man do not give a certain sound upon the trumpet the soldiers cannot prepare themselves for battle. But do we want trumpeters as well as soldiers? A man that gives an uncertain blast on the trumpet ruins the fight on his own side; the man whose trumpet is in tune, whose breath is equal to the occasion, who blows a blast that strikes inspiration into an army, is himself a crowd of soldiers. Just observe how we serve one another. Elisha was a man of thought—a man of prayer—a man of contemplation, and yet he sends warning to the king of Israel, and by a warning word he saves the king of Israel from the arrows of the Syrian assailants. Now there be some persons who cannot reckon up the influence of people who do nothing but talk, and teach, and pray, and warn. They have not got the true conception of work. Their conception of work is limited to the arms. Only give a man plenty to do with his hands and they claim him as a working man. But if a man so live as apparently to have nothing to do with his arms at all, then it is impossible for the people to whom I am now referring to consider the man as anybody working—whereas Elisha did more with his one warning word than if he had gone to the head of the Israelitish army and led the hosts into the thick of the fight. That is a word for you, mother—that is a word for you, sister—that is a word for you, letter-writer, you who only sit at home and write a few kind notes to your friends — for you, more public writer — for you, student—for you, minister—for you, praying soul. We can all serve one another. The men that came back from Jerusalem and spoke to Nehemiah had done nothing whatever themselves to repair the wall—they only told Nehemiah about it, and Nehemiah went and did it.

So Elisha heard of this, and warned the king of Israel, and saved him from a great battle with the Syrians. Use your influence; do what you can. You want greater power—use the talent you have. You shall see Rome also if you live faithfully in the cities and villages in which Providence appoints your place. Have you ever warned anybody? This Book excels all other books in this one particular—monition—warning—caution. Other books are always controverting, discovering, fighting illuminated battles, and registering things and putting things in order, and settling debates, and strifes, and contentions with some other book somewhere else in the world. But this dear old Book is full of warning, and sympathy, and direction, and practical counsel; it gets into the soul, it takes the language of our necessity, it prays with us, sings with us, gives us words wherewith to express our best emotions, helps our life upward and onward—a right positive Book, a grandly affirmative Book. Yes, if I could but listen to its voice—and you—we should always find ourselves on the right road, in the right temper, in the right spirit, with a very grateful heart and two very industrious hands, in the service of God. Don't, then, snub men who are not working in your own particular way. This is the great difficulty we have with one another. There is only a man here and there, a very rare man indeed, who sympathises with other people's way of working, who does not think if you don't do just what he does and nothing else, you are not working. But an ordinary man thinks if you go to his meeting, read his books, dance his dances, and fuss away in his little fussinesses, then you are working. But if you have any other conception of service, and are working from any other conception of stewardship in the sight of God which he cannot understand, you will very likely be troubled in your progress by his very small censure, by his vicious malediction. Oh that we could just know that we are all working in the way we can. I see a man yonder working in a way I cannot—I wish I could—but I must work in the way I can. Another says, I can only pray—that is, only move Omnipotence, only help to bring Almightiness to your side—only speak to God for you— it is a wonderful " only " that. You be faithful to that "only" and you will help all men, you will help the universe.

Now then Elisha, the quiet, contemplative, observant man, with an ear quick to all-but-infinite sensitiveness, hearing whisperings where any other man could hear nothing but a great silence, and he is warning and thus saving, teaching and thus delivering—and it will be a bad, black, woeful day for this England when you lose the teachers and the warners, the seers, the prophets who dream dreams and see visions, and can lift themselves up in all the erectness of a majesty higher than their own, to declare to men what they ought to do and what they ought not to attempt. Let us pray for our prophets, and say, " God bless our teachers, every one." "Therefore the heart of the king of Syria was sore troubled for this thing." There he is again—Oh that men should live on such poor flats, poor planes, low levels! The king is troubled and he calls his servants. Oh if he had only been a wise king, if he had only looked upward and inward, if he had only been quiet with a prayerful quietness and reverence, he might have done something more in that contest. But he lives among men, a social man, a chattering man, one of those people who could not spend an evening at home—one of those persons who always want to get away from their own company, one of those men who says, "you know—what I can do, sitting here? what can I do—I wish somebody would come in—I wonder where I can go to, I do so want to talk!" What do they do in life? Nothing—but make a noise. O my friend, when thou art in trouble, call upon God—call upon the Divine, call upon the Supernatural. It does you good to think that the firmament above, if it be but blue steel, brightened here and there with a patine of fine gold—it does you good to think you can catch hold of that great blue arch and lift yourself up an inch! That will do you good. But it is *this* motion that does you harm—getting down, as if the help were yonder. The help is never yonder. Whatever your perplexity or difficulty, the help is always up—never down, never lateral. There it is that religion, in any true and grand sense of it, does a man infinite good—just to get into his head the idea that there is a greater power than himself, if it be but the wind, or the great solemn thunder, or the mighty rolling stars and suns. To fall down on your knees and look up at the sun, clasping your hands in reverence before his brilliant image—that will do you good. It is this curse of always living on a low level that ruins us—calling in our equals, calling in our inferiors, calling in the people that are round about us. It is all right enough under given circumstances, as a secondary palliative and as a help in many a misery—all right enough. But there ought to be a supreme, glad, religious aspiration going out of the heart to find the big, the mighty, the *All*, the circumference of things. O my friend, if thou couldst but do that, everything would be under thy feet. Thou shouldst be calm, and happy, and very glad always; but as long as you look, and look, along the line of your eye—have everything hung so that you can get it there, you are dwarfing the universe, you are dwarfing yourself, limiting the infinite and forgetting the eternal. But in distress, in difficulty, call upon God—ay, and if He be but a wooden stick, a poor deaf, dumb stone, a blind thing thou hast thyself chiseled out of the forest, it will do thee good, if thou canst but lay hold, however dimly, of the idea that there is something greater than thyself, and out of that greatness thy help will come. How much more then to lay hold of the Father in Heaven—called with such infinite pathos and delicacy the God and Father of our Lord Jesus Christ. Oh how full these words! what sap, what juice, what blood, what life, what music, what light! The God—Oh how grand! The God and Father—more tender; equally majestic, but condescending: a King stooping. The God and Father of our Lord Jesus Christ—humanized, standing beside us, looking into our eyes, offering infinitude as our help and eternity as the grand duration of our growth and progress!

"And one of his servants said, No, my lord the king,"

you are quite wrong in your supposition—there is no treachery among your servants, "but Elisha, the prophet that is in Israel, telleth the king of Israel the words that thou speakest in thy bedchamber." Yes, it is this ghostly element in life that ought to make the highest man amongst us pause. I have often said this; I do not know why I should hesitate to say it again. If there was nothing but what we could see, nothing behind, above, beyond—begin here, pass over there, end yonder—if this were all, then I do not see why the old heathen programme should not be re-written in coloured ink on silken banners, waved over all the concourse of humanity everywhere—let us eat and drink, for to-morrow we die! Let us die fat, let us die drunk, let us die intoxicated with empoisoned delight; if we begin here, tarry there, fall yonder, up with the banner—eat and drink, to-morrow we die! But it is this ghostly element, the shaking of the veil, the unaccountable noise, the whistling in the window, the creaking on the floor, the upsetting of a whole scheme of probabilities we thought were built up together with something stronger than the strongest cement ever used in the uniting and cohesion of materials, the upsetting of our calculations, the shaking down of all our little plots, plans, schemes, and arrangements, the laying things down there, and saying we shall find them in the morning, and when the morning comes, they are gone!—saying, Good-bye, to a man, and hearing the man is dead in the morning! It is these ghostly things that make us uncertain and troubled and insecure, and that makes an atheist fit a clause of reservation in all his cold covenants and mercenary agreements. Even he must have his "if." O poor coward and fool—why not develop him, that he can put his arms around the whole firmament. "I hold it fast, and will do with it what I like"—why not? Develop him, and that great great God lets us get the tower a long way up, and then He comes and puts one foot on it, and down it goes.

"And the king of Syria was troubled," and the word rendered troubled is a very remarkable word—"tempested." There were in his spirit counterblasts of wind from the east, from the west, from the north, from the south, whirling, swirling, raging, roaring, storming his soul. He called his servants in—just what we do when we hear noises we do not like. We ring the bell—we are not afraid, you know, but we just like to see what this is. Are you not afraid, you lying man? If you had seen yourself two seconds ago with a face blanched as death, and now that your servants have come in you are looking as if you were never afraid in your life. Better make our account with these invisible presences, these incalculable quantities, these ghostly elements, these subtle unnameable, incalculable ministries that are about. He only has settled the account with them who has made his peace with God, and says, "God is our refuge and strength, therefore will I not fear though the mountains be carried into the midst of the sea. God is our refuge and strength, and a very present help in trouble. There is a river the streams whereof make glad the city of God." There have been men in that high calm, in that imperturbable peace, in that infinite tranquillity. Such peace have they, O God, who love and follow Thy holy law.

Well, the king of Syria having found out that this was the case, plucked up his courage again—said, I am not afraid—do not suppose it; if this is all, I will soon end it. Have you ever read the histories of the Welsh preachers, those grand old thunder-storms that spoke from the hill-sides to thousands of people and made them quail? One of these men, whose son is a Member of Parliament in our own House of Commons to-day, was preaching away, and saying as only a Welshman can say, and only say it in Welsh—"The day of judgment is come—the day of judgment is come!" And there was an orchard between him and a house in which dwelt a very ungodly squire, and this man heard through the trees this funereal voice—" The day of judgment is come—the day of judgment is come!" and he took down the prayer book at once and began to gabble over his prayers; rung the bell and called in his servant—Ben-hadad's old device, always get somebody up stairs to talk with—and he said, "John, don't you hear that strange voice—'The day of judgment is come'?" "Oh, no, sir, it's only old Mr. So and So, the Welsh preacher, preaching over there"—"Oh, that's it, is it—don't imagine there's anything the matter with me—that's it, is it?" And away went the prayer book. That is how it will be with you—some of you. I have seen you in a thunder-storm, getting down into the cellar,—into the coal-house, and shutting all the windows and bolting the doors, as if you could bolt out the lightning and exclude the infinite. And yet if all is right, what do you care? Ben-hadad said, Oh, that's it, is it? If that's the case, we'll have him. "Go and spy where he is, that I may send and fetch him." See! that is the plan; spy where he is and fetch him. Very good. "Therefore sent he thither horses, and chariots, and a great host; and they came by night and compassed the city round about."

That is one of the finest things in the history, and that is occurring every day. It is the unconscious tribute which the material is always paying to the spiritual, the unconscious homage which baffled men always pay to the Christianity they would destroy. Ay, how many Ben-hadads have sent horses and chariots and a great host to take the Cross? What a compliment to Elisha. We thought he would have said, "Here, you young whipper-snapper—the youngest of you—you can go—go and bring that man here —two of you run down and fetch him." No; it is an awkward thing, fetching a prophet; an awkward business, fighting the spiritual. So he sent horses and chariots and a great host, and told them—"Go by night and make a cordon round the city, and see that he does not escape you." Ben-hadad, why all this fuss about one man?—a quondam plough-boy, with nothing but the mantle upon his shoulder; why not send down anybody, any boy, any Bashi-Bazouk, to fetch him along? That is what they are always doing, and so we have shops opened to put down Christian teaching, and great hosts of people going to take the cross, and vast armies and crowds of assailants, saying, "Now then, this is the critical moment—this is the tremendous agony." And where is Christianity to-day? Where it is most wanted—in the aching heart; in the bruised, wounded spirit; in the contrite, self-accusing, self-renouncing soul, repeating all its old miracles, and none of its majesty is lost—none of its almightiness impaired. Always understand this, my friend, that the more people it requires to take a man, the greater that man is, in some way. But you have been quite surprised, you who did not know better, quite surprised how some people are exceedingly distressed and annoyed if they see so much as a single paragraph in a newspaper against a man. The finest thing would be to have the whole newspaper against you, and twenty more papers, and nearly all the papers. What would it mean? It would mean that there is some grit in you, some stuff in you, some quality in you. Don't suppose that all these people like to go and kick a gate post simply for the sake of kicking. So if it is only a gate post, why kick it? But the more men that are sent to take you, the more they sneer, the more they assail you, depend upon it, it is the unconscious tribute which a mean man must pay to the majestic—that the false man must pay to the true—that the disappointed man must pay to the man who is successful. And this teaching finds its supreme application in Christ and in His Church; for all the hosts of hell have been arrayed against Him, and no impression has yet been made upon the Rock upon which the Church has been founded.

And after Ben-hadad had sent all these things, "the servant of the man of God was risen early, and gone forth, behold, an host compassed the city both with horses and chariots. And his servant said unto him, Alas, my master! what shall we do?" Of course, a very natural question. I like to see a man natural; the man comes in and says, "It's all over—there's no mistake about it, I have seen it," and when a man has actually seen a thing what can you say? He only thinks he has seen it, but you can never persuade him better. Some people say, seeing is believing. There was never a more sophistical saying made, unless you define what seeing is; but seeing, in the ordinary sense of the term, is not believing. No man is so often befooled as through his own eyes, his own eyesight. He thinks he sees everything, and he sees nothing. And this man gave it up at once, and says, what shall we do? He does right, he comes to the master. Did Elisha send for the servant? No, the servant came to him. That is the way to live, live so that you will be master, whether you live in the parlour or the kitchen, whether you are master in sagacity, in knowledge, in sympathy, in reception of impressions, in grasp of details—have the mastery of the situation, whatever it is, because in the last result persons always send for the supreme mind.

Now this man says, "How shall we do?" First of all, Elisha says, "Fear not." Fear destroys power, fear takes a man's quality out of him; no man is himself who is under the chilling cloud of a fear. "Do not fear;" but why? For this reason: "they that be with us are more than they that be with them." And Elisha said, "Lord"—the servant came to the master, and the master went to his Master, that is the ascending line; and Elisha said, "Lord, open his eyes—open his eyes—that he may see." "But I have seen." "Oh, no, open his eyes that he may see." "Why, I have just been out, I got up early, I have seen." Oh, no; that is just the battle we have as Christian teachers, and as high teachers of any kind. Men think they see when they do not see. "What," a man says, "cannot I read the Bible for myself as well as you can?" No; if you are only reading the letter and I the spirit, you cannot. If you are only an etymologist and not a sympathetic reader of the word, you cannot read aright. Elisha's servant had been out early and had seen, and Elisha prays that his eyes may be opened that he may see. There is seeing and seeing, reading and reading, hearing and hearing. "And the Lord opened the eyes of the young man, and he saw; and, behold, the mountain was full of horses and chariots of fire round about Elisha," horse for horse, chariot for chariot, fire for fire, God *versus* Benhadad. It is a tremendous and terrible thing to fall into the hands of the living God. Another horse and another chariot from heaven till all your forces fall off in the cloudy perspective, and the inner concentric circle makes heaven round about you. Have you ever seen that flashing circle? I have, thank God—thank God. Have you never seen it—Providences that you could not explain on any other ground than merely kindness and beneficence—deliverances perfectly superhuman? Do you not know what it has been, lying between four quaternions of soldiers, with only six hours between you and the guillotine, and the angel of God coming and melting the irons and taking you out in the open air? I do. That is how I can read this dear old Book. If it is only to be read as a book taken off the shelf, I say, No, I cannot read such writing as that—I cannot understand it—I give it up. But I do not come to it like

L

that. You see, if I come to it thus—you know—in a kind of—sort of—semi-philosophical way; ah—with a kind of semi-philosophical eye-glass to look at it — then, of course, I shut it up. How do I come to it? Just in proportion as I can say—Thrice was I beaten with rods, a day and a night have I been in the deep—in perils in the city—in perils in the wilderness—in perils among the heathen—in perils among mine own countrymen—in cold, in weariness, in nakedness, in hunger—persecuted, cast down, perplexed, impoverished, embarrassed, dismantled, unmanned—death in the house, mother and child in one coffin—no bread in the cupboard, no coal in the grate, no friend outside! Ah, if I come to this good old Book through such processes, I say, "This is my Book." Are you not puzzled by the miracles? Puzzled by the miracles? I have lived them. I wanted this, these are the words I have been hunting for—yearning for—I know them all—it is my native tongue, it is the speech of my bleeding, triumphant heart. I see so many people bring up things like these, and they find them very burdensome; but if *you* can get down upon them out of a tragical, tremendous, awful experience, you will find them all written in plain language—you will need no interpreter to help you through them—your own gashed, half-dead heart has lived every syllable of the narrative—has gone through every throb of that strange, that tragic life!

J. P.

XVIII. Josiah. 2 Chron. xxxv. 21. "*Forbear thee from meddling with God.*"

JOSIAH was an excellent king of Judah. There had been none like him for many a long day. He was but an infant when he came unto the throne, that is to say, he was eight years old. The written law had been lost a very long time; Josiah had nothing by way of example to draw upon that could lift him up towards the true notion of worship and service to the real God. He was the son of a bad man, he was the son indeed of one of the worst men that ever lived in that time of the world's history. Being so young, what could he do? Well, he found something in his own heart, as we should humanly say, that started him on the right direction. He began in a very wonderful way to do very excellent things. He seemed to be a kind of instinctive or intuitional reformer; for the law was lost, and the priests and prophets seemed to be dumb, and the poor young king wrought away with such light as he had, and in the course of his working he did what you will do if you will try—he found the law.

You would find more if you sought for more: he that doeth the will shall know the doctrine: he who uses the little candle that is at his disposal shall be led out into solar light—twilight to begin with, but growing unceasingly and unchangeably up into the mid-day blaze of glory.

Josiah then found the law, had it read in his hearing, learned from it that every king of Judah and of Israel had been covenanted to keep that law with his own hand, and he felt that all the judgments prophesied against the house of Israel and of Judah would fall upon his own head, because he had not obeyed the letter of the word of the Lord. What was to be done? It was speedily discovered that the wardrobe-keeper had a wife in whom was the spirit of prophecy, and so to Huldah they went, and she sent comfortable messages to the young king: she said, "Thus saith the Lord to the man who hath acted so, because thine heart was tender and thou hast feared the Lord, none of these judgments shall fall upon thee, but thou shalt be gathered to thy fathers in peace, and after that there shall come a black day upon the black people." So Josiah took heart again, and it came into his mind to revive the old ceremonies and ritual of Israel, and to do wonderful things in the way of the Passover, and we read that there was no Passover like to that kept in Israel from the days of Samuel the prophet.

Now Josiah will go down to his fathers in peace—if he behave himself. He reigned one and thirty years, and in the last month of that last year he may be tripped up. You are not safe while you are on the water; though there be but eighteen inches between the ship and the land; there is room enough in eighteen inches to sink you down. Get on the land before you sing—be on the rock before you take the trumpet and put it to your lips: risk nothing of the detail of your life—an iota may ruin you, the miss of the smallest writing in all the minutest detail may lead to loss, to death, to hell. You are not saved by lumps of good behaviour, by breadths of possible morality: he that is unfaithful in the least will be unfaithful in the greatest. Even yet Josiah may be smitten from Heaven after his one and thirty years of very excellent service—so many people get wrong just at the last, so many people fall into the water just as they are stepping on land. What I say unto one, I say unto all—Watch.

The miscarriage in the case of Josiah came about in this way. There was a king of Egypt called Pharaoh Necho, an old foe of the Assyrian empire. He came up to fight against Charchemish, by Euphrates, and Josiah at his own instigation went out against Necho king of Egypt. "But Necho king of Egypt sent ambassadors unto him, saying, What have I to do with thee, thou king of Judah? I come not against thee this day, but against the house wherewith I have war; for God commanded me to make haste. Forbear thee from meddling with God who is with me, that He destroy thee not." A noble message—the man who can speak so calmly, solemnly, religiously, will fight well. Have no faith in the blustering assailant—dread the man who challenges thee when on his knees.

Josiah would not turn his face from Necho, but disguised himself that he might fight with him; he hearkened not unto the words of Necho from the mouth of God, and came to fight in the valley of Megiddo. And the archers shot at king Josiah, and the king said to his servants, "Have me away; for I am sore wounded." So he was put into his second chariot, and carried home. And he died, and was buried in one of the sepulchres of his fathers—he who might have been gathered to his fathers quietly, in the very peace, in the infinite sweetness of the benediction of God, was shot like a dog.

Are you priding yourself upon your quarter of a century's good behaviour? If there is a day yet left to you there is time enough for you to sponge out all the beauty of the past and to find your way into perdition. The question most deeply interesting to us is: what can we learn from the words of the king of Egypt that will help us to live a true and useful life?

Do we not learn from Necho—unfamiliar name, unaccustomed minister—that our life is not a series of unrelated accidents, but that it is a part of a Divine and immutable scheme? The king of Egypt said in effect to Josiah:—"This is no doing of mine; I am secondary in the matter; I am not following the lure of my own fancy; I am impelled by God; I am here as His servant—treat me as such, or God will cause His judgment to fall upon thee." This is the only solid ground to occupy, if life is to be more than a continual exasperation and a bitter disappointment. This is the great doctrine of Providence which Jesus Christ never ceased to teach, and never ceased to live. When He began His life what did He say? Oh, to catch the first words from those eloquent lips!—what was the first note in the anthem of that tragic life? "Wist ye not that I must be about my Father's business?" What was the last note in that same anthem? Will He be able to make His way around, so as to finish where He began? Hear Him on the cross: "Father into Thy hands I commend my spirit." Father at first, Father at last, and throughout all the teaching the same word glowed like a sun that kept all the inferior stars in their places.

Have you been centring in yourself, beginning with your own little individuality, carving out a small system of astronomy with your own shadow as a centre? Then I do not wonder that your faces are wrinkled, and that there is a murmur in your speech, a cloud in your sky, and that you are lost amid all the little, petty, fretful, vexatious details of life. You are wrong. We are invited in the Holy Scripture to believe that we are not our own creators; that we live because God wills it; that the very hairs of our head are all numbered; and that our steps are of the Lord's ordering; and that our downsitting and our uprising are noted in Heaven; that our outgoing is observed, and our returning regarded in the Heavenly books, and at the last our deeds and words will be judged by the wise God, whose strength and wisdom are the stay of the universe. If you accept that faith you cannot be troubled; if you have any other creed, the weather, the climate, will have you up and down according to the fickleness of its own movement.

The doctrine of the Bible is a doctrine of a Providential plan—a Divine scheme. Every page is rich with the promises of this doctrine, not a line is out of chord with its solemn music. Yea, the cross itself is part of the infinite plan, foreseen from eternity in every shadow of its gloom and every pang of its agony. So then, we who are Christians believe that God is over all, that the earth is in the hollow of His hand, and that nothing happens, even down to the falling out of its nest of the youngest sparrow in the early summer, without His notice. A grand conception, if it be nothing more—a marvellous poem if only a flash of fancy—an infinite rock if a Divine revelation. And yet I have people round about me—we all have—who pray to God but don't trust Him. Wonder ye that their prayers like birds with broken wings die on the threshold of the closet in which they were conceived? I don't. Any other outcoming of such prayer would vex me as a practical satire upon Providential ways. The great doctrine of Divine Providence is like the sun, distant, inaccessible; but the exemplification of that doctrine in personal and practical life is like the light which falls out of the sun, which makes morning upon our window and the abundant summer round about our houses. I propose therefore now turning from the great general doctrine which underlies the message which the king of Egypt addressed to Josiah, to look at some of the minute and special colourings of this doctrine which come to us through its personal trials and realizations.

I. In the first place the king of Egypt considered that the doctrine of a Providential plan was not inconsistent with difficulty, contention, loss, and suffering on the part of man. Does the king of Egypt say: "This is Providence, brother king Josiah, sitting on my throne, my head upon a pillow of down, my feet resting on velvet soft as moss, my whole house glowing with every light and every beauty"? No such foolish message does he send to the king of Judah. Necho has come up from his own land, come up to suffer, come up to fight, come up to shed blood: yet he says, "God sent me." It is so seldom we think God sends us to church on a wet Sunday: we think

He is so fearful of us taking cold that surely He would never be so unreasonable as to ask us to go out on a wet Sunday. In the old, old times, when heroes shook the earth with their majestic step, they were not afraid of insects and wet days—we are. "'Tis true, 'tis pity, pity 'tis 'tis true."

It was no holiday dream that had touched Necho's ambition or vanity: it was a service of severe discipline, anxious preparation, daily watching, mortal strife, and yet he saw God over it all, watching, directing, controlling. I believe there are some of us who believe in Providence when we are in a nice large boat and have the best seat and the softest cushion, and when the water is like molten silver, and the banks are near and green, and the sky far off and blue, with many a keen light lodging in its fleecy clouds. Then we say, "Ah,"—pious sigh!—" Ah, after all he must be blind who does not see God in this." It is sad, it is discouraging, it sometimes makes me impious. But to hear a poor woman—a widow—who has buried the one boy in the family that could work for its sustenance—to hear her say,—looking at all the little girls who are nearly helpless, taking up the corner of her apron to wipe off the tear from her poor eyes—"God's will be done: the Lord gave, and the Lord hath taken away, blessed be the name of the Lord"—that converts me, brings me home, makes me pray.

O full summer Christian, what art thou doing to bring lustre upon thy faith, to make the world wonder if it does not worship—stand aghast and amazed if it do not join thy psalm of resignation? If Christians carried out their creed, we should soon, by the blessing of God, convert the heathen.

II. In the next place the king of Egypt acknowledged and proclaimed the tender and ever comforting doctrine of a special personal, detailed Providence. Did he say to Josiah, "The Lord reigneth"? No. Did he refer Josiah to great abstract principles? He did not. What said Necho—man of the strange mouth and the unfamiliar voice?—He said, "God commanded me, God is with me." There is a deism which says that the whole is cared for, but the part must take care of itself. The king of Egypt reversed the doctrine, saw God caring for the part, and reasoned that therefore he cared for the whole. This is the very teaching of Christ: Christ hath some strange ministers, some irregular expositors, some preachers who did not come through the orthodox gate, and therefore much to be suspected by people who were cradled in orthodoxy and will be buried in it. Jesus Christ and Necho king of Egypt were at one in this high sweet note. Jesus said, "Wherefore," after having been looking at bird and lily, and small things accessible to all generally, "Wherefore, if God so clothe the grass of the field, which to-day is, and to-morrow is cast into the oven, shall He not much more clothe you?" If we believed that, the remainder of this day would be about the happiest portion of our life we have had, in the individual heart or at the family table, for many a long year.

My friend, God will take care of thee if thou dost live in Him and for Him, and dost love Him. He will not let thy grey hairs go down with sorrow to the grave, and He will find the key of that shut door, and He will search for a rod the shadow of which shall make the Red Sea sever in two parts, and thou shalt go through on dry land. Have faith in God—cast thyself upon Him and wait patiently His will and the revelation of His purpose, and if thou must perish, perish with thy belief upon thy lips. No man was ever wounded to death by that dart.

God cares for the individual, for the unit. Do you care for your family as an abstraction or as a reality? Do you care for your children as a whole, or do you care for them individually? Now how is it? If you lump them, speak of them as a poetical abstraction, I am very glad not to be under your patronage. But if you pick out the eldest, and the youngest, and the three or four or five between and care for each of them as if that were the only child, then it would be well to be one of the number. And so you do. Very well: "If ye then, being evil, know how to give good gifts unto your children, how much more shall your Father which is in heaven give good things to them that ask Him" —give the Holy Ghost to them that seek Him—give direction to every one of His children? Why, if one of them went astray, what would He do? He would leave the ninety and nine and would go after that which was gone astray. The God that gave that representation of

Himself is all the God I want. The tenderness of that suggestion shall stand for learning, for criticism, for history, for logic—it shall be all in all. You will find me there when heart and flesh do fail.

By constantly desiring to know and to do the will of God, we seem to link our small life to the great chariot of God's Providence; but when we take our life into our own keeping, we detach ourselves from that chariot and grope like cripples in the dark. By our faith we draw succour from the very root of God's own being, but by our unbelief and self-sufficiency we lose the sustenance, and perish, because we seek not to live on God's word but on our own. And to-day there are some people who imagine that they can get along pretty well without God: who are the people? Debtors to His mercy. Who are the people that have wounded you most keenly? The people to whom you have lent money and shown favours and been kind. Nobody else can thrust the knife so far into the heart. Barbarian and Scythian can give you an ugly thrust that shall tear the skin, but man of your own household, child of your own bones, friend that has sucked the blood of your love—he can thrust the blade up to the hilt.

When a man has been born in a Christian land, has been reared in a Christian atmosphere, and has had all the advantages of a Christian example and Christian training, it is impossible for that man to know exactly what he would have been and what he would have done but for those facts. Travelling the other day, I saw something which illustrated this graphically. I was standing in the railway station, and in there came a carriage, all by itself —no steam engine, just a carriage and nothing more. And the carriage said, "There is a notion abroad, an old-fashioned but mistaken and sometimes mischievous notion, that it is needful to have a steam engine in order to draw a carriage. Gentlemen," said the carriage, looking to the few persons on the platform, "if you seek an argument to disprove that fallacy, *circumspice*, look around." And we all looked around, and we all saw it, and we all said, "Carriage, this is very wonderful: you brought yourself into this station apparently, now take yourself out of it." And the carriage is standing there still, and will stand there till it rots,—it cannot turn a wheel. It was a detached carriage; the great engine that brought it along with mighty sweep went on, and this was left behind to spend its momentum, and it just came into the station so nicely and thought it had brought itself in. And there be many human detached carriages. They have had fathers, mothers, ministers, schools, lectures, books: they have been brought up under Christian culture, taken so far along the line: by some means or other become detached —asked to be detached, and in spending their dying momentum, they think they are using an original force. Be it mine to be drawn on by the great God: I would live and move and have my being in God; my smallest affairs I would spread before Him; I would ask Him to my bedchamber that He may give me sleep; I would see Him at my table as the Giver and Sanctifier of my daily bread. He shall keep my door lest an enemy enter or a friend go out—when I pass through the valley of the shadow of death I will ask no other comfort than His rod and staff.

The text is in 2 Chronicles xxxv. 21. It is very notable that we should have this great saying from the mouth of a king of Egypt. This would have come well from the lips of Jeremiah who prophesied in the days of Josiah king of Judah. It would have befitted the burning lips of Ezekiel—it would have fallen well from the eloquent mouth of Isaiah. But we get this doctrine from Necho king of Egypt. This is indeed water in an unexpected place—behold, a fair flower in a wide, bleak desert: hear the music of Heaven played upon a strange instrument.

But do you think it cannot be true because Necho the heathenish king of Egypt said it? Then you know not that it is part of the Divine plan to bring strange prophets into the ministry of the word. Were there not ten lepers cleansed? Yes. How many have returned to give glory to God? One. Who is he? A stranger. Did not one man stoop to pity the wounded traveller on the road, to pour in wine and oil, to set him on his beast, to bring him to his inn, and to take care of him? Yes. Who was it? A Samaritan. Was there not a woman who surprised the Son of God Himself by the abundance and vividness of her faith—did she not seem to turn back the going of the Eternal? She did. Who was she? A woman—a Syrophenician—no well dressed Jewess who was caught within the cordon of the old covenants and seemed to have a hereditary right to the Divine ministrations and privileges. Was there not a man who once said, preaching the gospel before the time, "it was expedient that one man die for the people"? Yes. Who was it—Peter? No. John? No. Who? Caiaphas. Certainly—it is God's way. If we hold our peace He will make the stones cry out. If we English Christians, stall-fed, if we hold our peace, He will make the stones cry out. If we who swallow three sermons a week, and would kill the finest preacher that ever breathed by drawing from him and never giving anything in return—if we hold our peace, He will make the stones cry out. If we who know about Nazareth and Bethlehem and Capernaum and Jerusalem and Golgotha and Bethany—if we who have seen the blood and felt the hot healing drops fall upon our guilt—if we are dumb, the heathen shall take our places and we shall be shut out.

J. P.

XIX. Job.

JOB i. 8, 9. *"And the Lord said unto Satan, Hast thou considered My servant Job, that there is none like him in the earth, a perfect and an upright man, one that feareth God, and escheweth evil? Then Satan answered the Lord, and said, Doth Job fear God for nought?"*

AMONG the mysteries of God's providence, there is, perhaps, no mystery greater than the law by which suffering is meted out in the world. It is not a mystery that sin should bring forth sorrow; it is not a mystery that pain, disease, and death should be the fruit of man's fall. He who has ever reflected on the nature of sin will not wonder, that, by God's irreversible law, sin should bring its own chastisement with it. There is such a moral heinousness in the defection of one made in the image of God, from the image of his Maker; there is something so appalling in the assertion of the will of the creature in independence of, and in opposition to, the will of the Creator, that we cannot question the justice of the sentence: "In the day thou eatest thereof, thou shalt surely die." The act of rebellion against a holy God must carry with it in its teeming womb the whole vast burden of human misery and pain. We feel that, were it otherwise, the moral majesty of God would be assailed. To introduce disorder into the moral order of God, to mar His works—that it should be possible for man to do this, is, no doubt, evidence of man's greatness; but could man do this with impunity, that would certainly be an indisputable proof, either that no God existed, or that the God of this world was not one whom His creatures could worship. The conscience of men in all ages—the heathen conscience as well as the Jewish conscience and the Christian conscience—has acquiesced in the justice of that great moral constitution of things by which sin becomes its own chastisement. The avenging furies haunt the evil-doer, and suffering is the expiation of guilt.

But the really difficult problem is not the problem of suffering in the abstract; it is the problem of the meting out of suffering on any theory of sin; it is the problem why the innocent are called upon to suffer, whilst the guilty too often escape; it is the problem why the purest, the saintliest of our race, should drain to the dregs the cup of sorrow, while the ungodly have more than heart could wish, and have neither afflictions in their life, nor bands in their death. This is the problem which comes before us in that grandest of all poems which has ever sounded the deeps of the human heart—the Book of Job.

Job is a righteous man, living in the fear of God, and eschewing evil. He is a man of large wealth and possessions; but he does not spend his wealth in selfish gratification. He is charitable to the poor, hospitable to the stranger, bountiful to all. He was not only the greatest of all the men of the East, he was, it would seem, the best. He not only sat as a king amongst the tribes of the Koreish, his heart was as comprehensive as his wealth; when the ear heard him, then it blessed him; when the eye beheld him, it gave witness to him. But in a moment, the sky of his prosperity is overcast; lightnings leap out upon him from the dark thunder-cloud; blow follows blow with fearful rapidity. Arab hordes sweep away his cattle, and plunder his homestead, and kill his servants. A hurricane destroys the house in which his children are feasting, and buries them in its fall. All this in a single day; and, as if this were not enough, he is smitten himself with a ghastly and loathsome form of leprosy; and then, that the last aggravation of his bitter trial may not be wanting, his wife, breaking down under the load of her misery, pours venom into the cup of his suffering, bidding him renounce his faith in that Being who was visiting such punishments upon the head of His servant, and die with a blasphemy upon his lips.

On what principle of justice is such a man made to suffer? Here is a man exemplary in his life, devout, pure, charitable, of sterling integrity, of pronounced piety, having a living and sincere faith in God. Why is he crushed with this awful suffering? This is the problem we have before us in this magnificent drama. Contrast the problem for one moment with that which meets us in the most impressive of Greek tragedies, with that drama of Æschylus the *Prometheus Vinctus*, of which the poet Coleridge said truly, that it was not so much a tragedy, as tragedy itself. Prometheus has been the benefactor of mankind. He has entered into a sublime conflict with Zeus, the supreme Deity. In his efforts for the good of the race, he is crushed by his adversary, and he dies with defiance on his lips. The conception, no doubt, is grand, but the chief element of grandeur lies in the fact that it is Power, and not Righteousness, which sits on the throne; and rebellion against supreme Power, which is not supreme Right, must always be grand. But the struggle in the history of Job is far nobler. He knows that the God he worships is not supreme Power only, but supreme Righteousness also. This it is that makes his trial so hard. With him the difficulty is to reconcile the God of his conscience and his faith, with the God who is Ruler of the world. On the throne of his heart sits One who is absolutely righteous. On the throne of the universe sits One who, judging by the facts of life, is not absolutely righteous. And the end of the struggle in the drama of Job is infinitely more instructive, and infinitely more consolatory, than the close of the *Prometheus*. It is not the defiance of Power, it is not the arrogant assertion of self-righteousness; it is the confession of ignorance of self, and ignorance of God; it is the submission of the sorely-tried man to the revelation of that God whose revelation he had longed for: "I have heard of thee by the hearing of the ear; but now mine eye seeth Thee. Wherefore I abhor myself, and repent in dust and ashes."

The problem of the book, as I have said, is that hardest of all problems to faith, as to unbelief,—the problem of innocent suffering. What is the solution of it? You have in this book the problem worked out, and three answers given. The first is the answer of the three friends who came to condole with Job in his affliction. They are evidently men of position, of education, of intelligence, of religious knowledge. As compared with their neighbours, they may be said to constitute the *élite*, the intellectual and social aristocracy of the country. There are representatives, moreover, of different modes of thought. Eliphaz is the man of prophetic insight; Bildad is the sage, familiar with ancient lore, well versed in the traditions of the fathers; Zophar is the average religious man of his day, orthodox, pious, sincere, but withal, bigoted, fanatical, uncharitable, a man who expects every one to agree with him, not only to believe what he believes,—neither more nor less,—but to express that belief exactly in the same rigid formula. But the three friends, though representing three different types of character, all concur in one thing: they all hold the same theory of the Divine government, and, on the strength of that theory, they all condemn Job. One after another, these officious friends take up their argument against Job; and one after another, they repeat the same commonplaces of their creed. God is just, and therefore God rewards the righteous, and punishes the wicked. If a man suffers, he suffers because he deserves it. If you do not concede this, they say you arraign the justice of God. Job may have been apparently moral, upright, religious, but he must have cherished some secret sin, and it is this which has called down upon him the vengeance of the Most High. This is their compendious system of theology. This was the system in which they had been been trained. This was the system with which they were content, because their experience had probably furnished them with no glaring violation of it; or because, like other good men in all ages, they shut their eyes to inconvenient facts which clashed with their system. But, like all compendious systems of theology, it breaks down. It is not large enough to cover the facts. You cannot sum in little the mysteries of the universe. You cannot still the anguish of beating hearts, crying out for God in their desolate misery, by giving them the dead dry sand of some formula which you presumptuously label as the truth. It is all too little; the facts of God's world are too broad for your system. "Who did sin, this man or his parents, that he was born blind? Neither did this man sin, nor his parents; but that the works of God might be made manifest in him." Centuries of teaching could not root out of men's minds the obstinate belief that the suffering is the measure of the sin. But the sufferer himself repudiates this. Job is stung to the quick; his spirit is roused at these insinuations, when he knows how unjust they are. He can accept the current theology in its generalities; he does not doubt that suffering is the fruit of sin; but that general principle does not touch his own case. God has not smitten him for his sin. His conscience is clear. He can look into his own heart, he can review his life, and he is sure that neither in thought nor in act has he departed willingly from God. Never has he been tempted by the idolatries around him. True and loving obedience to his Maker has been the law of his life. This, indeed, it is that makes his anguish so intense. This is the terrible dilemma in which he is placed. The righteousness of God, that is the fundamental article of his creed—*that*, nothing shall induce him to forego; and yet thence comes his greatest perplexity. The book is moistened, it has been truly said, with the bitterest tears that the human creature can shed —the tears of a wounded conscience. Job does not maintain his absolute freedom from sin. He admits the force of Bildad's statement that God will not cast away the perfect man, neither will He help the evil-doers. That is Job's theology too. "I know it is so of a truth, but how should man be just with God?" But this does not cover the facts. This does not explain why he, who had never wilfully transgressed, should be punished with such extreme severity. It is of no use to tell him that he has been a hypocrite and an evil-doer. He indignantly denies the accusation. This is not the explanation of his case. He will be true to God, and to the method of His justice so far as he knows it ; but he must be true to his conscience. He will not say, " I am guilty," when he knows that he is innocent.

Who does not feel the pathos of the cry as he exclaims, " Thou knowest that I am not wicked ; " and as he adds, trembling yet trusting, as in the grasp of one from whom there was no escape, " There is none that can deliver out of Thine hand ? " For a moment he is tempted, as who has not been tempted, to take refuge in a blind submission. " It is of no use ; He will give no account of any of His matters. I must take up my burden, and trudge on along the weary road to the end as well as I can." But, in spite of himself, his inmost heart cries out, " God must be righteous," and again and again there bursts from his lips the passionate desire that the eternal righteousness should be vindicated. He will not be beaten from his belief in that righteousness, though the darkness that shadows him be intolerable. " Though He slay me, yet will I trust in Him. I will maintain mine own ways before Him." And again: "Oh that I knew where I might find Him, that I might come even to His seat ! I would order my cause before Him, and fill my mouth with arguments." And so to the very last word he utters. He reviews his life, he describes in a strain of magnificent poetry the integrity of his career, and the happiness he had enjoyed, and, contrasting it with his present misery, he concludes with the same passionate assertion of his innocence, the same passionate appeal to God to come out of the darkness in which He is hidden : "Oh that one would hear me ! Behold, my desire is that the Almighty would answer me, and that mine adversary,"—so he boldly speaks of God,—" that mine adversary would write his accusation against me." And we know that Job was right, still needing, no doubt, as we all do, a deeper knowledge of God, a deeper knowledge of himself ; needing the lesson, above all, that his very righteousness was not his own :—but right in maintaining his innocence against his friends ; right in holding fast his integrity ; right in trusting God through all ; right in appealing to Him to declare His righteousness where it seemed to be hidden in cloud. God Himself bears witness to the sincerity of His servant, and condemns the specious but hollow theology of his friends. In His sight, a frank and loyal heterodoxy is of more worth than a strict, but hard and freezing orthodoxy, which would make God Himself the accomplice of its error. Job was learning his theology not from books, or from the traditions of the fathers, but in the midst of God's furnace, and by the teaching of God's Spirit; and, therefore, though it was defective, it was true.

But there is another theory of suffering, which approaches much more nearly to the truth, which is also given us in the Book of Job. When Job's three friends ceased to answer him, a fourth appears, who is indignant with Job for his obstinacy, and with them, because they failed so completely to vindicate the righteousness of God. Elihu has been taught, apparently, in a different school; at any rate, he has seen reason to question the received opinions; and, with many apologies for his want of experience and knowledge, he boldly assails them. He is the representative of a younger theology; and a younger theology, remember, is not necessarily worse than the old. It is often better, more generous, has a larger faith in God, and a wider grasp of the complex relations of the world. How narrow, how poor, how unfruitful, is the mere repetition of the past, even when it is true! What would the Church be now, if her children had never ventured beyond the interpretations of ancient doctors and fathers? How meagre, how poor would be her theology? And if the Church is true to the indwelling spirit within her, if that indwelling is a reality to be claimed and cherished by her children, then she will advance, not by a denial of the old fact, for that had its use and served its purpose, but by vindicating the genius of the old revelation in its ever new application to the emergencies of the time, and the contests in which she is engaged. She will gladly make use of the teaching of facts, and the lessons of experience, and as well fulfil her prophecies in the newness of the spirit and not the oldness of the letter. This was what Elihu did. His observation of life had been of service to him. He rejects the hard law of retribution. God's purpose in chastisement he declares to be the purification of His servants. If He puts those whom He loves into the crucible, it is to purge away their

M

dross, to cleanse them from past sins, and to keep them from falling in the future. Here, certainly, is a step in advance. We are standing on a loftier platform. We are breathing a purer atmosphere. To see a purpose of love in the affliction is to turn it into a blessing. Even if the conscience does not acknowledge it as merited, to be able to say, "It is a Father's hand that chastens, and He is wiser than I"—this is surely to rob chastisement of its sting. And you will observe that Job accepts in silence this interpretation of his suffering. Evidently it has wrought in him that submission which prepared him for the words of Jehovah, when He answers him out of the whirlwind, and for the humble confession that follows: "Behold, I am vile, what shall I answer Thee? I will lay mine hand upon my mouth!"

Let us pause for a moment on this aspect of suffering. Do you say: "Why have I been thus smitten? Why has sorrow so deep visited me? All God's waves and billows are gone over me. All that I loved most has been taken from me. I have eaten ashes for bread, and mingled my drink with weeping?" Do you say: "I have not sinned. I have been obedient to God's will, so far as I knew that will?" But was He supreme in your heart? Were there no idols usurping His place? Had you made no gods to go before you; no visible divinities to divide your heart; no wife or children whom you loved with a passionate love, for whose step you listened, whose voice made you gladder than all the music of earth and sky, with whom earth was heaven, without whom there was no heaven for you? And God put away your idol, and left you in your loneliness. Why? Not surely that He might wound and break your heart, but that He might draw you to Himself. He came to you amid the ruins of your earthly happiness, and He spoke with His penetrating voice; He put His hand upon your heart; He offered you His divine consolation. Then you said, like John the Baptist, "Verily, I knew Him not;" or, like Job, "I have heard of Thee by the hearing of the ear; but now mine eyes seeth Thee." You understood His word and His love better. His words assumed a deeper meaning for you, and now you know, as you never knew before, what treasures of strength and peace He was laying up for you; and you have found the promise true as you never found it before: "My peace I give unto you. Not as the world giveth give I unto you."

And then you are trained to a new obedience. Then, in the language of the Epistle to the Hebrews, God is making you a partaker of His holiness. He is transforming you to the image of His Son. For what is perfect holiness but perfect obedience; and where can this obedience be so fully learned as in the hour of affliction? Is it not then that we are compelled to confess that God's ways are not as our ways, nor His thoughts as our thoughts? In the presence of the great sorrow which has come upon us we quiver with agony; our soul is troubled in our Gethsemane. We are grappling with a terrible principle of contradiction. We may doubt God's love; but if then we are able to say from the bottom of the heart, "Thy will be done," we have gained the noblest victory of which man on earth is capable. When the day of that painful obedience dawned, though it dawned on the most terrible disaster, it was a day of infinite grandeur and beauty. You are raised to the very summit of moral life,—a rugged thunder-blasted summit like some Alpine peak, but one which pierces the clouds, on which there rests the light and the sunshine of God. One with Christ, a sharer in His Gethsemane, nailed to His cross, you become partaker of His holiness; and you confess that though the chastening for the present seemeth not to be joyous, but grievous; nevertheless, afterward it yieldeth the peaceable fruit of righteousness to them that are exercised thereby.

But the mystery of evil is not fully dispelled even when this purifying power is assigned it. The author of this sublime poem is made the instrument of revealing to us another purpose of affliction. He does not altogether deny a portion of the truth contained in the argument of Job's friends. There is a connection between sin and suffering; but there are cases to which neither of these explanations will apply. There is a suffering to which you cannot give the epithet of retributive; there is a suffering which is not even for the chastisement or the purification of the individual soul, but for the glory of God. If our attention has been fastened only on the earthward aspect of the problem, we should have missed this most important lesson; nay, the end of the story, if we were to read it only by the conclusion of the book, would bring us back to the old theology, that, in the long run, virtue has its reward here. But if we revert to the prologue of the book, we learn a far grander lesson. A door is opened in heaven. The great opposer of our race, the adversary who watches our conduct, presents himself before God in the midst of the heavenly hierarchy, and he insinuates that the piety of Job is a selfish piety. "Doth Job fear God for nought?" It is a mere bargain, it is a mere calculation. Honesty is the best policy; religion brings with it wealth, honours, position, length of life; therefore, it is worth while to be religious. Satan tells God to His face that His servants serve Him, not from disinterested motives, from sincere affection, but in the spirit of a hireling, on the lowest and most mercenary considerations. "Doth Job fear God for nought? Hast not Thou made an hedge about him, and about his house, and about all that he hath on every side? Thou hast blessed the work of his hands, and his substance is increased in the land. But put forth Thine hand now, and touch all that he hath, and he will curse Thee to Thy face." This is the challenge given. It is one that strikes at the honour of God Himself. It means this, that He is incapable of inspiring a genuine, disinterested affection. It means this, that those who worship Him, worship Him, not for what He is, but for what He gives; not because He is altogether lovely, but because in His right hand is length of days, and in His left hand riches and honour. And God accepts the challenge. "Go forth and do Thy worst. Take away all that is dearest to him. Rob him of wealth, of children, of happiness. Make his life bitter with sickness and sorrow, and let the issue be tried. Let it be seen whether he honours Me because he loves Me, or because he is prosperous in this world. Let it be seen if his homage is the homage of the heart, or the homage of a mercenary, servile adulation." This is the key to the enigma. Job knew nothing of this. The interpretation was not given to him. Enough for him to learn that he was in the hand of a wise and righteous and loving God. Enough for him to know that God was teaching him the hard lesson of obedience. Enough for him to come out of the trial as gold that is purified in the fire. But for us the veil is lifted. We are ushered into the inner sanctuary. God reveals to us His counsel. He bids us see that He may inflict suffering, not because there are sins to chastise, not because there are faults to correct, or evil tendencies to extirpate, but because God Himself is honoured in the trial. Surely no more honoured position could be assigned to man than thus to be the champion of God. Think of it, you who are called to endure long hours of agony; you to whom God has appointed days of pain and nights of sleepless suffering. Think of it, you who cannot comprehend His purpose, and your fainting heart asks, "Why is this?" That mother, who, for twenty years, has been laid on a bed of pain, deprived of the happiness of watching over and training her children; that honest and industrious father, whose strength is fading away under the protracted and excruciating torture of an incurable malady, and that at the very time his efforts are most needed for the support of his family; that upright merchant, that honest tradesman, who, because he would not consent to some fraud or some act of business dishonesty, sees himself and his children exposed to the shame of bankruptcy and to the privations of poverty: these no doubt will look into their hearts, they will interrogate their lives, they will beseech of God to show them if there be any way of wickedness in them; but if, when they have done all, they still find in their affliction that which they cannot fathom, then let them not doubt the justice, or question the love of Him that chastens. Can you not understand now, why it is that some of the purest and saintliest have had the largest share of suffering? They are God's elect. You marvel as you look at that pale face, which is like the face of an angel,—you marvel that it blesses the Lord: but you see that heaven is opened beyond; you see the accuser, and God the Judge of all; you see the triumph of Divine love in man. Yes, and by the light that shows you the cross, you see more,—you see One who did no sin, neither was guile found in His mouth, crushed beneath His weight of suffering. You see Him, who was the Son of the Father's bosom, learn obedience by the things which He suffered, made perfect through suffering. His trial, you know, was not the trial of punishment, or of purification from earthly dross, but it was the glory of God, it was the redemption of man. He gathered into His passionate embrace all our sins, and all our sorrows, that He might take them away. Is there no strength there? Is it not a sublime thing to be called on to share His suffering? And if an ungodly world still says, "Doth Job fear God for nought?" stretch out Thine hand, and see if Thou art worthy to inspire any heart of man with love? Will you not answer the question? Will you not be partakers with God, and cast that grievous burden into the arms of God, confessing that He has appointed it in love? They may mock at the Gospel and its promises; they may charge the followers of Christ with selfish aims and mercenary motives. One saint who knows that the glory of God is in his hands shall answer the sneer. His noble submission, his unwearied self-sacrifice, his love which takes upon it the burden of the world, will compel the world to confess that God is love, and that man loves God for Himself.

J. J. S. P.

XX. The Book of Job.—1.

I HAVE chosen the Book of Job as the subject of a short course of lectures, for more than one reason. First, and foremost of all, I would place its intrinsic, its marvellous interest and beauty. Why should I repeat to you what this man of genius or that man of letters has told us of his estimate of the book? Of this there can be no question. The story which ushers in what is after all the main substance of the book, is one of the most pathetic and tragical in all literature, and it is told with touch after touch of a simple and transparent eloquence which will never cease to move the hearts of men. The long dialogue which follows, and which contains, as I have said, the real problems with which the book deals, is often no doubt exceedingly obscure. It is difficult to read in our present translation many verses continuously without the sense breaking down, so to speak, under our feet, and leaving us in a path of perplexity. But it contains for all that, now isolated verses, now whole passages, which have taken their place—to say nothing more—in poetry of the highest order, among the permanent and enduring possessions of the human race. Whatever its difficulties, whatever its obscurities, no intelligent person could read our Authorised Version of the

Book of Job without something of a sigh to understand it more fully, to master its contents more correctly.

And secondly, I would add—and this in no spirit of undervaluing of the past—that the beauty and interest of the book have been greatly enhanced by the light of modern studies of the language in which the original is written. Every step which has been made towards a clearer and more correct rendering of the more difficult passages of the book has revealed fresh beauty. So much has been effected by the aid of many learned men who have devoted themselves to clearing away the difficulties which beset the reader, that the careful student may feel like one who has entered a gallery where picture after picture, long concealed by the accumulated dust and rubbish of centuries, has at last been revealed in something of its original significance and colour. If some time-honoured interpretations have been more than shaken, if one or two precious texts can no longer be quoted as a correct representation of the meaning of the original, a crowd of others which once were vague and meaningless have been recovered from obscurity, and riches have been disinterred that have long lain buried. Yet it is obvious that it is only the most general results, with such light as recent inquiries have thrown on the meaning of the book, that I should have to bring before you in this place. I shall certainly not detain you by discussions as to the meaning of this or that once obscure verse or still perplexing phrase.

And, thirdly, it is well that prevailing misconceptions as to the purport of the book should be discountenanced and corrected, not merely in small and learned circles, but as widely and publicly as possible. I shall rejoice if I can contribute, however humbly, to open to those who have little leisure for study and very few opportunities of access to the learned writers, the treasures which are locked up in one of the most instructive but least generally appreciated books of Holy Scripture. Let me say a word on this point at once. The general impression as to the substance is something—is it not?—of this kind: that it contains the history of one who was greatly tried, who showed under his trials the profoundest resignation; resisted, first the evil one, next the suggestions of his own wife, and, finally, maintained his ground in some vague way against his false friends. The popular conception of him is fairly represented in a picture of a patriarchal saint, with a halo round his head, seated on his ash-heap, putting to shame the tempter, rebuking his wife, bearing up against miserable comforters, and finally triumphing over all his sufferings and all his false advisers. So entirely has this view prevailed over all others, that it has been embodied in proverbs that are not confined to our own language, and which hold him up as a typical instance, now of destitution, now of patience. "As poor as Job," "As patient as Job," are expressions which have gone round the world, and with which we are all familiar. And yet nothing in the world could convey a more inadequate—I will not say a more false—idea of the teaching of the book than to look on it as merely a history of patient submission to overwhelming calamities. Its interest, its enduring, its main interest for us in modern days, lies in its subject being almost precisely the very opposite of this. I shall try and show you that it brings before us, not merely Job the patient, but Job the impatient, Job the perplexed, Job the questioner, Job the sceptic, Job the audacious, Job the all but rebellious; that ancient as this book is—so far removed in its surroundings, in its language, from our own day—yet it deals with problems that are as fresh, as undying, and as perplexing here and now in this modern life, and in the swarming streets of our crowded cities, as in the days when Roman civilization was in its cradle and the literature of Greece was in its infancy, and as when they are represented as pervading the heart of the Arabian patriarch beneath the skies of Asia.

Let me put before you in the very shortest and truest form the real contents of the book. It begins with two chapters written in prose. A man of the highest piety and the greatest wealth is suddenly bereft of all; he is left stripped of everything; plunged in bereavement, poverty, and disease. He refuses to despair, bears all with a supernatural sweetness and resignation. "The Lord gave," he says, "the Lord hath taken away." This is the prologue, and it ends with the arrival of three friends, and between these and himself there follows a long dialogue, and this dialogue, remember, is no longer in prose in the original, but in poetry. Even in the English you may trace that parallelism, as it is called, that succession of couplets, of two lines, each couplet with its rhyme, not of sound but of sentiment and idea, that is so characteristic of Hebrew poetry. Open any passage at random,—"There the wicked cease from troubling, and there the weary be at rest." So again, "There the prisoners rest together: the captives hear not the voice of the oppressor." And this dialogue between Job and his friends forms the bulk of the book— is the book itself, to which the two chapters are an introduction or prologue in prose; only we must notice that when the dialogue has been maintained through thirty-six chapters, a fresh speaker, or actor, as we might say, is introduced—a young friend, who takes up the dialogue where his elders have abandoned it. Six chapters later on, Jehovah Himself appears on the scene; and finally, when Job has uttered his last words, the poem ends, and a short narrative in prose is added, in which we are told of Job's justification by God—not for his patience, remember, that of course needed no justification at all; but we might say for, or in spite of, his impatience,—and of his renewed happiness and prosperity. You will see, then, that it is quite impossible to understand the meaning of the book if we omit the study of its longest and most important part—in fact, of the book itself—and only confine ourselves to the short passage which ushers in the real poem, the initial verses of the book, and those which follow to its completion, with a very short return, the narrative which introduces it. It is the poem itself, let me say once more even with a wearisome iteration, not its prose introduction, nor its prose conclusion, that supplies the main and the surpassing interest of the book. And what is the subject of the poem itself? I will only indicate it at present for a moment. It is the very greatest problem, the very sorest perplexity, with which the human soul can vex itself: "How is it that a good man can suffer undeserved affliction, if there is a good God in Heaven? Can the wise and righteous God leave evil in possession of the world?" "Impossible," say Job's friends. "You, sufferer, must have sinned; confess your sin and ask for forgiveness, and all will be well." But Job cannot say this; he protests his innocence. Remember the description of him in the prologue, as a man who feared God greatly, and eschewed evil, and so again and again he breaks out into audacious questionings of the whole government of the world, and into passionate pleadings with God as his persecutor. And while his friends plead, or seem to plead, for God, he pleads, or seems to plead, against Him, and after all God pronounced for him and against them. The poem, then, is one of the most moving, one of the most sacred and Divine, as well as one of the most human of all poems. It deals, as I have already said, with one of the most appalling of human problems. It is a meditation, so to speak, in the form of a dialogue, or a world of questioning about injustice and miseries. And Job represents not the calm and contented sayer of smooth things, but the bold questioner, in the agony of indignation of one who feels that the whole world is out of joint. Is it not to some of us a new thing to be told that such questionings cannot find a place, I might almost say an honoured place, between the covers of the Bible? Yet so it is, as we shall see further on; and the discovery may open the eyes of some of us to the treasures yet to be found in that ancient book, that unexhausted mine of teaching and wisdom.

I think a few words more on the general position of the book may possibly interest you. It belongs neither to the historical nor to the prophetical books of the Bible. The mere arrangement of our own Bibles will show you this. It stands side by side with the Psalms, the Proverbs, the Canticles, and Ecclesiastes; and between these two great divisions, like the four books I have named. It belongs to what we call the poetical books of the Old Testament, yet its poetry is not a series of detached hymns, the very highest teachings and uplifting of the human soul towards God, like the Book of Psalms; nor is it the common sense of the many embodied into maxims by the wisdom of the one, like so much of the Proverbs; nor meditations, often sweet meditations, on life, like the Ecclesiastes; nor poetry, half mystic, half idyllic, like the Songs of Solomon; it stands apart by itself, this great book of the Bible—apart, we might almost say, in the literature of the whole world. If it resembles the Book of Proverbs or Ecclesiastes as dealing with the great practical and speculative questions of human life, it differs from them both as gathering all its teaching round a single person who forms the centre of a group of speakers; and whatever the lessons it details, or the problems it raises, they come to us, never through the lips of the author of the book himself, but always of the individuals who, one after another, come forward on the stage to utter them. The author himself speaks only to introduce to us, if I may say so, the *dramatis personæ*, for so they are.

Yet drama we can hardly call it. For within the poem itself there is no action, no event, no movement. The action is not action in the common sense of the word; it is only the torture and the writhing and the agony, the movement, the swerving to and fro, and the doubts and the falling off, and the questionings, and the faith, between a single soul and the catastrophe of the coming face to face of that soul with its God. Nor is it a philosophical or didactic dialogue, advancing steadily towards a clear conclusion. The problem it deals with is too dark and complex, too high for this; and the teaching too varied, too conflicting, too merely suggestive. The solution, so far as solution is given, is left for the reader to draw for himself,—often remember, as is the case with so many of the great Teacher's parables,—it is left in the reader's hands to deal with as he can; and it is, or seems, strange how long and how constantly its true purport has been overlooked. Turn to many of the commentaries on the book, and you will find various views taken of him whose name it bears. Sometimes he is, as I said before, a model of submission, of resignation, which forms the popular estimate of his character, and all else that is characteristic of nine-tenths of his language is put into the background, or explained away. Sometimes he is represented as a merely mystical teacher of Christian truths—of truths not yet revealed to the world; sometimes he is looked on merely as the inspired and unconscious utterer of what to his hearers must have been quite unintelligible predictions; as a mere preacher before his time, of Jesus and the resurrection. Successive schools of thought have written themselves into his thoughts, and those of his interlocutors. It seems a bold assertion, yet it is, I venture to suggest, not quite unwarranted, to say that partly owing to the more profound study of the language in which he speaks, and of cognate languages, partly from a certain marked tendency in modern commentators, it has been reserved for the present generation to read the book in something, at all events, more nearly the sense of him to whom it was given to produce it ;—that modern study often presumptuous, often decried, often frowned upon, has been rewarded by bringing to light a fresh and almost untouched vein of thought in those unexhausted, those inexhaustible treasures of the Scriptures.

One word more may add to the interest which some here may possibly bring to the fresh perusal of so little studied a portion of Scripture. In what age, we may naturally ask, and in what country was the book written? Who was its author? I need hardly say that on such questions we have no authoritative guide of any kind. The dictum of this or that Jewish Rabbi, this or that Father of the Christian Church, may be received with due respect, but it is impossible to find any sure ground in the vague traditions or later theories that came into being centuries after the book had been—we know not exactly when—placed in the roll of the Hebrew canonical books. We must look for any answer in the book itself—not outside the book. the reader who has with moderate attention gone through those forty-two chapters, may be inclined to ask, "How came this book in the Hebrew Scriptures at all?" There is nothing, we may say, saving that it is written in Hebrew, and in confessedly difficult Hebrew, that points to the Hebrew nation, or to the land in which that nation dwelt, or to its history, or traditions, or institutions, or ceremonies, or mode of life, or ideas, or law. Where is Moses or the law of Moses here? Where is there any mention of the land of promise or of the heroes who won that land, or of the kings who ruled it, or of the patriarchs to whom it was promised? Where is the yearning love for Jerusalem or for the Temple, that burns now so fiercely, now so tenderly, through so many Psalms? The author of the book passes by all these things and persons in entire and absolute silence. Palestine and its great history; Jacob and his twelve children; Moses and his law, might never have existed so far as an allusion can be detected to them from the first chapter to the forty-second. Instead of these persons, and events, and places, we have a background very different, as we may see in any further study of the book. The great plains of Asia, traversed by the slow caravans, swept over from time to time by marauding tribes like those plundering, and, as we know, too often murderous Bedouins of modern days, yet inhabited by nations with a civilization and government of their own, and families with the ideas that belong to people among whom the administration of justice and the value of free deliberation and a sense of the value of human rights and liberties have made some way—these form the scene of the drama, if drama we may call it. And above it were those lucid skies which bent over those Asiatic plains, skies from which the stars glittered with a brilliancy unknown in these Northern climes, the land in which astronomy and astrology alike had their birth. And those who tread the stage speak not only of the poetry and legends of those heavenly bodies, but of the ancient and marvellous land of Egypt once the centre of the civilization of the world. They are familiar with palm trees, bulrushes, with the hippopotamus and the crocodile; they are familiar with smelting of metals, the driving of mines through the bowels of the earth, with the pilgrim stories of far-off lands, with the war horse of the desert, and with the animal creation. How or when could an inhabitant of Palestine, a child of the covenant, who looked with scorn on the uncircumcised, uncovenanted world —how, we might say, independently of the Jewish character of his world, could he have written a book steeped in a Gentile atmosphere with every allusion to the land of his forefathers studiously, it would seem, excluded? The question is a very interesting one. Many of the ancient writers cut the knot at once. Job, they said, taking him for granted as the author of the book, lived before the days of Moses, and the book was written some even say by Moses himself before the revelation of the law from Sinai, so that it is the oldest book in the Bible, perhaps in the world, and has come down to us from a dim, prehistoric, immemorial antiquity. It is, I need not say, a very attractive and interesting theory. It is almost with reluctance that we listen to arguments which seem fatal to ascribing to the book so vastly remote a date. The language, we are told, the grammar, the vocabulary, above all the style of the original, are fatal to the supposition. Such an evidence, if it rests on sufficient grounds; is almost unanswerable. If the analogy holds good, we could not for a moment suppose that Milton could have written before the age of Chaucer; but besides this we must remember, account for it how we may, that the same absence of peculiar Jewish allusions and ideas may be found elsewhere in the Old Testament. Many of the Psalms, almost the whole of the Book of Proverbs and Ecclesiastes, bear no trace of Hebrew scenery, or of allusions to Palestine, and, finally, and what will interest us all perhaps far more, the great problem of the book, the great riddle that vexes Job, is not one that springs into life with the earlier stage of human progress. Those awful questionings as to the mysteries of life, its strange inequalities and seeming injustices, they are the offspring of a more confused and tangled social web than that of the primæval and simple life of a patriarchal family. They would have found no voice, no echo, in the times of Isaac, Abraham, Jethro, or of Jacob, and God's Spirit does not transport men out of their own epoch. Great and lofty as are the utterances of the book, they would have been wholly unnatural and inconceivable till the problems with which they deal had been brought home to the hearts of men by a series of unexplained sufferings, much meditation, long and painful questionings. We may, therefore, accept what we may call now the generally received view, that the author of the book lived late enough to have seen woe after woe fall upon God's people; to have pondered over those sufferings, as falling not on the most evil, as national chastisements for national sins, but as miseries, undeserved miseries, of good and God-fearing men, and that he found no sufficient answer to the doubts that stirred within his breast as to the simple faiths of his forefathers, which only tell him that the righteous were always prosperous and the wicked always afflicted. He had travelled, it may be, far, and had seen with his own eyes, or heard from the lips of others, much of the great world into which adventurous Jews were steadily pushing their way; and when at last God's Spirit stirred him to his great task, he was guided to lay the scene of the marvellous poem in which his meditations were to be embodied, in a scene far from the narrowing associations of his own race, and to

> "Rise to the height of his great argument,"

above the limits of the law of Moses to the serener heights, from which his words might go forth and be judged on their own merits, divested as far as possible from any direct connection with the traditions or tenets of his own countrymen; and if this be true, we have in him one who, almost more than any other Old Testament speaker, was able to breathe air in which the Saviour, and he who walked so closely in his Saviour's steps, lived, worked, and died,—to grasp the truth that the Jehovah he speaks of in his poem, and whose Spirit spoke to his own heart, was a God, not as many of his countrymen believed before, and with him, of a single nation, but the God and Father of the whole human family. And whatever its exact date, whether he lived, as may well have been the case, at the fall of Samaria and the crash of the northern kingdom, and before the destruction of Jerusalem and the Babylonian captivity, or was removed from this time by a few generations, we may hail him as in this sense, though in this sense only, as one who "died in faith, not having received the promises, but having seen them afar off, and been persuaded of them, and embraced them"; and thus going in his measure before his Lord to prepare His way before Him.

G. G. B.

XXI. The Book of Job.—2.

I PURPOSE to bring before you that which I have already spoken of as the introduction in prose, the prologue so to speak, to the poem;—in a limited sense, I have already explained, we may venture to call it, the *dramatic* poem of the Book of Job. It is, remember, only an introduction; yet for all that, it is a thoroughly integral and essential feature of the book, which could not possibly be dispensed with. It gives not merely tone and colour and emphasis, but its whole meaning and significance to all that follows. Yet our work to-day is simple. The greatest and darkest problems of the book will not meet us. Yet I have no fear of any lack of interest at any step. The opening words of the first chapter are the key to much that follows : " There was a man in the land of Uz, whose name was Job ; and that man was perfect and upright, and one that feared God and eschewed evil." The scene is the land of Uz. I will not detain you for one moment with a description of its precise locality. It is important, however, to remind you that it is far beyond the confines of the Holy Land, and if much of the Book of Proverbs, much of Ecclesiastes, many of the Psalms, are so far unlike the rest of the Bible that they have no local colouring at all, are not redolent with the air of Palestine, this book, with all— every word—that is contained in it, is so distinctly removed from the confines of that land, that its atmosphere is not merely non-Jewish but distinctly and positively something other than Jewish,—truly Gentile. It is the only book of the Old Testament which, not indirectly but directly, from the very first word to the very last, anticipates the words of St. Peter, that God is no respecter of persons ; but that in every nation, he that feareth Him and worketh righteousness is accepted of Him. The history, so far as it is a history, is that of a Gentile patriarch. Here, then, in this Gentile land dwelt Job, who is fearlessly described as " perfect and upright ; " though the word perfect means rather whole-hearted, sound, sincere, than technically or theologically without sin, and words are added to show that this was no skin-deep or pharisaical uprightness— " one that feared God and eschewed evil." This, remember, this high and blameless character of Job before God and before man is a necessary element in the tragedy that is to come.

His goodness, then, is the first element in the story, and the second is his well-doing. He was rich in all the wealth of that early world. First he is rich in sons and daughters —above all, we remember, in that far-off world of the East, in the former,—seven sons and three daughters. He is rich also in the possessions that mark the stage—the transitional stage—of civilization in which this great parable is placed ;—a mingling of some traces of the nomadic life with the pastoral on the one hand, and settled and agricultural, and even city life, on the other—in thousands of sheep, in camels, in oxen, and in asses. Rich also in slaves :

in a very great household and retinue, of his treatment and bearing towards whom he himself speaks later on. " If I despise the cause of my bondsmen, what shall I do when God riseth up, and when He visiteth, what shall I answer Him? Did not He that made me make him? and did not one God fashion us both in the womb?" He speaks as no Greek or Roman could; I might almost say, as no slave-master has ever spoken. He is one that respecteth his brother man: who, in the Apostle's words, "honoured all men." And his position is summed up in the third verse as that of the very greatest sons of the East, a term often applied to the Arab races; kindred to, but not of the same family as the sons of Jacob, and who lived between the Nile and the Euphrates. And the story goes on to tell us of the mutual festivities and gatherings of his children. This touch brings out, and it is meant to bring out, the picture of affluence and prosperity; it is not merely this, for the next touch is one other of the two marked features of Job's early career :—his affluence, his blamelessness,—his more than blamelessness,—his active affection and piety. As he thinks of his feasting children he would commend them to God.

There is some obscurity in the translation, but there is nothing to mar the picture of fatherly love. Probably he sends for his children, and bids them join him in some acts of ceremonial performed at his home. Certainly he rises early, when the feast is done, and stands by the altar side. You see at once how far we have travelled from the Levitical or Aaronic priesthood. And this Gentile and layman (to use modern language) offers to God his sacrifice for each child in turn, interceding, in the simple faith of his day and region, for any chance or secret utterance of sin or folly. He sums up all in the words, "It may be that they have cursed God in their hearts, and sinned." The form of worship may be the form of the religion of the land of Uz. But who does not see beneath it, the Christian parent pleading with the same God for the unguarded hours of unwatchful and thoughtless youth?

But now the scene shifts at once from the land of Uz, and we are carried upwards, as in a vision, to the halls of heaven; and there Jehovah holds His court like an Oriental sovereign, and His sons—His creatures of other than human mould come before Him; and among them is one malignant spirit, called Satan, or the accuser, the denouncer. He represents himself as fresh from travelling to and fro on the face of the earth, and spying out evil therein. And Jehovah calls his attention to His own servant Job, and bears His testimony, a more than human testimony, to his goodness, repeating the very words in which the author had introduced him—"There is none like him on the earth, perfect and upright, one that feareth God and escheweth evil." But the evil spirit hath his answer ready: "Doth Job fear God for nought?" He represents at once that only too common view in the world, that there is no such a thing as disinterested goodness. Such a question as the spirit asked is not confined, be sure, to such evil spirits, or to the story of the man of Uz. It was one of the questions which had already been raised when this book was written, we know not when. It is one of the questions with which this book is meant to deal. You have heard it raised, you may hear it raised again, in the chance conversation in which you join with a fellow-traveller. There is no such thing, it is said, as the love of goodness for its own sake; there is always some ulterior, some selfish motive. Or even religion, you will be told, is merely a matter of self-interest; it means nothing more than this, even if it is sincere; it means nothing more than a desire to escape pain, and to enjoy happiness hereafter. "Doth Job serve God for nought?" Can men or women care for goodness and righteousness and truth for their own sakes? Can they feel, can God, can Christ inspire, a disinterested love? Happy those who can answer such a question, from something of the experience of their own hearts, or from the lives of those whom they have known through and through.

But the Evil One proceeds to describe God's favour to Job. "Thou hast made an hedge about him," he says, "to shield him from all trial." "How easy," says the modern satirist, "to be good on an abundant income. Let a man live in a crowded lodging-house, let him know not where to-morrow's bread is to come, where will his goodness be?" "Thou hast blessed the work of his hands, and his substance is increased in the land." No doubt, therefore, he is perfect and upright; "but put forth Thy hand and touch all that he hath, and he will curse Thee to Thy face." The challenge is accepted by the good man's friend, and power is given to Satan (who is represented here, you will observe, not at all as the tempter to or suggester of evil to the human heart, but, as more than once in the New Testament, as a being whose power to inflict pain is derived from One who is his master), to torment upright and perfect Job with the loss of that on the possession of which, the accuser says, his seeming goodness is based: power, not in the first place over Job himself, but over all that belongs to him.

And once more we are upon the earth, in the land of Uz, on a festal day, with the children of happy Job. Blow falls after blow: the message comes that a wild tribe has burst into the cultivated land, and carried away all his oxen and his asses and slain his labourers. " I only," says the bringer of evil tidings, "am escaped to tell thee." And another tells of the destruction of his grazing flocks and shepherds by the terrific lightning. The fire of God has fallen on them from heaven. And even as he was yet speaking another comes to say that the still wilder tribe, the Chaldeans, the Kurds of to-day, had made a foray from the highlands, and, divided like skilled marauders into three bands, had swept away his wealth of camels, and slain their guardians, and all his wealth is gone from him at once;—three kinds of wealth, representing as it were three stages in the growth of early human progress; and sorrows come not singly, but in full battalions. They come on even as he is listening to these terrible tidings; worse, far worse follows.

The scorching wind that sweeps over the desert plains of Asia has buried his children, one and all, in the ruins of their eldest brother's house. All are dead; the messenger alone survives; and the man of wealth is stripped of all his riches, and the happy father is left bereaved and childless. It is like the close of some dark, brief tragedy, coming in its opening scene. And Job arose, we are told. The news tore his heart. There was no need to tell him, like the bereaved father in Macbeth, to give his sorrow words. He made no attempt to smile impassively, or to bear it like a stoic. He rent his clothes and shaved his head, like a true son of the East, in overwhelming grief. But this was not all. His past life bore its fruits. Accumulated years of service to God stood him in good stead, as they have stood others. In this sudden tempest of bereavement, he resigned himself to the hand that afflicted him: in the memorable words that rise at once from prose to poetry, and in which the Church tries to guide the hearts of sorrowing mourners, "Naked came I from my mother's womb, naked shall I return to mother earth: the Lord gave, and the Lord hath taken away; blessed be the name of the Lord."

The Evil One, then, was foiled, and Job's innocence and sincerity were vindicated even at this terrible price. But the story does not end here. The trial is to be renewed after an interval, how long, how short, we know not. Once more we have a vision of the courts of heaven, and once more we see the sons of God presenting themselves before Jehovah, and, as before, with the repetition of the same words, that remind us for an instant of the simplicity of Homer, Satan is questioned whence he comes, gives his answer, is told to turn his eyes to the blamelessness of God's servant, who still, in spite of all his causeless woe, holdeth fast his integrity. And Satan's answer is in the same spirit as before: "Skin for skin," he says. The phrase is not easily explained. Possibly it has some such meaning as, anything in the way of a bargain man will submit to: all that he hath will he give away cheerfully to redeem his life. But he challenges Him that, as He has allowed all these successive waves of woe to fall upon His own servant's head, to go one step farther. "Do what Thou hast not yet done; touch," he says, "his own person, his bone and his flesh, and he will curse Thee to Thy face." And once more the challenge is accepted, and the fiat goes forth: "Behold, he is in thy hand; but save his life."

And we are brought back once more to Job: from the sole of his foot to the crown of his head, he is attacked with the direst form of the sorest of Eastern diseases, the terrible leprosy. Into all that is told of its horrors by Eastern travellers, dreadful stories of horrors which you may look for in vain in the wards of a London hospital, I will not enter. He cowers among the ashes, loathsome alike to others and to himself. His cup seems full. One further turn of the rack, so to speak, is yet possible: it is not spared him. From the one human quarter from whence comfort might have come, comes only a suggestion of despair. "Dost thou still," said his wife, who comes across the scene only to heighten for one moment the tragical impression of her husband's wretchedness, "dost thou still retain thine integrity?" (that is, thy blamelessness). "Curse God," she says, "and die." "Renounce this God who thus leaves thee to such a fate, and quit life, life that has nothing left to live for." It seems hard indeed, hard above all to those who have known Christian or English homes, that such a suggestion should have come from such a quarter. It pains us with an unwelcome shock. Let me remind you that when the poet-painter drew, nearly sixty years ago, some wonderfully powerful illustrations to the Book of Job, the English husband of the most loyal and affectionate of wives refused to follow the detail of the narrative in this terrible feature. All the rest could be pourtrayed step by step; but here his love for his own wife stayed the painter's hand, and those who have ever seen his drawings will see Job's wife kneeling beside her husband, sharing his misery with him through all his trials that are yet to come, and restored with him to happiness at the end. There was something in the roll of Job's suffering too remote, may we not thankfully say, from the accumulated experience of English and Christian married life, something too keen for the poet and the artist, often on the borderland where genius runs into madness, to bear to reproduce. It well might be so. The depth of human agony seemed sounded. How many might, in more senses than one, have cursed God and died? A Roman might have turned upon those unjust gods, and died by his own hand with defiance on his lips; left the world in which he felt he was nobler than they. *Victrix causa Diis placuit, sed victa Catoni.* Others might have sought refuge in dull despair: not so Job. "What," he says, "shall we receive good at the hands of God, and shall we not receive evil?" " In all this," says the writer, who so rarely speaks a word in his own person, "in all this did not Job sin with his lips." We have here, then, the highest and most perfect type of patience in the sense of human resignation; the calm, untroubled, and profound acquiescence in the will of God which (in words which are not my own) is one of the qualities which marked Eastern religions when to the West they were still quite unknown, and which even now is more remarkably exhibited by Eastern nations than among ourselves. " Thy will be done," is a prayer which lies at the root of all religion. It stands among the foremost petitions in the Lord's Prayer, and it is deeply engraven in the whole religious spirit of the sons of Abraham, even of the race of Ishmael. In the words "God is great," it expresses the best side of Mohammedanism, the submission to the will of the Heavenly Father. Yes, we can feel that to be ready to leave all in God's hands, not merely because He is great and powerful, but because we hold Him wise and good, is the very essence of religion in its highest form; and the great English divine, Butler, has well said, that though such a passive virtue may have no development in itself, no fitting sphere in another and a better world, yet the frame of mind which it produces, and of which it is the sign, is the very frame, of all others, to fit men to be active fellow-workers with God in a larger sphere and with higher faculties. And the very highest type of such entire submission we have thus far in Job: poor as he now is, he is rich in trust and in nearness to God, and pious souls will feel that if there is a God and a Father above us, and if there is another life inconceivably more enduring, and with a larger range than this, that it is better to have felt as he felt, than to be the lord of many slaves and many herds and flocks, and the possessor of unending happiness on a happy earth.

And here ends the introduction properly so-called. It ends with Job miserable but resigned, and patient on his dung-heap. Had the story ended there, it might have remained in our memories as, it may be, an overdrawn, an excessive ideal, yet not wholly an impossible picture of what is sometimes seen, or something like it, in real life—trouble after trouble coming upon some human soul. We may have turned aside from the picture, yet it may have recurred to us once and again in the course of life's experience, as after all, a type of tragedies that are in their way possible in this tangled world, a type of many an over-true story. But the story does not end here. We have only passed within the portal of the book, not yet entered the gallery of conflicting thoughts that we have to tread, and one more touch comes, the transition to all that follows.

Three of Job's friends—their name and race is given—men, it would seem, of the race of Abraham though not of Jacob, have heard of his calamity and have come from far to comfort him; but as they raised their eyes and saw the change, the horrors and the miseries of that spectacle overcame them. They lifted up their voice and wept, we read, and used every sign of Eastern lamentation, and then they found no phrase to comfort him. How should they? They sat by him in silence, says the story, seven days and nights, for they saw that his grief was very great. If the imagery is of the East, Eastern, the sentiment that underlies it is neither of the East nor of the West, but something world-wide. There are troubles in which we can show our sympathies best, not by idle words, but by silence and by sorrow.

So far, my friends, we may draw our own lessons from Job's submission, and Job's patience, and from the mute sympathy of those who visited him. They preach, surely, their own sermon, if we had come, as we did not come, to hear a sermon.

Before I close, let me bring clearly before you the results of what we have thus far reached. As we read, the narrative has tended in one direction to heighten the growing and growing contrast between Job's deserts—if I may dare to use such an expression—and Job's lot in life. The two are brought before us in the opening verses of the first chapter as in entire and absolute harmony; but from that moment they have parted company, parted at every step, and have become more divergent. If he was, when the story opens, perfect and upright, fearing God and hating evil, how much more does he deserve such a description now—now, when the sad, sweet uses of adversity have done their best work upon him, and when he comes before us purified in the furnace of such sore affliction, his fear of God and his hatred of evil proved and tried to the very uttermost; yet, on the other hand, the shadows that had begun to darken the happiness of his life have grown at every verse, not longer only, but thicker and blacker. The spectacle before us is that of one who combined the highest and most beautiful piety and love of God of which the human soul was then capable, with the darkest and most tragic misery. Such a spectacle would be perplexing to the advanced and most enlightened Christians. The Book of Job, I need scarcely remind you, does not come within range of New Testament teaching. What a problem must such a spectacle have seemed to the pious Hebrew,—to one who had no further Gospel as yet than that the Lord ordereth a good man's going, that God shows mercy unto thousands of those that fear Him, that the righteous are never forsaken, that even in this life men are rewarded for their righteous dealing, that whatsoever the good man doeth shall prosper, that it is the ungodly whose prosperity is like chaff which the wind scattereth away, that it is on those that delight in wickedness that God rains down snares, fire and brimstone, storm and tempest,—all the woes and sorrows that have fallen on the head of Job. Surely it might well seem to such that the foundations were cast down—the very foundations of their faith; surely they might well say, "What hath the righteous done?" Such is the problem that will come before us when next we meet. We leave Job and his friends seated in silence, yet we feel that the sky above them is troubled, and that there is thunder in the air. We shall hear the storm break as we pursue our course through the book.

G. G. B.

XXII. The Book of Job.—3.

WE have considered the two opening chapters of the Book of Job. I shall remind you once more that, interesting in themselves as these chapters are, and important and direct as is their bearing on what follows, yet that they are not, as is sometimes supposed, the main portion of the work, followed by a long appendix, but that they are simply an introduction, the best of introductions, let me say once more, to the great poem that follows. At their close we left Job crouching in utter misery, yet calm and patient, the very model of resignation and acquiescence in the will of an unseen Master. In no single instance do we read that he sinned with his lips; and of this attitude of resignation as an element in the Christian and religious life I have spoken fully. Friends, too, you remember, were by his side, who sympathized with, and respected his heavy calamities. They sat silent, and none spake a word unto him, for they saw that his grief was very great. And now we close the introduction and open the book itself. We turn to its opening verses and all is changed. Job's silence is turned to loud and clamorous outcries. He was Job the patient; he is now Job the impatient. Indeed, the whole of the third chapter is one long wail. He curses, in all the wealth of wild but measured and elaborate Eastern poetry, the day of his conception—the day of his birth. In another stanza, so to speak, he craves for death as the one sovereign anodyne to human woe; as the great leveller that brings alike the hope of rest to kings and councillors in their solitary and stately tombs, and the sleep of freedom to the slave. "Wherefore," he cries, "is light given to him that is in misery, and life to the bitter in soul; which long for death but it cometh not; and dig for it more than for hidden treasures?" It is a very moving chapter The obscurities of language are comparatively few. The very intensity and passion of feeling seem as it were to fuse them away. It flows on in one broad and human current even in its agony. One of its phrases has passed, as we know, just as it stands, into recent poetry; but parallels to others abound. And it is very true, essentially true, to nature. Great calamities, great losses, are sometimes not fully felt by communities, by nations, or by churches, at the first blow, at the moment they fall. The loss of the wise counsellor, or the guiding brain, is felt more keenly later. So it is still more with individual sorrows. Some griefs men can meet bravely at the very first shock. They do not fathom their full depth of bitterness till later on. "God's will be done," men have said at the graveside, but the waking of the morrow has brought, perhaps, other feelings. Some here, perhaps, may have learned that sad lesson.

But moving and natural as the chapter is, it is a symbol of, and a key to, much that follows. It shows us at once that the main and substantial portion of the book on which we have now entered, is separated, as by a great gulf, from that which came before; that we breathe another, a more troubled, and a more stormy atmosphere. All there was calm and still, even if the skies were sombre. But now, the winds begin to moan, and the thunder to roll, and the change is not confined to Job. Eliphaz the Temanite, or Arabian chief, the eldest, doubtless, of his friends, breaks his long and kindly silence, and his words, though he saw but a little way into the depths of that troubled heart, are not unkindly words, and are not meant to be so. They also are the key to all that follows, on the side of him and of his friends; though in form they are different. Mild as yet, they are well weighed and dignified, even apologetic in tone. "Wilt thou be grieved," he says, "if we essay to commune with thee?" He was shocked at Job's wild words of despair. "Once," he says, "thou didst instruct and strengthen and uphold others, and now, lo; when evil toucheth thee, thou faintest and art troubled." And having said this, he handles for a moment tenderly, and half indirectly, the barbed arrow which is soon to rive the very heart of Job, and to bring to him a pang, even greater than any which has yet torn and tried him. "Who ever," he says, "perished being innocent? When were the righteous cut off?" His own experience in that simple Arab life tells him that the proverb is true, that they that plough iniquity and sow wickedness reap the same. But he speaks oracularly, and relates in striking language, how in the visions of the night, when deep sleep falleth upon men, a shape, if shape it were where shape was none—a formless spirit, passed before him, and awe fell upon him as a mysterious voice came forth, telling of human blindness, and human weakness; and he darkly hints that his friend should forbear from calling too bitterly on that great and wise Being, which doeth great and wise things, and unsearchable; the Lord of creation who giveth rain upon the earth, and sendeth water on the fields; the Ruler of creation, who disappointeth the devices of the crafty, and taketh the wise in their own cunning; who saveth, he tells him, the poor, and sets on high the lowly. He bids him commit his case to Him, accept His corrections as a blessing, and despise not His chastisement, for His chastisement is correction. It is the only light in which he can view his friend's misery, and if he does this, he promises him in a series of Eastern images, that typify all the forces of nature once more enlisted on his side, God's renewed favour, all the blessings of a prolonged life that He shall give to His servant, so that he shall come to his grave in a full age, like to a shock of corn gathered in his season. But his language, however well meant, falls wide of its mark. It prepares the way for, though it does not yet provoke, the fierce explosions that come later on. At all events it brings little comfort to his afflicted friend. How could it?

And, once more, in the sixth and seventh chapters, Job returns, not exactly to the exceeding loud and bitter cry of his first utterance, yet to the prolonged moan of sorrow. "Not without reason," he says, "do I lift up my voice. The wild ass brays not, even the very ox lows not when fully satisfied; and my cries come from a wounded heart, from a deep sense of agony." And once, once more he turns from his friends to his Maker and prays for death; that it would please God, he says, to let loose His hand and cut him off; that He would give him the rest in death for which he sighs, as a slave toiling beneath the sun of Asia longs to claim his freedom, as the labourer looks for the wages of his work; and then, in full tone, he pleads against his sufferings, the mystery of life and the terrible finality of death. "Oh! remember," he says, "that my life is but breath or wind, and that as a cloud is dissolved and is no more seen—so he that dies returns no more from the under-world to the home he has left, neither shall his ancient place know him any more." And then he recounts his weary night when he craves for the dawn of the day that passes without hope; he resents the unsympathizing words of the oldest of his friends, friends who are to him in the hour of his sore need like a treacherous torrent that dries up in the sultry desert, and turns to despair the hopes of the thirsty traveller; and then he half angrily pleads once more with his God to remove from him these haunting visions, and these wearying bonds: "Pardon so frail a being, pardon, oh! Thou Watcher of mankind, pardon, ere he dies in sin that he has committed, ere it be too late." Its imagery is very plaintive—and it is wholly natural. But it is far removed from Mohammedan resignation—further still removed from that Christian hope of those who out of weakness are made strong, and who in the very valley of humiliation, in the valley of the shadow of death, feel God's hand leading and supporting.

And now in the eighth chapter, the second friend, Bildad the Shuhite, of another Arabian tribe, stands forward. He, like the first speaker, puts himself in the attitude of pleading before his God, and of rebuking one whose faith is weak. "Doth God pervert judgment; or doth the Almighty warp justice?"

And he too offers a suggestion, shocking to us, but which gives force to the view against which so much of the teaching of this book is directed, the suggestion that Job's children suffered for the sins of their father. He appeals no longer to the revelation made in the vision, but to tradition, to the authority of a primitive and a wiser age, against one whose words are rash. He cannot too soon turn to God and make supplication to the Almighty. God, he assures him, will not cast away the perfect man; but neither will He accept evil-doers. Job finds scanty comfort in these words. The mighty stream of misery is sweeping him to his grave, and his friends are merely throwing him straws. "How," he says, "can I vindicate myself with God. The thoughts that burn within me, how dare I bring them out to Him? He removes the mountains and He shakes the earth, He stays the sun, and seals up the starlight, and gives their lights to the bright spheres. Were I never so convinced of the justice of my cause, I dare not plead with Him. Better to condemn myself than answer Him."

See how his soul sways to and fro in his misery. "This one thing," he says, "I see that He destroys the righteous with the wicked, that evil is triumphant on the earth, that if I prove my innocence to be white as snow, this mighty Being can plunge me, as it were, in foulness, and there is no superior judge," he cries, "to decide between us." Alas! no mediator between God and man. "Oh, that He would take away these heavy woes, and let me plead my cause fairly." And after these audacious words he turns to God in the very bitterness of his soul, and "Show me," he says, "wherefore Thou contendest with me. Thy hands have made me and fashioned me long ago. Why, like a malignant human foe, dost Thou deal so cruelly with Thine own creature, one whose innocence Thou knowest. Oh, why didst Thou give me the gift of this weary life? Having given it, why not give me some respite that I may take comfort some little before I go where I shall never return, to the land of darkness and the shadow of death, a land of darkness as darkness itself, without any order—where the light is as darkness—from the sunlight to the sunless land."

There is not, you see, one word, as it were, left of resignation or patience. Only a moan, now loud, now low, of one who feels himself wronged, deserted of the God who loves him, who lifts up his cry for mercy and relief. Neither is there, so far, a word of hope for redress beyond the grave. His friends' words seem full to overflowing of the even current of pious and indisputable truths; his much the reverse. Yet somehow, as we read, our hearts go, and seem meant to go, with him, rather than with them.

And now the third friend speaks. It is in the same key as those that went before. His language is sharp and stern. He deals no longer in hints and suggestions: "Should thy falsehoods," he says, "make other men silent?" He taxes Job with self-flattery, self-righteousness, with the sin even of profanity in saying to his Maker "I am clean in Thine eyes." He declares to him that whatever his sufferings, God is exacting from him less than he deserves, and then, after dwelling in striking language on the holy, mysterious nature of Him whom he is charging by his loud cries, he bids him put iniquity far away, and then he shall forget all his miseries, then the rush of sorrow shall pass away, and he shall be restored to the noonday of God's favour, and therefore to happiness. It is too much for Job. The whole world is against him. He stands alone in his doubts and in his misery.

These three friends represent, not the majority only, but the sum total of the religious thought, the religious world, the Church, we may say, of his day—the *quod semper, quod ubique, quod ab omnibus;* and they no more share his anxious questionings than they share his bodily pangs. In the twelfth and two following chapters, he bursts forth afresh in a strain of sorrow and upbraiding that dies away into despair as he turns away from them to the God who has so afflicted him. "No doubt," he says, "ye are the people, ye represent the whole world, and wisdom, doubtless, will die with you. And me—me whose footsteps are slipping on life's hard course, you who sit at ease can scorn. Would you tell me of God's greatness? All creation knows and all history teaches, the beasts, the fowls, the fishes, earth and sea, kingdoms and nations tell us of His power. What ye know, I know also. Sorrowful counsellors are ye all, poor pleaders for your God." And then bidding them hold their peace, he declares that, come what will, he will yet plead with God. "Though He slay me, yet will I so far trust Him as to plead before Him." And then, with another sad appeal to his Maker, to withdraw that heavy hand and let him plead face to face, he implores Him again to let him know what is his transgression, what is his sin. "Wherefore hidest Thou Thy face, and holdest me for Thine enemy? Thou writest bitter things against me." We see that the imagery here, as elsewhere, is drawn from the formal processes of the registers and deeds of judicial courts in no uncivilized land, and it makes him still responsible for the forgotten iniquities of his youth. And then his spirit dies within him, and in the fourteenth chapter we have one of the most wonderful of utterances that ever passed from human lips: "Man that is born of a woman is of few days, and is full of trouble. He cometh forth like a flower, and is cut down; he fleeth as the shadow, and continueth not." And can God enter into conflict with one so frail; or expect strength and perfection from so poor a weed? Let him rest till his short day is over. And then in words of solemn and sustained hopelessness he paints man's ephemeral nature in images which poet after poet have scarcely yet exhausted—"there is hope of a tree," he says, "that if it be cut down it will spring up again, at the scent of water." How natural the language! At one vivifying touch of rain in the sunburnt East, it will bud forth and bourgeon. "But man lieth down and riseth no more; till the heaven of heavens above be no more the dead shall not awake nor be raised out of their sleep." What a chill and despairing cry. Then a sort of faint gleam of hope! He breathes a prayer that God would hide him for awhile in the grave till the storm of His wrath were over. "Let me, let me wait even in death, for a better time," till his Maker should yearn over the creature to whom he had given his being. But no; the hope vanishes as soon as seized. God's sentence is gone against him.

It is sealed and fixed. And he turns in utter agony to the great Creator as the great destroyer. "The solid mountains," he says, "come to nought; the waters wear the stones." If the words are those of an Arabian patriarch, the thoughts are those of one who in the light of modern science sees the slow action of the dissolving rains and the rushing torrents of the broad river, sowing the dust of continents to be.

Nature, he says, as well as life, tell us the same sad tale. Change, and decay, and destruction are everywhere; the individual withers and the world is more and more. "Thou destroyest the hope of man; Thou prevailest for ever against him; Thou changest his countenance and sendest him away. His sons come to honour, and he knoweth it not; they are brought low, but he perceiveth it not. The same doom is over all Thy works." His language is the very reverse of the psalmist's words: "All Thy works praise Thee, and Thy saints give thanks to Thee." "All Thy works pass away, and thou regardest them not."

Once more, then, we have pleading, agony, contention, questioning, despair. We have everything in the world, we might say, except patience; and the climax is not reached even yet. The dialogue is resumed. Each of the three friends rises in turn to speak once more, and each is followed in due course by Job. And yet again, two out of the three return to the argument, and are followed by a long soliloquy, as we might call it, from Job himself.

It would clearly detain us far too long to go, as we have thus far done, chapter after chapter through the whole dialogue. Let me summarize—it is easily done—the position maintained by those whom Job calls in his bitterness his miserable comforters. They represent, and are obviously meant to represent, the class of good and God-fearing men who do not feel at all acutely the perplexities and the problems of life, and who resent as merely mischievous and misleading the doubts which these perplexities and problems suggest. Much of what they say is most striking. It is not until they are shocked and pained at Job's presumption that they plead, and seem to have a right to plead, that the wisdom of antiquity is all on their side;

what wise men had told from their fathers' day were genuine traditions better than the mere idle tale of some passing stranger, and that they bring against him the wisdom, and thought, and experience of grey-headed and very aged men, much older than his father. Much, also, that they say is very true as well as very striking, on God's greatness, the greatness and omniscience of Him in whose sight not even the very heavens are clean. On human weakness and sinfulness they enlarge in language which will never lose its force. So, too, on God's readiness to receive those who will turn to Him under chastening they preach almost as preachers of the Gospel before the Gospel came; and for a most striking picture of the force and power of an evil conscience haunting the evildoer even in the height of prosperity, a dreadful sound ringing in his ears, a voice within telling him that a sword is waiting him in the darkness, and an inward trouble and anguish causing him more terror than kings arrayed against him in battle, we may turn to the second speech of Eliphaz in the fifteenth chapter. Throughout all these runs the unshaken and unfailing conviction that God hates evil and loves good, that the Divine power is a power that works, and works actively for righteousness.

The cursory reader, nay, the attentive reader, may naturally as he reads, anticipate the close, and ask himself how is it possible that men who speak so wisely and so well, and who evidently are full of the conviction of what they say, who are doing their very utmost to rise to the height of the greatest of all arguments, to justify the ways of God to men, are at the end of the book rebuked, while Job, of whose bold questionings and repinings and doubts and murmurs we have only yet heard a part, is justified.

Let me end this with one more word on the attitude of the three friends, true friends as their visit showed, devout men as their language showed, orthodox men after the prevailing belief of their day, as their entire agreement with each other, and their appeals to the consent of the good and the aged shows,—yet, after all, utterly mistaken men. In the first place their sympathy with him with whom they reason soon left them. "Who is weak and I am not weak? who is offended, and I burn not?"

That Divine cry of sympathy was not their language. On the contrary, the tempests in Job's soul only lower him in the eyes of the men who sat watching him safely on the mainland. They were shocked at his failure in faith, as it seemed to them, and they soon began to upbraid and to denounce him. They set an example which Christian controversialists have been only too ready to follow; they tried to break that much-bruised reed, to quench that smoking flax. Their language grows harsh and stern just where harshness and sternness were most wholly out of place.

And secondly they were in possession of certain undoubted truths, truths which I have already indicated, and to utter these in season and out of season seemed enough. Whether they were the truths needed for the special trial with which they had to deal did not matter to them; it was enough that they were true; and the result was what was to be expected. The wholesome medicine became poison in their unskilful hands, the remedy only aggravated the disease. How often and with what evil results have good Christian men and women trodden in their steps, and repeated the same error!

And finally, all that they said was tainted with one fundamental error, that error against which the whole of the book is one long protest. God was teaching the world in the sufferings of Job a truth new to the early world, and very hard, as we see centuries later, for the Hebrew world to realize. One great object of the book is to announce the truth that God's hand may be heavy, very heavy, on those whom He dearly loves; that individual suffering is no proof of individual wrongdoing. The words, "Think ye that those on whom the tower of Siloam fell, were sinners above all men?" or again, our Lord's answer to those who asked Him "Whether did this man sin or his parents, that he was born blind?" were addressed to men who still clung to the belief that personal suffering proved personal guilt. They were the true heirs, the spiritual children of those in this book, who, beginning with gentle hints could end with taxing their friend, to whose blameless life before his trials came, God and man alike had borne their witness, with a life of hypocrisy and double dealing, and infinite injustices and meannesses,—with having in the midst of all his wealth taken a pledge, as one said, from his brother, and of having stripped the naked of their clothing. It is the conflict of these narrow ideas with the new and Divine light dawning as sunlight on the summit of Alpine mountains in some solitary hut, the light that was to gather one day round the Cross of Calvary, and was to gild many a bitter hour of poverty, of failure, of bereavement, of humiliation, of sickness, and of the hour of death, that lies at the very root of all these reiterated arguments, all of this that seems to us a long monotony of protest and appeal that makes up this book.

G. G. B.

XXIII. The Book of Job.—4.

I so far anticipated what still lies before us in my last lecture, as to give you a general summary of the language of Job's three friends, at the supreme moment when, at the opening of the thirty-second chapter, we are told that they ceased to answer him because he was righteous in his own eyes. What had been meantime the effect of their arguments on one whose despairing words at the close of the fourteenth chapter we noticed in our last? What had he gained from their well-meant counsels? They had convinced him at least that there was no human consoler left him. He felt this keenly; and in answer to the words —the often eloquent and often true, but still inopportune words—of the gentlest of his interlocutors, he drily replied: "I have heard many such things; miserable comforters are ye all." And so again in answer to another, "How long will ye vex my soul and break me in pieces with your words?" "Not so," he says very touchingly, would he have treated them. "Had your souls been in my soul's place, I would have strengthened you with my mouth, and the moving of my lips should have assuaged your grief;" but for the rest he turns his back on those ill-judging friends, and pleads (pleads for his very life) no more with them, but with the God who is afflicting him. I shall put before you samples only, but they shall be fair samples, of his language.

First, what I have already spoken of as his long wail is

not yet over; it breaks forth, rising to the surface like a bitter spring, from time to time, in various forms and expressions, under various, often very curious and interesting figures, almost to the end of all that he says; and the careful reader will find much that is exceedingly interesting and suggestive in these hymns, if I may so call them, of pain and suffering, often seeming to have little direct reference to Job's actual state, which passed, from time to time, from his lips. Read, for instance, that which begins with the 6th and ends with the 22nd verse, chap. xix.; it will remind you, verse after verse, of some of the very saddest and most solemn of all the psalms, pointing onwards, even as they do, to One whose sorrow was above all human sorrow. "He hath put my friends far from me; and my familiar friends have forgotten me;" and ending with the heart-rending appeal, "Have pity upon me, have pity upon me, oh ye, my friends, for the hand of God hath touched me." Read, again, that strange description of some lower and conquered aboriginal race, whose fathers had ranked, he says, in his eyes below the very dogs of his father's flocks, which ushers in the thirtieth chapter. How vivid, how life-like the picture of the scanty and scorned tribe, thinned by want and famine—driven from the haunts of civilized man—cried after as thieves when they passed men's doors—dwelling in caves, and amongst the rocks, and feeding on wild roots—braying, as he says, in their unintelligible half-articulate chatter among the bushes, where, viler than common clay, they crouched, as he says once more, with the lower animals!

But the whole book is full of vivid pictures, vivid touches of the life of that early world, often lying covered up beneath the obscurity of our version as—I used, I think, the figure before—as the treasures of Pompeii under the ashes of Vesuvius. If I were to follow them, I should lead you aside from the broad human highway of the book into its strange by-ways and interesting recesses. Let me go back to the one thread which runs clear and strong through the twisted and tangled strand, alike in its earlier and its later subjects; the quivering sense of pain, the cry, the complaint, the outspoken agony.

Secondly—side by side, with this—there is another stream of thought that heightens and gives poignancy to his other pangs. It is the moral pain, the spiritual torture, the bewildering sense that these woes, which God has laid upon him—for never for a moment does he doubt that they come from God—are causeless, unaccountable; that he has not merited such terrible, such signal, such exceptional chastisement. " If I am to lie down in misery that makes me cry for death, if I am to go in unrelieved misery down to the land of darkness, it is for no act of injustice that soils my hands." "My prayer," he cries, "is pure;" and then, goaded with a sense of wrong— " Earth, earth," he cries,—there seems to be (I will not speak too positively) a rare allusion to the Book of Genesis, a reference to the innocent blood of Abel, crying from the ground,—" earth," he says, " cover not my blood, hide not my cry. I cry out for my wrong, but I am not heard; and I cry aloud, but I have no redress," and he appeals to his Sovereign to bear witness whether he has gone back from His commands, whether he has not esteemed the words of His mouth as dearer than his daily bread; nay, he feels bound to assert his innocence against the charges of his accusers. " My righteousness I will hold fast, and I will not let it go." And then in a chapter, the twenty-ninth, more pathetic, more moving, if I may say so, than words of mere lamentation, he recalls the happy days of the golden past, when the " candle of God shone upon my head, and by His light I walked through the darkness of life; when the Almighty was yet with me, and my lost children were about me;" and he recalls those days as not merely days of well-being, but of well-doing. It was not only, you will see if you read that chapter, that the young men, and the aged princes and nobles had done him honour, but he could add that " When the ear heard me, then it blessed me; and the eye when it saw me, gave witness to me." And why? " Because I delivered the poor that cried, the fatherless, and him that had no helper; because I won the blessing of him that was ready to perish, and caused the widow's heart to sing for joy. Because I was a righteous judge, and because I rejected not the stranger's plea. I searched out to do him justice, and so I dwelt," he says, " among men as a king among his host, as a beneficent king, as one that comforteth the mourners." And so, later on, " Did not I weep for him that was in trouble?" "Was not my soul grieved for the poor?" And in his last appeal, in the thirty-first chapter, to the God who sees his woes, and counts all his steps, he asserted his innocence of sins of the flesh, of niggardliness, of fraud, of avarice, of oppression, of deadness to the woes of others. The very slave, he says, he regarded and treated as his fellow-creature. "Did not He that made him make me?" The fleeces of his sheep had warmed the loins of the poor Never has he eaten the fruits of his land without due payment to his labourer. Never has he exulted in the sorrows of his ill wishers. Never has he cursed his adversary. Never has he eaten his food alone and left the orphan unfed. Never has the generous Arab allowed the stranger to lodge beneath the cold night sky. Never, again, has the sun when it shined, or the moon walking in its brightness through that transparent sky, tempted his heart to worship or his hand to do homage. Never has he denied the God who so afflicts him. We, who have been elevated, by the slow process of God's Spirit speaking to us through the ages, to a higher level; we who have been born into the dispensation of that Spirit that was to convince the world, not only of righteousness, but also of sin; we may be startled by such broad and unflinching assertions of human innocence; but the sequel shows that in one sense, and that a very essential sense, they were well founded, the whole book would be meaningless if they were false. Yet they do have in all of them an element of error and imperfection, and it is the mingling of these two currents that forms the keenest and most searching of his trials, and yet perhaps the very one into which it is most easy for many here, and now, thoroughly to enter. His wealth had gone from him, we know, in a moment; but great riches are, after all, exceptional, and the sudden transition from opulence to utter destitution is the lot of few. His children, whom He so dearly loved, had been swept away at a stroke, sudden and signal. Such has had its parallels, its sad and its very rare parallels in modern experience. Health had gone and his frame was racked with sore diseases. It is an accumulation of woes on a single head, such as we may say is seldom or never seen on the stage of daily and of practical life. Yet all this he had borne with a profound, an absolute submission to Him who gives and takes away the joys of life, our life itself. It recalls to us, as I said before, not only Christian submission, but that which forms the true greatness, the redeeming feature in the life of the pious Mohammedan, who when wealth and children and health had gone, something yet remained to him; he walked with unseen glory crowned in a sense of his dependence on his Maker and his God. But now the rebukes of his unwise friends had given birth to something not from without, but from within, that made the solid earth reel beneath his weary frame. Their hard and ready dogmatism had forced upon him a question for which his soul travailed in vain to find an answer. This mighty, this almighty Being, whose greatness, and whose justice, and whose omniscience they discussed so fully, was he after all a righteous Being? was the ruler of the world a just Ruler? Did the Judge of mankind judge rightly? Powerful He is, no doubt. Nature, he feels, tells His power. In His hand, he says himself, is the life of every human being, the health of all mankind. History, such as he knows it, tells His power. Nations, he says, rise and fall, and kings exchange the royal girdle for the cord that encircles the loins of the captive horde. What if all this power is wielded by one who looks with indifference on right and wrong, and smiles alike on the good cause and the bad; who leaves the world to be misgoverned, pain and pleasure to flow through creation at random, or, worse still, to be distributed in the interest of wrong-doing; and all the wise saws of his friends intensify the agony of this doubt. They tell him that from of old, from the day when men were first placed on the earth, the triumph of the wicked has been short; that God had been invariably and at all hours the good man's friend; that he himself is paying the penalty due to his hypocrisy and ill living, and he knows that this is false, and dark thoughts stir within him, and bitter doubts—doubts that have tried many a heart that have never tasted of his exceptional and tragic cup of misery—fill his brain, and shake the faith that Satan's malice had vainly tried. "Mark me," he says in the twenty-first chapter, "and be astonished, and lay your hands upon your mouths." The thought that stirs within that pious patriarch he hardly dares to utter. "Even when I remember Him I am afraid, and a trembling takes hold of my flesh." Yet speak he must. He looks out with changed eyes on the spectacle of life, and beneath the dress of the patriarch of the Old Testament, honoured in all the Churches, the friend of God, we see the questioner of the most fundamental of all religious, of all moral truths. "Wherefore," he says, "do the wicked live and become mighty in power?" Their seed is established; their families, as we should say, are founded under their eyes; all goes well with them. Their wealth increases, and all prospers. They send forth their little ones like a flock; and their children dance to the timbrel and the harp. We see beneath that Eastern imagery the prosperous family in all ages founded on wrong-doing. They spend their days in wealth; in a moment, in due time, they go down unpunished to their graves. Where is the God that rules the world with righteousness? And he tries to find satisfaction for his doubts in retribution falling one day on their posterity. But no, he comes back uncomforted to the same question, the inequalities, the injustices of life. One dieth in his full strength, being wholly at ease and quiet; another dieth in the bitterness of his soul, and never eateth bread with pleasure. They lie down alike in the dust, and the worms cover them. It is the opening scene of Dives and Lazarus, without its sequel. The rich man died; the beggar died also. And we, my friends, need not go through Job's preliminary tortures to feel the problem that vexed him. An hour's walk in London, a day, it may be, in a country village, may stir the same question; and think, too, how much darker and more cruel the world must have seemed, when thus regarded, to one who lived in the religious atmosphere which Job breathed. Not one word all his friends whispered to him of the world beyond the grave. Amidst all the visions that haunted him, there is none of One who tasted shame and desolation and death, and was in all points tempted like as we are, yet was He infinitely dear to His God, to His father, and lives at God's right hand. The voice that spake of a life to come, was not wholly, absolutely dumb. If he dare not cherish that full embodiment of the Christian hope which meets all that is mortal of our friends, high or low, as we bear them to their graves, yet through its darkness and obscurity, there is at the very least, a looking forward to the sight of God, when the bodily frame must return to dust; and once or twice we hear the accents of that better voice, but its accents are faint and low and overborne by that louder voice, the dreary touch of the simple sense that speaks of death as the final and eternal end of each human soul.

And so he stands at bay. He has to face the spectres of his mind; his foes are indeed those of his own household—his wife, his friends, the teaching of his age, the traditions of the past, his own sorrows, his own experiences, his own tumultuous thoughts; and what is left him, what severs him from the mere cynical denier of God's providence and God's goodness, or from him who smiles at all distinctions between right and wrong? What is it that gives him his place in the roll of God's servants? Much is left him still, much that in all times it is well to remember is dear to God. There is the eager, the passionate desire for truth, "Give me light and let me die"; and there is the firm persistance in calling on his God to reveal that truth to him. Through all the darkness that surrounds him, does not the search for God still haunt his soul? He thirsts for the living God, for God and His truth. "Behold, I go forward, but He is not there; and backward, but I cannot perceive Him; on the left hand, but I cannot behold Him; He hideth Himself on the right hand that I cannot see Him," and so "Oh, that I knew where I might find Him, that I might go even to His throne." He tries to comfort himself by drawing pictures, even as his friends had done, magnificent pictures of the greatness of Him at whose reproof the pillars of the heavens tremble and are astonished, and he lays his fingers for a moment on the immortal truth, that all these are but parts of His ways, that we hear but a small portion, that we see, in modern language, but the skirts of creation, and he speaks of truth and wisdom as sorely hard to find; as hidden from the eye, as veins of metal which can only be reached by the dark miner's path; a hidden path like that beneath the earth, which the vulture's eye hath not seen, the lion's whelps have not trodden, nor hath the fierce lion passed by it. Yet for all that, he speaks of human wisdom as consisting in the fear of God and avoidance of evil; and he cannot believe that to do justice, and to love mercy, and

to walk humbly with God, can alienate a man from God.
And just before his last words had died away, he breaks
forth into one last piteous appeal, obscured though it be
in our rendering of his imagery, that the God who seemed
his adversary would reveal to him His will, would only hear
and answer him. "The words of Job are ended." Such is
the close of the thirty-first chapter. That most eloquent
of voices is hushed. His friends who listened to him were
pained and shocked, and they forebore to argue with him
any more, because he was righteous in his own eyes. But
we may feel as we read through the book, that it was not
only the full, the desperate, the proud avowal of the integrity of his early life that silenced these representatives,
as I have called them before, of the religious thought of
the age of Job. It was the upheaval of a new stratum of
ideas, if I may so speak, that revolted them. The question
that Job had stirred was one that had disarranged all their
hereditary creed. He was the teacher, the unconscious,
the half-articulate teacher, of a doctrine that would cut
across all their views of the government of the world,—of
a doctrine that would one day be a very Gospel of life,—
that God might be the friend, the living friend of one
sorely afflicted, and who was not therefore to be listened
to or argued with longer. Their feelings were very natural.
We, as I said before, feel that there is something that is
not of the very highest type of religious thought even in
those simple and moving appeals to his blameless life
which fell from the lips of Job; and, at all events, we can
sympathize in the outcries of the men whose creed contained few articles, but among them one to which they
clung as the fundamental article of their faith—that suffering was always and invariably the sign of sin, great and
overwhelming calamity a sure sign of great and signal
criminality. And if Job's assertions of innocence were
well founded, a well-ordered universe would be resolved
into chaos. With such questions they might well fail to
sympathize. The very foundations of the great deep
seemed broken up; and their creed must dissolve and
construct itself afresh. It is not the first time in the
history of the world that the majority of religious professors have been wrong. The solitary thinker, the philosopher, the heretic, the forlorn monk, the rejected of their

day, have been sometimes, even in spite of many errors, in the right. That little group in the unknown land of Uz, who tried to silence the one among them who was in his world like the herald and the apostle of a truth that was one day to be embodied in the symbol of Christ's religion, may warn us against thinking that truth is always to be found on the side of numbers—that the God of truth marches always with the largest battalions. How startling to those who heard it, how instructive to those who read it, are the words which we shall find when next we meet! "Ye, ye, who have been so earnest, so rigid in justifying My ways and asserting your righteousness, ye have not spoken the thing that is right, as My servant Job hath." And surely a new meaning must be found for the word patience, as elsewhere in the New Testament, so also in the words, which some will remember, of St. James: "Ye have heard of the patience of Job, and ye know the end of the Lord, that the Lord is very pitiful and of tender mercy." There may be a higher patience than that of submissiveness; a holding out of a corner of the fortress against desperate odds—the resistance of a charge by a handful may determine the issues of a campaign. He that shall endure to the end, said a greater than the Apostle James, shall be saved. "If ye have faith as a grain of mustard seed, ye shall remove mountains;" remove, and raise, and elevate what is more precious than a mountain, the human soul.

G. G. B.

XXIV. The Book of Job.—5.

WE are reaching the closing scene. We are in sight of what may be called the catastrophe of the Book of Job. The three friends are silenced; the words of Job are ended; the ground seems clear. But before the close, there comes what appears to be an episode, a pause in, a diversion from, the main progress of the story. A fresh character under the name of Elihu appears on the scene. He was unmentioned before; he will be unnoticed at the close, where all but himself are passed in review, and receive their meed of praise or blame. And there are many who, from various reasons, hold that the chapters devoted to him—the thirty-second to the thirty-seventh inclusive—are not parts of the original Book of Job, but were added later on, possibly by the writer himself, to mitigate the shock produced on pious readers by the sudden reversal, by the judgment of God, of the judgment of what almost might be called the Church of the day as represented by the friends of Job.

I need not enter into so vexed, and thorny, and difficult a question. Yet you would wish me, I feel sure, to glance at the substance of the new speaker's words, and to indicate his attitude, which seems to me to go far to explain his words. He is younger than those who have yet spoken. He has listened to the words of his elders with that outward deference shown by a true son of the East to age and experience. "I am young," he says expressly of himself, "and ye are old; wherefore I was afraid, and durst not show to you mine opinion." Yet, as he listened, his anger, we read, was kindled against Job, because he justified himself against God; also against the three friends was his anger kindled, because they had found no answer, and yet had condemned Job. He represents, it would appear, something different; a younger generation, more open to new ideas, less resolutely set against fresh shapes of truth, and more fit to be the means of transition from one stage of religious knowledge and spiritual life to another. So much we may fairly say. And it is well that we who are older should remember that if youth is often presumptuous, age is almost invariably averse to change; somewhat intolerant of what seems novel, and therefore revolutionary; and as slow to do justice to the new forms in which God may be fulfilling Himself, as were Job's friends to bear with the new truth to which his, as it seemed to them, profane and daring language was the prelude.

Into the full details of his long discourse I, of course, shall not enter. We must not look for the carefully constructed argument of a Platonic dialogue. The accents of the last human speaker in this book are, we must allow, correctly described as somewhat trembling and hesitating; the argument is somewhat confused and complicated. Doubtless he too, like his friends, censures Job for speaking of himself as clean and without transgression, and as treating God as his enemy; and he speaks of pain and suffering as a discipline, and of God as raising up the penitent from the very edge of death to be enlightened once more with the light of the living; yet for all this, he does not do much to lift them out of the difficulty. He is shocked at the thought that he attributes to Job, that it profiteth a man nothing that he should delight himself with God; "God forbid," he says. "The work of a man will God render unto him, and cause every man to find at last according to his ways." "Yea, surely," he says (the words, my brethren, are sure words), "God will not do wickedly; neither will the Almighty pervert justice." "Shall," he asks, "he that hateth right govern?" "Shall the Judge of the whole world do wrong?" we read elsewhere; "and wilt thou condemn Him that is most just?" He has not felt (how should youth have felt?) Job's trials; and he cannot sympathize, therefore, with Job's anxious questionings. So far, also, as we understand his language, he seems to miss the real and vital core of the problem that Job's case has brought to light. He speaks, or seems to speak, as though, because God was so great and high, therefore Job's righteousness, or Job's innocence, or Job's guilt, however important in the sight of man, mattered little. Yet it may be that we are wrong in judging thus, and that he is only obscurely indicating the surpassing greatness of God, of whom he says very strikingly in his closing words, that, unsearchable as He is, and past finding out, yet that He is certainly excellent, not in power only, but also in judgment and in abundance of justice, and that He will not afflict His children.

With these words he passes from the scene which he has merely traversed, to speak once with a kind of balanced judgment,—that may remind us, perhaps, of more than one utterance of the chorus in some Greek tragedy,—which a hasty critic would scarcely wish to cancel; and then, when human advisers and human censors have done their best and done their worst, God answers Job out of the Whirlwind.

And what is that answer? How eagerly may we lean forward, as it were, to listen! Those who have in any way followed Job's sad history and feverish pleading might well have hoped that, with such a knot to untie, the voice of God would not have been heard at all unless to solve the whole enigma for him and for us. But it is not so in fact. "God speaks, but it is not"—I quote the words, or nearly the words, of a recent and excellent English commentator—"it is not to say, Let there be light, where all was darkness;" and when He has spoken, you and I must close the book with the sense that the question of questions, as it seems to us, has received no full, entire, adequate solution. What is the answer that Job receives in reply to his repeated, his clamorous, appeals that God would speak to him? In the first place, it is much to him that his appeal is answered at all. As he hears the words, "Gird up thy loins like a man, for I will demand of thee, and answer thou Me," he feels at least that he is no longer forsaken of his ancient Friend; he is no longer left alone in a world ruled by evil or ruled by chance. And what next? He is asked the solution of one riddle—his own hard destiny. "Can," he says, "that Voice read other mysteries? Is this the only dark spot in a world radiant and transparent elsewhere with light? or is he not rather surrounded on all sides by clouds which he cannot pierce, riddles which he cannot read? He has darkened counsel—that is, misread God's designs by words without knowledge on one point. Can he read the mysteries of the universe, of creation, of all the varied forms of life, fair or monstrous, that swarm around him? Can he," he is asked later on, "abase the proud, tread down the wicked? Has he penetrated into the secrets of the government of the world, and seated himself in the centre of the great forces that rule the distribution of good and of evil? Or is he not rather weak and ignorant, able to read only a fragment of the mighty laws which shape alike the courses of the stars and the destinies of mankind?"

Such seems the substance of the answer that he receives, when we strip it of its noble scenery and its splendid illustrations. Let us glance at it more closely for a moment. Job is called on to consider the greatness, the immensity of nature; not, I need scarcely say, of the forces, as we call them, of nature, as seen and interpreted with modern eyes, but still of the awful and overpowering phenomena of nature and of life as they were revealed to Job. He is carried back to the regions of earth and sea and light, and with each question comes, as it were, a lightning flash of poetic beauty. We hear the angelic host, the morning stars, the stars of dawn, fitly hailing the dawn of life in a new-born world, " when the morning stars sang together and all the sons of God shouted for joy ; " or the wild and capricious sea subjected to law and order—" Hitherto shalt thou come, and no further, and here shall thy proud waves be stayed ; " or we see the sudden sunrise in a land of briefest twilight flash on the dark earth, and its scenery, coming out sharp and clear, as the shapeless clay receives the impress of a seal. The sunshine even there hath a glorious birth. " Where wast thou," said the Voice, " when these things had their birth ?" and then his brain is, as it were, made dizzy by challenges to penetrate, now the homes of light and of darkness ; now the regions of stored and accumulated snows ; now the clouds feeding here the streams that, swift or slow, mould the mountains and shape the earth, now falling on the broad desert steppes in beneficent and fertilising rain ; now the realms of ice, the frozen seas ; now the majestic heavens and the laws that move the stars. " Where is thy hand ? what is thy knowledge among these things ?" he is asked.

And then he—and Job, remember, is here the type of all our race, though the language used to him is couched of course in a form suited to his day and generation—is bidden to look upon the forms of wild, untamed, untameable life that filled in those early days so vast a portion of the earth's surface. He is called to look upon those kingly lions that needed not the aid of man ; on the wild ravens whose cry, to the poet's ear, went up as a very prayer to the Father of all life ; and the rock goats and the wild ass, creatures so strong, so vigorous, so rude, so free, rejoicing in a noble liberty, scorning, he is told, the multitudes of the city, neither regarding the cry of the driver ; then on the mighty and primeval buffalo, unfortunately rendered by the meaningless heraldic unicorn, whom none can train to draw the plough, none force to carry home the garnered wheat ; then the sullen ostrich, so dull to natural feeling, so hardened against her young ones, yet able to put to scorn the steed and its rider. Then the words, " Hast thou given the horse strength ? Hast thou clothed his neck with thunder ?" usher in the stirring, the splendid description of the horse, not as with the Greek poet, the servant of man, but in the form known to Hebrew or Arab or Egyptian, as the fiery, neighing, snorting warhorse of the Arabians, "who saith among the trumpets, Ha, Ha! who smelleth the battle afar off." And the list of pictures which began with the king of beasts ends with that of the queen of birds, who builds her nest upon the rock, upon the crags of the rocks, her young ones also suck her blood, and where the slain ones are there is she; and once more, after a few simple words from Job, there follow, too, elaborate pictures of monstrous untameable creatures, the behemoth and the leviathan, the hippopotamus and the crocodile of the sea-like river of Egypt.

The language, we all feel, if we read it, reaches the very high-water mark of poetic beauty. Nothing in the world can excel its dignity, its force, its majesty, or the freshness of its pictures of nature and of life. But what next? we ask. No answer, we may say here, to Job's agonized questionings, no answer to the sore riddles and problems of life which still vex ourselves. Quite true. There is at least no direct answer at all. Even those partial answers which have been touched on from time to time by speaker after speaker, are not glanced at in those final words. It is as though the voice of God did not care to repeat that His power works on the side of righteousness. He only hints it. Nor does He enforce, but leaves for the present where it stands, the undying truth, already mooted in this book, that sorrow does its best work when it purifies and raises the human soul; nor is any light thrown on that faint and feeble glimmer of hope, that streak of light not yet fully born into the world, of a life beyond the grave, where there shall be no more sorrow and sighing, where Rachel and her lost children, Job and his lost sons and daughters, shall be once more reunited. The thoughts that we should have most looked for are not here.

One other thought and one only is brought forward into the foreground, one lesson; it is this: The world is full of mysteries, strange, unapproachable, overpowering, insoluble, that we cannot read. Trust, trust, in the power, in the wisdom, in the goodness of Him who rules it. Turn from the problem of your own destiny; good men have said their best, wise men have said their wisest; we are still left to bear the discipline of questions too hard for us to solve. We cannot answer them. Turn to the belief that all is good, all is wise, and that one day, not here, the riddle will be read ; that behind the veil which we cannot pierce lies its solution in the hands of God.

And yet, strange as it may seem, to Job this answer, which may appear to many so inadequate, was ample and sufficient.

It was much, as I said before, that God had answered him ; and his tortured heart is calmed, and he turns trustfully to his Answerer. "I know," he says, "that Thou art Lord of all, and knowest all wisdom. I have uttered things beyond my knowledge. I know Thee better now. I feel Thee nearer to me ; mine eye seems to see Thee. Before it was only the hearing of the ear, and to know Thee here and by me is all I need. I have misjudged Thee. I repent my rash words," he says ; "do Thou forgive them." And Job is reconciled to his God, and his friends are censured. All the truths, the many truths in what they had said, did not compensate for their hasty, their coarse, we may call it, and ill-judged application of these truths to God's afflicted servant. And Job's wild words and audacious questionings are freely forgiven for the sake of his firm conviction that righteousness and mercy were, and must be, dear to God ; that if under any pretext or under any system they were not dear to God, it would be a hideous universe under an unjust master ; for it is after all by goodness, and in virtue of goodness, that God is God. Is it not so, that if God were not good, not all power, not all wisdom, would make him God ?

"Ye have not spoken of Me," says that God, "the thing that is right, like My servant Job ;" for even when he seemed to assail his Divine Friend, he was pleading for His unchangeable, His dearest attributes of justice and of goodness. And God's unfailing love for His afflicted servant, over whom His heart had yearned in all his sufferings and in all his outcries, and not less in all his doubts, is shown by his renewed prosperity, of which we read at the end— restored life, greater riches, other sons and daughters, other friends, honoured and lengthened days. By all the accumulated conditions of human happiness, the Lord blessed the latter end of Job more than the beginning.

These things, as I said before, prove God's love for one who had suffered much, and they do something also to relieve the tension, the pang that we should all have felt at Job being left to die, whether in resignation, or in patience, or in sadness on his dunghill. But they do not, we all feel, undo his sufferings. The lost child does not come back; "the vanished hand," "the voice that is still," are not, and were not to be replaced; and the world is full of instances where the clouds and shadows of life are not followed by such countervailing sunshine. Hence, it is, perhaps, that in the very ancient version of the book which formed for a very large portion of the Jewish race even in our Lord's day their authorised version of the Old Testament, we find a verse added in quite another key and by a later hand. It is written, that Job will rise again with those whom the Lord raiseth.

One word more before we part. We close the book with a sense of its treasures, not exhausted, of interest and beauty; but also, it may be, with something of a natural disappointment that it contains no direct, complete, and cheering answer to questions against which the human soul has beaten itself from Job's days to ours. It stirs, if we choose to say so, great doubts that it does not answer. We see Job, as it were, led to the verge of a sea-shore; a great and limitless and pathless ocean which he cannot pass is before him; he can go no further, see but a little way on; he must rest where he is and trust. All that he is told is, that God most surely loved him; that He will not answer his eager and passionate questions, but that through them all, and in spite of them all, he is dear to Him because he had loved righteousness and hated iniquity, and that for these things God cares, and cares infinitely; and in the sense of this and of God's power and wisdom, he must rest content. And he is told also that trouble and affliction do not prove God's displeasure; that the very heaviest, the most overwhelming blows may come from a Maker who is full of love to him on whom they fall; may come, as did Job's, from causes far beyond his power to comprehend or guess, and that he need not look on God as his persecutor or his enemy—not shrink from Him, but draw closer and closer to Him in his trouble, and trust Him more wholly.

And his story reminds us also of God's mercy and forbearance to those who are under sorrow; of the larger, the other eyes with which He may look on the impatience, the bewilderment, the fretfulness, even the doubts and questionings, of His servants. The impatience, as it seems to us, of Job is answered by the patience and pitifulness of Job's God:—" The Lord is very pitiful, and of tender mercy "—and this, surely, is much.

The book marks, as I have said before, an era, an epoch, a stage of progress in God's education of His people. It suggests lessons that must have been precious beyond words to those who had been trained to identify suffering with sin.

We, my friends, who have long left behind us that simple answer to life's hard problem which satisfied Job's friends, and well-nigh broke Job's heart, we feel our darkness still; yet as we take our place by his side, whether in his anguish, or in his restored brightness of life, we feel that we have light given to us which was denied to him. The whole revelation of the Christian life, of the life of Christ, the upward course, the forward course, of One who was despised and humiliated and scourged and slain, " made perfect through suffering," has brought a new ideal into the world like vernal airs on to a frozen soil,—something which the age of Job could hardly have conceived of, and which the Jewish nation later on steadfastly rejected. It has leavened race after race with the sense that the highest, the divinest life, may be compatible with sorrow, and rests upon pain and self-sacrifice. How many thousands has it taught that the truest use of pain is to brace us to do work for God and man ! And even as the life of Christ would be meaningless if the other world of which He spoke were a mere delusion ; if God, whose nature He reveals to us, had suffered His Holy One to see corruption and final extinction, so to us these difficulties and mysteries are inseparably linked with the sense, not only of God's undying love for the human race, but with the hope which in that love He holds out to us of another and a larger and an unseen world, of a greater dispensation, of which this life's puzzles and wounds are only a part. Even as it is, prophets and kings and patriarchs have desired to see even the truths that we see so dimly, and have not seen them, and we, too, must be content to look forward for larger light. " What I do thou knowest not now, but thou shalt know hereafter."

Meanwhile, we must repose in the sense of God's love and goodness, as in that of His power and wisdom.

G. G. B.

XXV. The Second Psalm. Psalm ii. *"Why do the heathen rage, and the people imagine a vain thing? The kings of the earth, etc."*

I PURPOSE to deal with the whole of this psalm. The 1st and *this* 2nd psalm form a kind of prelude to the whole of the Psalter, and taken together, contain the two tones to which the rest give voice. The two great ideas of the Old Testament considered as revelation are: first, Law; second, Prophecy. The two elements of the Old Testament religion then are: first, loving obedience to the law; second, faithful anticipation of the prophecies. And the 1st psalm deals with the picture of the good man, and the bad man, in their attitude respectively to the law of God; while this 2nd psalm, with the other great element of Old Testament revelation—the Old Testament religion, with the great promises that men were called upon to trust; and sets forth the antagonism and opposition which rages upon earth against God, and the firm purpose of the unalterable Will, which sets its "King upon the holy hill of Zion." So the two psalms together fitly stand as preface and introduction to the whole of the Psalter, and sound the tones which are ever echoing throughout its whole range. I must necessarily deal with it superficially and briefly here, and must, therefore, put the general case of it, rather than any specific portion of it.

You will see that it falls very artistically and regularly into four very distinct parts, vividly separate from each other. First of all, in the first three verses the picture of the hurry and bustle of the conspiracy of the rebels down here upon earth. And then there comes crashing into the midst of that, in the next three verses, the contemptuous ease with which the fixed Divine purpose crushes all that swarming bustle of the little ant-hill down below. And then there comes into the next three verses, breaking into the very middle of this, the first attestation of the Divine King. And then there comes the psalmist himself, or the prophet himself, speaking, in the final triad of verses, the summons to surrender. First of all then, we get, what I have ventured to call the picture of the futile conspiracy of the busy rebels down below there. The psalmist, the seer, has before him the picture. He does not describe it, but with true artistic and dramatic power he brings forth the question : " Why do the heathen rage " and band themselves together. Why do they mutter and meditate a vain thing. The kings of the earth, and people and the rulers taking counsel together. What is the meaning of this universal laying of their heads together, all bending themselves and whispering, and setting themselves in antagonism, and consulting for a thing of naught against the Lord and against His anointed ? So he sees the whole of the conspiracy hatching, the eager antagonism which is being developed, in which all classes and all ranks unite, and that it has all no reason, no issue. What are they doing it for ? There is no ground for it. To what end are they doing it ? It is a vain thing. It will go up in smoke, and all come to nothing. The conspiracy against the dominion, which is not twofold, but one—the Lord and His Anointed—the dominion of the Jehovah exercised through His Son, saying, " Let us break their bands asunder, and cast away their cords from us." So they are rebels, and their opposition is rebellion ; and they are attempting to shake off the yoke which exists, to get to a freedom which they do not now possess. These are the outlines of this chapter : first, the antagonism of the kingdom of God as against the existing kingdom. That is to say, you and I,—by His love, His mercy, His sweetness, His goodness, His grace, by His Christ, and by His passion,—we have been made the subjects of His loving realm ; and for us to lift up our puny wills in opposition to that great throne and Sovereign Will, is not merely warfare, but revolt ; not merely opposition, but rebellion. And then, the other two points upon which I do not touch, but simply mention, are these : this antagonism, every single act of opposition between my will and God's will, is, first of all, truly absurd and groundless ; and, secondly, perfectly futile, perfectly vain. It is the paradox of human history, the one unanswerable question of the whole universe—Wherefore do the people set themselves against the Lord ? No reason that will stand for a moment can be given to the question, Why does the creature lift itself against God. No answer is possible except the one answer—Because we are fools! Wherefore do the people rage? The existence of evil, the existence of sin, my opposition, is the unanswerable mystery of all human history; the one standing puzzle of the whole universe is the possibility of antagonism, and still more the reality. There is nothing so strangely unreasonable in the whole history of man, as man setting himself against God. The other thought also, is vehemently expressed in this first picture; that not only is this antagonism wanting in all basis and reasonable explanation, so that it can never be reconciled with common sense; but also it is wanting in all issue; it will all come to nothing. They set themselves and band themselves together, and according to the vivid saying of the old hymn triumphal, "The Lord, the Lord did blow upon them, and they were scattered, they sank, etc." We may hurt ourselves, we may rob ourselves of the sweetness of entering into His will and finding rest, but we can make no impression upon that kingdom,—" the people imagine a vain thing."

So I come to the second stage, the phase of this vision which comes into the next three verses, where in picturesque and vivid opposition to the busy multitude down in the world, we get the one figure " He that sitteth in the heavens shall laugh, etc.;" "Yet have I set My King upon My holy hill of Zion." So there is something that seems very grand and very full in that contrast. On the one hand, the gathering opposition, the whispering conspiracy, the vehement banding together of the multitudes; and, on the other, the calm King sitting throned there in the heavens, and not even arising from His throne, nor stretching out His hand, and meeting it all with but a God-like smile upon His face, which means no favour, but which expresses the Divine recognition of the utter futility and nothingness of all that is going on below, the boldness, the audacity of the conflict; and the very incongruity between the thoughts of the rebels, and the calmness of the Divine Nature and such a love as that, is intended to strengthen and impress not only the essential ludicrousness of antagonism to His will, but the calmness with which that Divine power contemplates it all. And then notice, that just as the climax of the conspiracy was given us by the quotation of the whispered words that were passed from lip to lip amongst the rebels, so the climax of the Divine calm antagonism is given by the quotation of the Divine words, "Yet have I set My King upon My holy hill of Zion." That is to say, to put it into more abstract words, the one weapon of antagonism to all that human opposition to the Divine kingdom, is only, the Word—the Word of God—the utterance of His Will. That is all that is needed to crush it into nothingness. I need not, then, notice the thought, what tremendous force there is put against the busy multitudes,—the one single Personality. And what a power and grandeur there is in the "yet *I*"—we can easily fill up the ellipsis. "I" have set My King, in spite of all the opposition, notwithstanding all the antagonism, "*yet I*" have set My King. That is to say, one Divine purpose, one sovereign Divine purpose, stands there erect, and the antagonism of men, and of kingdoms, of individuals, of social systems, of schools of thought, of forms of life, and of the world in all its varied forms, hurled against that rocky purpose, is broken up into feathery spray, and falls back into the tossing sea. There stands the throne, one great hand holds it up, and the only answer that is given to all the conspiracy heat and enmity is, "I" have set My King upon My holy hill of Zion.

And so, still further, look now for a moment at the third phase here. We get next, coming in with startling suddenness, without prelude, we get another voice speaking, the voice of the King seated upon the holy hill,—what I may call the *self-attestation* of the King. "I will declare the decree: the Lord hath said unto Me, Thou art My Son; this day have I begotten Thee. Ask of Me, and I shall give Thee the heathen for Thine inheritance, and the uttermost parts of the earth for Thy possession." So suppose the King set upon the holy hill of Zion; and I am not going to enter into the question whether the words of it may have applied to some historical king of Israel—whether it be so or not, does not matter, in my judgment, to the truly pure Messianic character of the psalm. There is the great promise to the house of David, which is so often heard of in the psalms, which is, in fact, but a version and explanation of that great promise which applies simply to Jesus Christ Himself. So let me just try to bring out the three great main ideas which lie here in the self-attestation. There is first of all Sonship. If you go back to the original passage in the Book of Samuel, you will find there the conception of the day of the Son's birth does not mean the beginning of the man's life, but the day of the coronation of the King; the day of His entrance into His Kingdom; the day of His birth in reality is exactly the day of His resurrection from the dead. Turn to the thirteenth of the Acts of the Apostles and you will find that Paul quotes the words of my text as having a distinct bearing upon the resurrection of our Lord; and so what I want to fix upon for one moment is, that the sonship which is here set forth is our Lord's exaltation in His humanity by the resurrection from the dead, and the visible and manifest dominion in His human nature over earth and hell. We do not sufficiently remember that when Christ rose from the dead He arose with His human body, and His human nature was lifted to the royalty of the universe. And that is that which is here specially referred to.

The next point is, the universal and the delegated dominion: "Ask of Me, and I shall give Thee the heathen for Thine inheritance, and the uttermost parts of the earth for Thy possession." That is a world too wide for any human monarch that ever reigned, or ever could hope to reign, over the little strip of sea-board on the Mediterranean; and yet here is the Divine, not the universal, monarchy received from the Father. That is to say, Christ's reign and God's reign. Christ's reign—delegated dominion that is vested upon Him. And these words are the last words that He Himself spoke: "All power is given to Me upon earth, go ye and preach, etc."

The last point is the destructive energy of this great King; "Thou shalt break them with a rod of iron; Thou shalt dash them in pieces like a potter's vessel." "Ay," people say, "that is the Old Testament idea of a vengeful and warlike king." It is the idea of the King that smites, and that is Old Testament, and it is New Testament, too. Do not let us forget that the difference between the Old and New Testament is not that the New weakens or reverses the Old, but that it adds another thought to it, leaving the Old intact, but completing and supplementing it by another. Christ the King is the King whose mission it is to break and dash in pieces as well as to complete and build up. Thank God that it is so. There are plenty of things in this world that cannot be sanctified, and therefore must be altered. The task is, to break and bring to naught that which obstinately and ultimately sets itself against Him. Therefore we rejoice that sin,—social, political and individual evils, are all to be crushed and broken by the iron sceptre of the Universal King. Lift up your heads, redemption draweth nigh, and the ancient tyrannies—blood-cemented—that have been builded up through all the generations of the earth, are tottering to their fall. And so there comes the final word, the summons to surrender: "Be wise now therefore, O ye kings"—things being so—and "be instructed, O ye judges of the earth." All opposition is folly. Wisdom points to surrender, and that surrender is twofold; one in reference to the Lord, and one in reference to the Anointed. "Serve the Lord with fear, and rejoice with trembling. Kiss the Son." And, though I do not think that anything doctrinal depends upon it, I take it we have to read here, as our Bible has it, "Do homage to that Son lest He be angry, for His wrath is swiftly kindled." And then after that solemn warning—beautiful and tender—how wonderfully the whole psalm rises to another height, "Blessed are all ye that put your trust in Him." The religious emotions of faith and confidence which in the Old Testament belong to Jehovah, are transferred to that Anointed. And so the iron sceptre and the dominion are all explained, or rather elevated into a higher region, and we can trust the love, and nestle close to it, and enter with glad submission into the dominion of the King, and find that they that trust Him need never to know the weight of His iron sceptre and the terror of His wrath. Brother, let us crown Him King in our lives, as well as share with Him in His monarchy and His rest.

A. M.

XXVI. The Preaching of King David in the Psalms.
Psalm xxvii. 8. *"My heart hath talked of Thee, seek ye My face; Thy face, Lord, will I seek."* Psalm xxxvi. 1. *"My heart showeth me the wickedness of the ungodly."*

I suppose that, if any of us were asked, from which of the books of the Old Testament he had learned the most about his own heart, about the nature of sin, its effects and cure, about the faithfulness and forgivingness of God, he would answer without hesitation that it was from the Psalms. No book of the Old Testament has had really half as much influence upon the religious thought of the world as this most wonderful collection of the spiritual songs of Israel. And that, not only because for nearly three thousand years the voice of prayer and praise has gone up to God from the dwellings of the righteous, articulated in these forms, first in the Jewish Church and then in the Christian Church; not only because in ages, in which all or nearly all the other books of the Bible were in a measure sealed up in strange tongues, this book was made familiar and put into the hands of all who learned to pray; not only because by reason of this use, the psalms may be said to have moulded religious thought itself, and not merely expressed it; to have led man to the footstool of the Most High as well as placed words in his mouth when he reached it; the cause is deeper still, and the words are found to fit in with the case of the man who is just turning to God, as well as with his who has set God always before him. It is surely because is there a revelation in them of the heart of man to itself, a glimpse, seen as God sees it, of what is in the heart of the sinner, the penitent, and the saint. And is not this as great a wonder as any of the other miracles of inspiration? For, taking the Psalms of David alone, and excluding from the list all that either ancient tradition or modern criticism claims for other ages and other writers, setting aside the direct prophecies of the Messianic Psalms, and even those utterances which we are justified by our Lord's own application of them in believing to be prophetic, and to contain prophetic reference by type and shadow to his own work, his sufferings, and exaltation.

there is enough in what we may call the experimental psalms to deserve the name of a miracle of inspiration. They at least are David's; the words of the sweet singer of Israel.

And then when we look again on David himself, they are yet more wonderful. What was there in his lot, in even his varied history, in the condition of his age, in the society in which he lived, to suggest such thoughts? A shepherd boy, a royal favourite, a banished man, outcast and fugitive, a rising prince, at the last a mighty, comparatively powerful, king; a great offender against laws human and divine, a great penitent, humbled by trouble and shame and by the sins and shame of his children, at last restored to good conscience and peace, and dying in old age, disquieted still by domestic alarms, and outliving mental and physical strength. In all this there is variety of experience, it is true; but of what experience? Of a state of society most difficult for us to realize; perhaps more like that of a modern chieftain of some wandering Asiatic tribe than of a Christian prince; the companion of rude, rough, cruel men, standing on a border line between ancient and most corrupt civilizations, such as those of Egypt and Assyria, and an absolutely wild shepherd-life like that of the nomad races which people the same border lands to this day; inheriting the prophecies and traditions of Moses and the priesthood and the tabernacle, and a conviction, in itself exceptional and miraculous, of the destiny of the people;—but how little more, and how little at all and altogether, unless that conviction be regarded as itself a miracle. Yet this wild, wanton, ruthless chieftain, not less than his fellows a man of blood, a rough man, impulsive, hasty, generous, thoughtless, a very Esau, a very Ishmael, is the teacher of self-knowledge to all the world; to the Jew of the kingdom, the cultivated and civilized philosophers of the age of Solomon, to the long generations of ritual-worshippers in the temple that he had not been holy enough to build. That is conceivable; we can look on him as a great educator of his nation with awe but without astonishment; but when we look farther ahead, and into the Christian ages, and into the spiritual city and kingdom of which he could have known only by revelation of God; and for whose citizens he, singing a thousand years before, prepared a body of spiritual thoughts which seem to become the spontaneous language of the redeemed people; when we look on to the far regions which contain so little of the forms that mould the imagery of the pastoral poetry of Judah, to the civilizations that pride themselves on having cast away all that is old and barbarous, ay and to the opening, widening future of the Church in far-off lands, where as soon as the word is heard and received, it calls forth thoughts and words that admit no readier, no more perfectly fitting dress than this; what say we, what can we say, but this is the Lord's doing, and, much as we know of His other dealings, accustomed as we are to the wonderful workings of His hand, here is an ever fresh wonder, it is marvellous in our eyes.

David is the great preacher of the Old Testament, first to his own nation, then to the whole world; ages before Homer he sings the national songs that mark out his nation from all other people of the earth; ages before Socrates and Plato he reveals the mysteries of self-knowledge, conscience, and immortality, in language that needs no interpreter. "David the son of Jesse said, and the man who was raised up on high, the anointed of the God of Jacob, and the sweet psalmist of Israel said: The Spirit of the Lord spake by me, and His word was in my tongue."

How was this, and how is it exemplified?

We ask the question, not doubting the direct action of God in the action of His servants. Out of the mouth of babes and sucklings He ordaineth strength; He chose the ass to reprove the madness of Balaam; but ordinarily He allows us to see the fitness of His messenger to deliver the message. And so here. David's first and foremost, continuous, characteristic was a sense that God was by his side and before him. "I have set God always before me," he says in the 16th Psalm. And that not only in that he trusted in Him as a defender, although that profound conviction is the key-note of many of the psalms, and makes us look on David's whole career as one great lesson of faith and faithfulness between his Lord and himself; but in the direct and general sense, he felt that he was living before God. Sometimes we think that all the people of whom we read in the Bible share this characteristic, and that in this consists the main difference between the lives of the men of old and the lives of the men of to-day, so that David may be only a more prominent example of what may have been a general type. Possibly we may be wrong in such a generalisation, for, reading God's account of men's deeds as He tells them in His Revealed Word, naturally we come in some degree to look on them chiefly in their relation to Him, and so regard them through the medium of an atmosphere of which they were hardly conscious.

But allowing for this in the case of the general rule, it does not affect the case of David, of whom we know, from his own mouth and from the minute record of the Books of Samuel, so much more than we know of the others. In every detail of his life we see him living before God. It was not an equal, uniform, or consistent life: there was in it, as I said, much sin and shame, sorrow and trouble, too, as well as success. If it had not been so varied, David could scarcely have been so fit a preacher for all time. But, throughout it, he lives consciously before his Lord. In his troubles he rests in the Lord; in his labour he works in and for his Lord; his very sins present themselves to his mind as sins done against the Lord, against the love of the Faithful Guardian and Good Shepherd. This, I think, is clear and important; for, if it is true, it justifies us in regarding David as one of the first and greatest of our teachers of morals. Sin in his mind is not so much an offence against law, although the law of God is an undefiled law converting the soul, and although the law of God in many of the Psalms is practically and equivalent for the presence of God or influence of God upon the conscience; still, it is not so much against a positive enacted and published law, as against the ever-instant presence of the Almighty that he sins. If he has forgotten his God's presence for a moment and fallen, a moment's thought both brings back the sense of it and brings the penitence that the sin required. It is not so much, then, the notion that sin has weakened his moral nature, or has involved offence to his neighbour, or that it entails remorse or deserves punishment, as that it is an offence against a loving Presence. And I cannot help thinking that this, which, as it marks the psalmist's sense of sin, more clearly and distinctly still marks his sense of God's protection and guidance, his delight in God's service, his faith in justifying God's ways, his hope, long and far-reaching, of ends that God will bring about in due time, his certain looking for of pardon and rest, and awaking in the Divine image; I cannot help thinking that this is one of the chief things that are meant when David is spoken of as the man after God's own heart. Certainly it cannot mean that his whole life was ordered in conformity with God's commandments; that it assuredly was not. Holy Scripture itself tells the story of many lives far more innocent and holier than David's, and far more like our Saviour's. On the other hand it must mean more than that David was a chosen instrument in God's hand for performing work that was in His heart, a chosen founder for the monarchy of the chosen race, and a type of the royalty of the Son, the Redeemer. It was in the consciousness of the Divine presence, the continuance in that measure of the law of liberty that was imparted to him, the ruling desire, not always prevailing, nor always unthwarted, nor always absolute and alone, but still the ruling desire, to keep his heart right with his Lord's. This then, being as it seems the chief feature of David's life as revealed to us in the history, is the first of the great qualities that fits him to preach to us. It is not holiness, not example, not direct admonition, not circumstantial and particular direction, but a profound feeling of God all around him; the sense of being before and in God.

The second great mark is that which the opening words of the 36th psalm more especially illustrate, the psalmist's knowledge of the heart of man; that, scarcely less than the other, looks like a revelation; from the study of his own heart, from the study of his heart under the illumination of God's presence, he has a sympathetic and most real knowledge of what is in men's hearts. A sympathetic knowledge, I say; that is a knowledge of the heart of others gained by knowledge of his own; of their desires learned by his desires, of their sins learned by his own sins, of their self-deception and defiance of God, learned by his own self-deceptions and defiance of God. I do not say that very much sympathy with other men's sins appears in the psalms; though there is sympathy with penitence and renewed effort after purity and holiness: rather the psalmist treats sinners as God's enemies and his own, and there are denunciations of vengeance that show far more of the judicial than of the mediatorial side of the dealings of Jesus with us. The mystery, the whole mystery of godliness is not revealed even to the man after God's own heart. Prophets and kings desired to see the things that we see, and did not see them; and to hear the things that we hear, and did not hear them. To bear our sins and carry our sorrows was a depth of love that could be showed only by the Saviour Himself. It cost more than David could count to redeem our souls. But short of that Divine compassion, by means of which there were laid upon Him the iniquities of us all; short of that feeling of our infirmity with which surely none but the High Priest, who Himself was without infirmity, could be so touched, there is in the psalms a very distinct realization of what is in the heart of man. We read in them, if we will look for it, an analysis of the origin and development and full growth of men's sins; of our sins. We see exemplified, in the very penitential forms in which David rehearses his story, how lust when it is conceived bringeth forth sin, and sin when it is finished bringeth forth death. The original inclination, the resistance to good influences, the secret growth of evil desire; "My heart showeth it me, the wickedness of the ungodly:" the weakness of the betraying will; "There is no fear of God before his eyes:" the self deception; "I can go on up to a certain point, and then stop short, stop short before my evil has taken the actual form of sin;" "God is afar off and He will never see it;" or He is such a one as myself, why has He made me fit and inclined to the thing I long for, and then forbid me to enjoy. So the thought dwells on the thing forbidden, until it seems not to be forbidden: the words of the tempter, "Yea, hath God said, Ye shall not eat of every tree of the garden; ye shall not surely die;" are echoed in the heart, "Tush, the Lord will not see." And then the sin is done. And there follows, perhaps first a surprised and bewildering sense of humiliation; what a fool I was to yield: and then the sense of the loss of God's blessing; "Thou didst turn Thy face from me and I was troubled:" and then the self-abhorrent mortification, "I abhor myself and repent in dust and ashes;" and as yet perhaps no more: for penitence does not always in one impulse complete its perfect work, and there is a sorrow of the world that worketh death. It may be that the temptation recurs, and the self-deception betrays the soul again, and the sin and the mortification return again and again, until the fear of God no more works to retard it, and the sinner flatters himself in his own sight that God has forgotten him or does not regard his sin as sin. And then comes the awakening; for, in all David's knowledge of the heart, we must remember that we have to trace the record of the sin through the record of the penitence, and the sorrow of the sinner through the joy of the pardoned and restored child: and so on until we can realize the full meaning of both halves of the 51st psalm; "Have mercy upon me, O Lord," and "Thou shalt open my lips, O Lord, and my mouth shall show Thy praise."

He who would struggle with temptation, he who having fallen, would rise from his sin, he who, having been strengthened to rise, wants still more strength to stand, to stand without presuming and yet without morbid fear of another fall: he who has awakened to the misery of separation from God and yet cannot free himself altogether from lingering and longing looks after the things that would separate him from Him; he who has learned the wretchedness of this state and has not yet come to know the love, so freely bestowed, of Him who died to deliver not only from the penalty but from the nature and working and effects of sin on the conscience; he who is learning the virtue of the great and only sacrifice, not merely to save from a hell whose torments must be everywhere where God is not—for the heart that God made for Himself cannot but without Him breed the worm undying and the fire unquenchable; not merely to save from death eternal, but to win wholly the affections, and to content the affections which if they are given to anything else but Him must lead to death; to purify the soul, "purge me with hyssop and I shall be clean," cleansing the desires; to purify the memory, enabling it to cast aside the remembrance of sin for all purposes but to enhance the love of the deliverer; to purify the conscience, that it shall bear true witness how the old things have passed away, and all things become new; the love of Jesus has won the heart, and the Holy Spirit rules, creating, prompting, assisting, and perfecting the holy desires, good councils and just works, that as by new nature form the habits of the new-born :—every man who passes through any or all of these experiences, finds a voice and a guide in the Psalms.

Beloved, David is the preacher of all the phases of repentance. Mark him well; the busiest man of the whole Bible; and in this respect certainly scarcely below the greatest.

May He who has put the words of this Book into our hands for our daily lessons, and so wonderfully adapted them to all the forms and phases and stages of the life of our souls, so open our hearts that we may realize the full import of them. "Open Thou our lips, O Lord, and our mouths shall show forth Thy praise."

To have God always before us, to learn the windings and waverings of our own hearts, two chief points of the Christian's safeguard over himself, must be supplemented still with that crowning power of faith, the certain consciousness that no self-knowledge of ours, no knowledge even of our God, is enough to keep us from falling without His constant help, His perpetual watching and guarding. And where can we find a better mould and model for the thought that would rest and rely wholly on Him, than in the words in which the Saviour Himself, when He, in His own Person, and for our sins, realized on the cross the nature and lot and offence and penalty of all men, found expression for His sorrow and trust: "Into Thy hands I commend My spirit;" and we add, with the fullest of full conclusions, "For Thou hast redeemed me, O Lord, Thou God of Truth."

W. S.

XXVII. **Penitence.** PSALM li. 5. "*Behold, Thou desirest truth in the inward parts: and in the hidden part Thou shalt make me to know wisdom.*"

ALL sin, as distinguished from mere error, consists essentially in the violation of some dictate of our conscience. That is what it really comes to when we go to the root of it instead of attempting to disguise its character by dwelling on the temptations which led to it. But that dictate of the conscience is interpreted in the Scriptures as the voice of the living God speaking to us as person to person. The Scriptures draw back the veil from the invisible world and reveal to us the character of those great spiritual influences of which our hearts and consciences are sensible. Thus we learn that the human spirit is in constant union with the Divine spirit, and that in God we move and live and have our moral as well as physical being. This is confirmed by the deepest moral reflections. It is this conviction alone which exhibits the evil and taint of sin to those who have had the truth brought home to them.

That men should recognise that a living God is calling upon them to obey His voice, and to do His will, and that they should, nevertheless, allow themselves to be attracted away to thoughts, and words, and deeds, which they know to be repugnant to Him, ought to evoke from our hearts contrition like that of the psalmist: "For I acknowledge my transgressions: and my sin is ever before me." This acknowledgment of sin is the first step to repentance, and the psalmist proceeds to lead us to see its relation to God and ourselves. "Against Thee, Thee only, have I sinned, and done this evil in Thy sight: that Thou mightest be justified when Thou speakest, and be clear when Thou judgest." In other words, if the expression may be allowed, it is the confession of God's justice in the matter of our sins. It recognises that all His influence upon us has been in support of what is righteous and true, and that it is our sin alone which is responsible for our sorrow. And here we may consider what St. Paul says, "Yea, let God be true, but every man a liar; as it is written, That Thou mightest be justified in Thy sayings, and mightest overcome when Thou art judged." The moral history of mankind is only read aright, when we recognise on the one side a perfectly true and holy and righteous God, and on the other side, men and women false to their consciences, and in this sense all liars, all untrue. Such considerations throw a not less vivid light on the struggles and sufferings of mankind. They offer a profound problem, almost impossible of solution with our imperfect knowledge of our own nature. When we consider them in connection with the utterance of St. Paul, it is all the more forcible. Being so, what marvel is it that this untruth of our nature has involved us in the misery under which we labour? Let us look at our own experience, and consider it multiplied in the race which live and have lived. Let us consider that every individual member of the race has been in a more or less degree false to the laws of his condition, and is it not a wonder that mankind should be making such progress as it has? Not merely for the purposes of our private opinions, but for the sake of the efforts to remedy the sufferings of the world, it would be well if we started more generally from the acknowledgment that God is justified when He speaks, and is clear when He judges. If we acted on the words of St. Paul, and concentrated our efforts by the example of our Lord, we should pray with greater hope and greater success.

The psalmist accordingly goes on to recognise that the evil of which he is thus conscious is rooted in his very nature and that of his fellows. "Behold, I was shapen in iniquity; and in sin did my mother conceive me." The statement is not made as an excuse, for every excuse has been cast away in the words, "Against Thee, Thee only, have I sinned;"—it is simply a recognition of the fact that the nature which he inherits is involved in the common fall, and, to a great extent, in a common responsibility.

A clear acknowledgment of this truth is the next step we are to take if we are to advance to any hope of remedy. We have to recognise the fact that no effectual means of recovery can be found in human nature itself. After every one of the springs of conscience have been examined we see that we are shapen in iniquity, in so far that our moral nature has the seeds of corruption within it. The child may be innocent of pollution or sin, but when the temptation comes the conscience is disregarded and the will yields. If this be the case, if the very nature of man be corrupt and weak at the source, what possibility can there be of any regeneration by its own efforts?

But now it will be seen in what manner this brings us to the true remedy for the evil, and how the psalmist is rooted to his only hope. "Though every man be a liar" the blessed reality remains that God is still true, and He will make men true like Himself if they will but follow Him. The two experiences are contrasted in the very form of the expression, "Behold, Thou desirest truth in the inward parts: and in the hidden part Thou shalt make me to know wisdom;" as much as to say, Although I and the nature from which I spring, and the men around me, are tainted with untruth and folly, yet Thou desirest to see Thy truth in the very secret recesses of my heart, and I can call upon Thee for this truth and righteousness. The very nature of our sin thus reveals the means of our deliverance. It is the revolt against the righteous influence of a loving God, who, although grieved at it, does not love us less, and still desires to see us true in our inward parts. To that love and that gracious purpose of His we can at all times appeal. We are always privileged to utter the prayer, "Search me, O God, and know my heart; try me, and know my thoughts. And see if there be any wicked way in me, and lead me in the way everlasting."

Contemplate man standing alone. Let us imagine our own souls left to themselves, and what hope could we have of truth and wisdom in the inward parts? It has been observed that men are disposed to urge that forgiveness may be granted to us without the Gospel. Allow it for a moment. Is that *all* that the soul desires? Could any one of us be content with mere forgiveness, if we were allowed to remain in the imperfect condition to which sin has brought us? What we need is truth and wisdom in the very root of the soul. If there is to be any peace for us in the presence of the righteous God, what we need is to have all the corruptions of our soul cleansed away, and some influence brought to bear upon us which could make us new creatures. This, my brethren, is the blessing held out to us in the text that God will grant truth in the inward part and in the hidden part wisdom.

There is another point of great practical importance. The Gospel brings us not only in contact with humanity but with divinity; and brings all the influence of an absolutely perfect nature, alike human and Divine, to bear upon our hearts and lives. In short, it makes the prayer possible—we may almost say necessary—"Create in me a clean heart, and renew a right spirit within me."

Of the various methods by which this purification is wrought I do not speak now. But there is one specially important—it is the force of the perfect example of the Saviour, not only in His life, but especially in His death upon the cross. If we could but remember the exceeding great love of our Master; could we bear in mind the blood He shed, and that His very life's blood is eternally sprinkled upon all things that are pure and just and true—then, and not till then, shall we derive an adequate motive for the higher life, and conquer those affections for evil which are our weakness and our shame. What a force is introduced into the world when by our struggles to be pure we stand with our Saviour Jesus Christ! If we regarded the matter from a merely moral point of view, that struggle has been stamped with the highest importance to those around us. We have of late become only too familiar—God grant that we may not become more familiar still!—with the manner in which scenes of pain and bloodshed have harrowed the soul. If we realized that in every impatient or sinful word, act, or desire, we despised the blood of Jesus Christ, should we not shrink from sin? Consider Him now as living, and that each day, each moment, the righteous spirit within you pleading for you to be pure and true and holy is that of the suffering Lord Jesus, and is there a heart to resist the appeal? It is scarcely conceivable. All our sins have been committed in the absence of any such realization. To the apostles and other immediate followers of Jesus it was always present. The blood of Jesus Christ was not only an atonement, but was ever present in their thoughts; it was sprinkled upon the entrance of their souls, so that the enemy of souls could not enter. It is the privilege of Christians to sanctify every duty however humble, to intensify every dictate of the conscience however slight, by considering it as united with the passion and death of Christ. The atoning efficacy of that sacrifice is revealed to us as a fact. No mystery veils its relation to ourselves. It imparts into our moral and spiritual life, and every thought and act of that life, the most intense and vivid of all natural influences, immeasurably heightened by the supernatural relation in which we stand to the person who exercises it. Let the power of Christ in His person and suffering be understood by us, and in the appeal of the apostle, "Let this mind be in you, which was in Christ Jesus," and it will possess an almost irresistible force.

H. W.

XXVIII. Trust and Waiting. Psalm lxii. 1, 2.

"Truly my soul waiteth upon God: from Him cometh my salvation. He only is my rock and my salvation; He is my defence; I shall not be greatly moved."

WHENEVER and by whomsoever this psalm was written, the circumstances which gave rise to it are plainly marked upon its very face. The writer is surrounded by enemies who have long been hypocritically professing to be his friends, but have at last cast off the mask, and have now manifestly confessed themselves and sought to cast him down from some position of dignity and to destroy him. These intentions fit of course most naturally to the superscription of the psalm, which states it to be the composition of David, probably taking its rise from the persecution of Absalom. But whether or no, this sweet psalm stands very high indeed amongst those in the Psalter which express triumph and quiet confidence in God even in the face of much that might tempt to the opposite disposition. And my purpose is rather to take the whole of it, and try to set before you the striking and lovely characters which run through it.

If you will look at the psalm you will see that it is divided obviously into three equal portions by the intervention of "Selah," which comes at the end of the fourth and the eighth verses. There are thus three portions in the psalm, and I name the leading ideas of it here at the commencement.

The first clause seems to me to set before us: the soul in waiting upon God. The second section sets before us: the waiting soul encouraging itself to wait. And the last section sets before us: the triumphant confidence to which, by waiting, the soul attains. I will then notice these three points as they come up before us in the words of the psalm.

The first section: the soul waiting upon God. There follows upon the words of our text the opposite picture: the psalmist turns away for a time, and conjures up the enemies running round him, and has it—what is in our version I venture to alter, without defending the alteration of the third verse—"how long will ye rush in upon a man?" and then you will observe that in the next clauses of the verse, with a very slight alteration of the original, we shall get a continuation of the question, instead of the imprecation, which seems here to be out of place: "how long will ye rush upon a man? how long will ye press against him?" the image being that of a hostile pressure against a man; supposing he were ready to fall and to slip, they only consult to cast him down from dignity. There are two portions here: the trustful contemplation of God, broken in upon by the trembling thought of the enemies. You should follow that order in your thoughts about your troubles. It makes all the difference whether you begin with God, or whether you begin with men. If these things had been turned round the other way it would have been very hard for him to have been found waiting upon God. But when we start from God, we can venture to think, in the second place, of the foes round about us. And now about his confidence: that "truly" with which the psalm begins recurs over and over again in this psalm, and does not mean "truly" so much as "only"—"my soul waiteth upon *none* but God."

And then there is a beautiful literality, which is missed in our Bible: "my soul is silent," or perhaps even "my soul is *silence* unto God." *Waiting upon* Him, no doubt, is the meaning of the expression, but the force of that literal rendering we shall all perceive. What a lovely simple description it is of the quiet spirit, that with no influence of earthly passion, with no loud voices of human will, with no buzzings and whisperings of its own desires, has calmly settled itself in His presence and stands there like an awe-struck priest in the presence of Divinity! "I will hear what God the Lord shall speak," my soul is all one great silence in His presence, and in that silence I catch the utterances of His will. And if you and I rush into His presence with the hot voices of earthly imprecations and human desires, and these rebellious wills of ours clamouring and bellowing all round about us, what chance is there that we shall ever catch the secret of His voice who "strives not, nor cries, neither causes His voice to be heard in the streets"—"my soul is silence before God." And then, following upon the attitude of dumb submission to the Lord, but in an equally beautiful metaphor: "my soul, wait thou only upon God, for my expectation is from Him. He only is my rock and my salvation: He is my defence; I shall not be moved."

In general one would say about that repetition over and over again of names and thoughts that are nearly synonymous, that it is not even tautology, although at first sight it may seem so. Just as you and I in our homes, father and children, mother and child, will dwell with reiteration on tender names, so all true affection and all vivid trust delights to turn the object of its love round and round, so to speak, and to look at it from all points of view, and to lavish names which may not have much difference of meaning between them, but which in their accumulations express the depth and security of affection. So the psalmist, with like emotion and fondness of thought, deals with the great and blessed contemplation, and repeats over and over again those sweet names. Like that sevenfold repetition of them in the psalm where he seems to lose his breath in saying over and over again all that the Lord is to him, and a cold-blooded critic steps in and says, Oh! you are saying the same thing over and over again. Yes, but no repeating of the epithets can reach half-way up to what He is to me, for my soul is silent before Him. And yet is not all reiteration, there is a very lovely progress of thought in these words. Notice: "from Him cometh my salvation." Well that is a great deal, that deliverance shall flow from His hand; but that is not all, there is something a great deal more than that—"from Him cometh my salvation," not what I am giving to you, a gift, not as a man may give to another something that is separable from him: "He only is my rock and my salvation." And salvation is much that comes from Him, but it is shallow compared with the depth of the scriptural idea, in which He is not only the giver and the source, but is Himself the essence of the salvation which He giveth: "He only is my rock and my salvation." And then as a consequence of that loving contemplation of the realities of the refuge that he has in God, there comes the assurance which he utters, "I shall not be greatly moved." A modest confidence to be built on so broad a foundation. He recognises the likelihood that he shall be moved, but he hopes that he shall not be much moved, either in the sense of being overwhelmed, or agitated, or swept away from his refuge: bending like the willow, and blown by enemy and wind, he is sure that he will not be like the chaff in the threshing-floor, which the wind drives away; but when the tempest is past the fluttering leaves and feeble branches will come back to the upright position, and he "shall not be greatly moved." Our hearts and lives will be like one of those Cornish rocking-stones, that a child's finger can set in motion, but which moves only through a very puny arc, and comes back certainly to be poised on its central point of rest: "I shall not be greatly moved." And then, as if the very thought of his stability in the face of the trouble brought up the trouble again in all its dreadfulness before him, there comes storming in upon his quiet confidence the opposite sound and picture. Look at the contrast between the two halves of the first section of our text,—the holy stillness and the rapt vision of God that is granted to the quiet spirit in the first two verses; and the hurly-burly, the tempest and antagonism, and the bitterness and the lying and enmity, the pressing upon him who is ready to fall, in the second half. So your life and mine has got these two halves, the still rest, the end of the sorrow and trouble, and the tossing and the seething in this sea of troubles; and no exercise of quiet confidence makes facts other than they are, or annihilates this outer ring of darkness and trouble that lies round about us all: and so we have the two halves of the life to deal with, and we all know how into the midst of our happiness and most faithful moments of religious consideration and quiet confidence, there force themselves, weed-like, dark thoughts and care and trouble.

Turn now to the second section of this psalm, which, as I said, is the waiting soul encouraging itself to wait upon God. The first section began "only on God waiteth my soul," the second section, "only upon God wait thou my soul;" and so the psalmist stirs himself up to do the thing he says he is doing, and animates and encourages his spirit to continue in the posture of silent expectation which he has already declared is his posture. A very plain and simple lesson we want to draw from that, from the juxtaposition of these two things, and it is just this: the firmest confidence, the happiest communion, the quietest submission has no guarantee in itself for its own continuance, and needs a distinct and definite effort on our part in order that it shall be continued by being repeated and shall last because it is renewed. External things come to sweep us away from our most rooted confidence, and our sins darken so as to hide our clearest vision. I have seen a great rainbow span the eastern sky near sunset, bright and vivid with its prismatic rays. But all at once there came storming up from the west a great black rain-cloud and smote against the bright crown of the arches, and all disappeared but the two broken fragments; and so the visible bow that is thrown athwart the stormy sky of our lives is ever being smote upon by strong clouds of tempest, and unless we take a leaf from the psalmist's book here, and instead of saying, "my soul, waitest thou upon God?" say, "my soul, wait thou upon God," all the confidence will be dissipated into fear.

So, then, the next point to notice is how this confidence which the psalmist makes the effort to repeat is most surely preserved and strengthened by the simple method of renewed contemplation of the great truth on which it rests: "my soul, wait thou only upon God; for my expectation is from Him. He only is my rock and my salvation: I shall not be moved." That is the first and second sections over again, word for word, with two very significant alterations: instead of "salvation" in the first, we read "hope" in the second; and instead of "greatly moved" in the first, "I shall not be moved" in the second. You and I want to get our silence of spirit, our high confidence, and our calm hope. The only way to do it is to go back over and over again to the old simple truth on which it rests, and to lose all thought of fear and unrest in thinking upon the face of God. And thus while the continuance of the confidence needs perpetual effort, just as a fire is sure to go out unless it be stirred and tended, the issue of such discipline is a very much increased confidence and quietness. The psalmist begins with "I shall not be greatly moved," but in the second expression he has got far in advance of that, he has left out that word greatly—"I shall not be moved" at all. So has trust grown by the renewed contemplation of the greater truth on which he has built. And instead of the picture of the enemies, who came storming in and disturbing his contemplation before, there comes only the continuance of the quiet thought of what God is to him. He has got to a point far higher up than he was before, and his devout expectation is not broken and dashed by the tremulous remembrance of what lay outside there. It is there all the same and he knows that, but he does not need to think about it now, he passes it by as not needful to speak of. "I shall not be moved," and the fact that I am not moved is shown in this, that all the noise of the enemies is storming all round about the gate where I sit, yet here I sit, thinking not about them but about Him. "In God is my salvation: the rock of my salvation and strength and refuge is in God." Well, notice that is the old language over again. He has already said, "my rock and my salvation." This time he says more, he takes each of these two words and he enlarges them: "In God is my salvation and my glory." When I began, it was as much as I could do to get hold of the half certain confidence that He would deliver me, but I have got far in advance of that this time. My salvation and my glory; not bare deliverance, but enriching me with something far higher than that: from Him will come not merely an escape from the trouble, but radiant lustre of joy, of rights eousness, and of peace. These words lend themselve beautifully to the old Christian thought: "whom He justified them He also glorified." "In God is my salvation;" and not merely the negative side, but "from God is my glory, and from Him shall I be clothed with strength in Christ, and all my darkness made radiant with the light of His perfect likeness, and my life left in possession of His love." Such is the effect of that thought until he has found out something more than that. And although it may perhaps be fanciful, I cannot help thinking there is some dim suggestion or anticipation of a great thought, that God is certainly the rock on which we build and are safe, the deliverer and the defender, but that most mysteriously and most really there comes up from the rock, into us building on the rock, the strength from the rock; and He is the rock, not merely because His strong hand is our deliverance, but because He infuses into us something of

His own strength, His Spirit in the inner man. That is better than outward deliverance: "My refuge is in God." And so the spirit encouraging itself to wait and continue waiting upon God, turns itself now to the men standing round about him, to his little band of followers—if this be David in one of his experiences of Saul's persecution—with the words: "God is my refuge." That is to say, when a man has once been in silence and waiting submission before God, has deeply infixed into his spirit the confidence that God is his refuge and his rock, the next thing that is sure to come to him, is the desire that the brethren and friends may share with him the safe place, and so encouraging he next exhorts the men who stand round about him. How wonderful that is! that one poor man's experience, ours if we choose, may be so deep, our conviction of the all-sufficiency of God's power so strong, as that we shall be saying, "He is my refuge," and then turn round to the whole world and say, "God is a refuge for all the world." And then whosoever has incorporated into his own spirit the conviction that God is sufficient for his joy and peace, that man's lips must needs break into exhortation; and not far from the utterance of his own personal confidence to God will be the utterance of His message to man. And notice how in simple and beautiful words there comes out here the setting forth of the conditions on which God is a refuge to all men. Trust Him at all times; pour out your hearts before him, in the frankness of humble trust, in the lowliness of humble confession, acknowledging your weaknesses, and doing it all in the simple confidence that He is by our side to comfort.

And then there follows the last section, in which we have the picture of the grateful sense of insight into the temporal realities which comes to that waiting heart. The reward of this waiting spirit is a profound conviction of the absolute nothingness of human power, be it for me or be it against me; gather the whole mass up together and put it into the scale, and put a *breath* into the other, and it kicks the beam. It is because the man has seen the strength and the power of God that everything has dwindled to nothing. As George Fox used to say in his quaint mystical way, "He has seen every man and all the world, and has ascertained how hollow they are; friends and foes, it matters not, there is no help in one, there is no danger in the other." And then follows, "trust not in oppression, and become not vain in robbery; if riches increase, set not your heart upon them," upon the nothingness of all material wealth, the external props and supports.

And then follows the great voice that tells us whom we are to trust. "God, my soul is silence before Thee," the psalm begins; and the psalm ends, "God hath spoken once; yea twice have I heard," and I heard it because I was silent before Thee. And this is the double proclamation that he heard: "power belongeth unto Thee, O God; also unto Thee, O Lord, belongeth mercy."

These are the two things which God is—a God of power, so trust; a God of mercy, so trust: a God of power before whom all the accumulated forces of humanity, high and low, are less than nothing; then a God of mercy, and therefore safe for us to wait before Him. If thou wilt thou canst, if thou canst thou wilt. Power without mercy is brutish force, mercy without power is a shadow that no man trusts; but bring them together and they make the firm will on which we may hang, nor fear that stand will ever fail. And the demonstration of both the one and the other lies in that great fact of the righteous retribution to enemies and friends, wherein they that set themselves against His power shall know His power; and they that trust themselves in His mercy shall find His mercy; and the paradox is solved for you and me that can say, "In Christ is my righteousness, and in Christ the Judge is mercy for us." The psalm halts far short of the blessed New Testament proclamation wherein we can say, "we may have boldness before Him in the Day of Judgment;" and although He judgeth every man according to his works, we sinners shall find mercy in the Lord in that day, and be found in Him, not having our own righteousness but that which is of God. "Unto Thee belongeth power, unto Thee mercy." Trust in Him at all times. God is a refuge.

A. M.

XXIX. Waiting. PSALM lxii. 5, 6. *"My soul, wait thou only upon God; for my expectation is from Him. He only is my rock and my salvation: He is my defence; I shall not be moved."*

ATHANASIUS says: "In all trial of the body, in all trial of the faith, in all trial from men and devils, in all trial of temptation, in all trial of defamation, sing the 62nd psalm." The subject of this psalm is "Wait upon God," and this is the special subject, epitomised, of the two verses of the text. The general subject is waiting for God, and this is in particular ways. Let me go through the particulars, not so much in the logical connection and sequence, as here uttered by David. Next notice to whom the psalmist speaks—"my soul." If you look through the psalms, you will find many illustrations of this principle. Generally we shall find the psalmist is a leader of praise. In the 146th psalm he says: "Praise ye the Lord"—and then in the same verse he simply continues; as soon as he has said this to the people, he goes on, "Praise the Lord, *O my soul.*" If you want to awaken an oratorio in other souls, see that you get the chords of your own soul in the right tune. But he speaks also as a preacher. George Whitefield said he had never preached a sermon to his congregation before he had preached it to George Whitefield. It would be a good thing for us if each one would speak to his own soul first for a congregation. What word represents multitude as this word soul? An army in one, a great congregation of faculties and vitalities and forces. Speak to that congregation first for your own sake, for I speak to you individually. Let the soul be wrong and the lips will be wrong —everything will be wrong. For your own sakes, I repeat, speak to yourselves first; but also for the sake of others.

This is a peculiarity of David's writing—he starts from himself. His words express not only what he ought to express but what he himself feels. How wonderful it is that these songs which we sing were written perhaps in some leafy covert where David was hiding from his enemies, alone; in these psalms where he pours out his soul to God we are permitted to hear him speak. Now when David speaks to his own soul, all the world hears him, and let us now hear him for our profit. Let us catch the spirit of his words, and copy the example of his utterance as he says: "*My* soul, wait thou only upon God."

Next note the word "wait." The word does not mean spiritual laziness, but the most active of all activities. It is difficult for persons of active nature to wait. Wait in faith first. Let my faith wait upon God as the bough upon the tree, waiting alway; wait as the house waits upon the foundation; so may my faith wait upon God. This is what Christ tells us—"Abide in Me." Wait in patience. God is never behind time. God hastes to perform His word. You recollect the words addressed by the great Inspirer to the prophet: when the latter said, "I cannot speak; for I am a child," the Lord said, "Say not, I am a child; for thou shalt go to all that I shall send thee, and whatsoever I command thee, thou shalt speak." Later on we read, "Moreover, the word of the Lord came unto me, saying, Jeremiah, what seest thou? And I said, I see a root of an almond-tree." The Hebrew word for almond-tree is "hasting" tree. God hastes to fulfil what He speaks, and so that almond-tree, though you look in the winter and see it with no sign of a bud on it and looking as if it never would bud, that tree is the first tree to bud: while the white grass crackles under foot, long before the other trees burst forth into buds and flowers, this almond-tree puts forth its buds and blossoms. So God's promises are the blossoms of God's almond-tree.

However, God's haste is not like man's hurry, of which we say "The more haste, the less speed." It takes a century sometimes for God to make haste. It is a long time measured by the clock, and so we are sometimes out of patience in waiting. David felt that tendency, and so he said to his soul "wait." God never forgets; God hastes His word to fulfil it. Look at human life in its merely secular aspect: you see two persons, one old and one young, waiting for a certain thing. The old person does not look like a person in impatience. Look at the youth: he wonders how it is the thing is so long. He looks at the clock and is filled with impatience. So in spiritual things, we are a long time learning to wait.

God speaks about it in this word. *We* may say the same to our souls as David said. This also implies expectancy. He goes on to say, "My soul, wait thou only upon God; *for my expectancy is from Him.*" Sometimes we wait expecting very vividly what we are waiting for, and yet we know that after a night of waiting and peril the morning will come; but it seems a long time. You wait expecting. You wait, and you notice keenly the first bark of the dog, the rumble of the waggon, and the sun with its glory lighting up the black sky. The first Moravian missionaries who went to South Africa, found that the ship was becalmed. It was death to be stricken with that stillness there. They waited upon God in that trial, and one prayed, "Help us in our journey, Thou who ridest upon the waves and wind." He was joyful after that, and said, "We shall have that for which we have prayed" Shortly after one of the sailors said to the helmsman: "It does not look like a wind;" but in half an hour the wind came and the ship was enabled to proceed on her way. I do not say that a prayer for certain weather will bring that weather; but I know as a rule prayer is designed to get the blessing God gives, and if it is one of the things He wished to give, pray. Just try and expect. This is a summary of what can be said for that word "wait."

The next word I would call your attention to is "only" —"wait only;" and you notice how frequently this word "only" occurs in the Bible, especially in relation to God: "Thou art the Lord, Thou only;" "Thou only makest me to dwell in safety." These are only two instances out of a multitude. This psalm used to be called by certain Hebrew scribes "The Psalm of the Onlies," as some of the psalms used to be called "The Psalms of the Morning." In Hebrew the word occurs six times, but in our English translation only four times. In fact, however, it occurs six times, once being translated "truly." Sometimes when a great stroke of trouble comes, when health and fortune and friendship goes, you are ready to say, "I have now only God left." What would you have? *Only* God! If you could but realize what that means, you would not feel poor to have only God. To have *only* God: why you have infinite perfection and love. Do you want to mix up anything with that which is *only* perfection? The sun *only* gives light: would it give light if you mixed up something else with it? Your pure water: would you mix up anything with that? Say in full confidence, "My soul, wait thou *only* upon God." Do you want two Gods, do you want two Christs, do you want two infinite friends? Does your soul want two husbands? Trust only in the one God; trust in Him who is the only God, and trust not partially but totally. Some old divine, I think it is Father Trapp, says: "When a man stands with one foot on the edge of the cliff and one foot on the air with equal pressure, he is sure to go down." You might as well stand with both feet on the empty air. Trust God only, why?

Why, in the next place: you say because "He only is my rock and my salvation: He is my defence; I shall not be moved." The whole of these meanings we have summed up in that word "rock." The Book of Deuteronomy is the first book of all the Bible in which God is spoken of as a rock. In the early ages the word used for God was "rock:" because a rock is real, it is not like a mist; because a rock is settled, you build upon a rock, not upon sand; a rock is high above the commotion of the world. So it was natural for the first men to speak of what they trusted as God, to speak of Him as a rock. So you find that Moses in that grand passage in Deuteronomy, with grandest of all words of command, with grandest sum of all experience, speaks several times of God as a rock, and says: "How should one chase a thousand, and two put ten thousand to flight, except their rock had sold them, and the Lord had shut them up? For their rock is not as our rock." Their rock he says, *has sold them*. We use that expression in reference to persons who are not to be trusted.

But to bring out the entire meaning you must of course interpret the early part of the Bible by the final part. Our rock is Christ: He is the fulfilment of that word "rock." When David said: "God is my rock and my salvation," he had a prominent reference to the rock that yielded water in the wilderness. Moses, when he spoke so much about God as the rock, had of course that in his mind. He looked back upon a series of wonders, and one of the most wonderful was that rock that yielded water. Travellers point out a certain green cliff in the land of Tyre, and they say, there is the rock from whence the water burst forth; and there the water is trickling now. Whether that be or not, we know that God did get Moses to strike the rock, and that stands for ever as the type of what Jesus Christ is. Our "rock was stricken," and out of our stricken rock came all salvation. Our salvation, all that makes refreshment to our souls—all that came from the stricken Christ: He was stricken for us, and now through Him we drink strength and beauty, as of old the Israelites refreshed themselves at the rock that Moses struck. So when you wait only on God, you wait only upon the rock, Christ, that you may have the water of salvation.

But further, this was not only so for the Jew but for the heathen. Theologians speak of the Supreme in reference to a rock. In the very heart of the American forests the Indians used to make a rock their castles or defences: the Jews did so. David makes frequent references to a rock in this way. Sometimes this same word is translated "strength" or "refuge." All this is realized in Jesus Christ. He is our castle. We have not to go far for Him. In time of war the person had to run sometimes a long way, but we have not to do so: Jesus our castle is very near, and He is waiting.

All life has its foes. The life of the flower has a fight with the blight, and the life of the child has a fight with the sicknesses of childhood. There are deadly enemies about. Run into the refuge: Jesus Christ only is our rock and our salvation: He is our defence; we shall not be moved. When the law points its guns and Satan assaults us with his armies, run unto Christ and you are beyond the reach of harm, and you can say, "The Lord is my salvation." Also the Hebrews spoke about the rock as being a place of shelter from the heat, a shadow from the heat. Men journeying over the burning sand, fire above and below and all around, feeling faint and ready to drop under the blinding rays, feeling the heart nigh to stop: then they see a rock, and in the shadow of that rock they fling themselves down and get refreshment. You have that ready at hand: it is not that which is wanting—"My soul, wait thou only upon God; for my expectation is from Him. He only is my rock and my salvation."

One word more: this is unlike all other rocks. David said, "Our rock is not like other rocks," our rock Jesus Christ is a rock all feeling, all sympathy. This startles us —it is one of the paradoxes of the Bible. Who would cry out to a rock? Why, David did. He prayed to the rock, a certain rock, a rock so kind, so sympathetic that he was astonished that no answer once came to his prayer, and he said: "O God my rock, hast Thou forgotten me?" When we have sorrow, our rock is sorry for us; when men are cold to us, our rock has a warm heart; when we are not able to help ourselves, our rock will help us.

Trust in Him at all times: He is our strength. You can take these words of strength and consolation. Trust in Him at all times, all ye people: in times of weakness, in times of strength, in times of sickness, in times of health, in times of indifference: in all times, times of the night, times of the day, times of girding on the sword, times of striking with it, and times of dealing the blow back again; weeping times, dying times, working times, wrestling times, trusting Him at all times. O ye people, pour out your hearts to God in complete trust, in perfect faith. Amen.

C. S.

XXX. A Song for the New Year. PSALM cxxi.
"I will lift up mine eyes unto the hills, from whence cometh my help."

IT seems to me that this psalm is one which we may well take for our encouragement and our strength at the beginning of another year.

Always in season, it is especially seasonable at such a time as this; and in itself it is so comprehensive, covering the whole ground of our necessities, that instead of isolating a verse of it and talking about that, I would rather just take the whole psalm, and try to bring out more of the meaning than perhaps a superficial examination might convey.

"I will lift up mine eyes to the hills," says some one; we do not know who, we do not know under what circumstances. Some people say an exile away in Babylon, looking across the desert to the horizon, behind which lay the mountains of his native land. Some people say a pilgrim, going up to the city, and catching the first sight of "the mountains that are round about Jerusalem."

It matters very little which of the two ideas we adopt; in either case the hills to which the eyes were lifted are a symbol of the strength of the lofty, eternal God who is the true helper of His people—"I will lift up mine eyes to the hills." And then the next clause has far more force in the original than in our Bible, for it is a question there,—"Whence does my help come?" He looks to the mountains, and a question springs to his lips which may be a question of longing, but I think is rather a question of, almost, doubt. "Does my help come from them? I do not see any help coming." And then he lifts his eyes higher than the hills, up above all symbols, away from all material things, high up;—not to the hills but to the heavens.

"My help cometh from the Lord, which made heaven and earth." That is a loftier glance than to "the hills that are round about Jerusalem;" beyond symbols, above the material, far in advance of everything creatural, however strong, however lofty, however firmly rooted,—we must look there if we are to look to the place from which our true help comes. It is well when we can look to the hills, but it is needful that we should look to the heavens. And when a questioning soul can answer its own question, that is a soul that is at rest.

When a man asks where his help is to come from, it is a weariness and a misery for him unless he can give the answer with that full-toned triumphant confidence, and say: "from the Lord' which made heaven and earth." And then look how, in this exercise of faith, lifting up the eyes above all the material, up to the infinite Father, look how the man gets confidence and gladness from the one thought, the thought of who it is into whose arms he is flinging himself: "The Lord! which made heaven and earth."

He grasps in that idea these two things,—Eternal Being, which is implied in the name Jehovah, and infinite creative power, which is implied in the Maker of the lofty universe and of this low earth. These two things are the basis of the confidence that his help will come from Him.

If it be true that between me and One who loves for

ever, unchanging and undecaying, and who, by the breath of His lips—His almighty respiration, if I may so say—breathed out all this great universe; if it be true that between Him and me there are relations of sonship and love and Fatherhood, then my help is sure, whatever befals. Let us let the full sunlight of that thought, of how dear God is, flood our hearts, that He is "the same yesterday, to-day, and for ever;" that everything that is, or that ever has been, or that ever shall be, is but the issue of His will, and then we can stand in the centre and feel that we have got to the heart of things, and that all that lives round about us is living for our good, and that it is according to His will by whose strength we stand. "'Up to the hills?" No! that is too low. Up to the hills if we look only, we are only dwelling in the region of questions, but if we look up into the heavens we are dwelling in the region of affirmation and assurance.

And so, if you notice, after this first verse the psalm seems to change its tone, and a new speaker comes. Instead of reading about the "I" and "my," we read about "He" and "thee." "He will not suffer thy foot to be moved; He that keepeth thee will not slumber." And so on. What is the meaning of this change of tone? We cannot exactly say that it is intended to represent two different speakers, but we may come very near it. It is the man communing with himself after a different fashion. He began with that weary cry as of a man whose eyes have long been looking for help, and who has said a hundred times:—"Do you see anybody coming?" He begins with a voice of longing that quickly passes into the voice of confidence; and then he makes a pause, and in the silence of his own spirit there rises up the assurance, so deep, so vivid, so certain, that he is sure it cannot be his own imagination, but somebody else that is speaking to him.

That is to say:—if we will wait patiently before God, and try in the midst of our troubles and conflicts and doubts to fix our thoughts and our hopes upon Him, there will presently be heard in our hearts a voice which, though it be our own, is charged with a message from some one else than ourselves, and speaks to us what is not our own imaginations but is felt to be God's faithful word. And so the man that says: "My help cometh from the Lord," and then says: "Speak, Lord! Thy servant heareth!" will hear a still small voice, diviner than his own, whispering to him: "He will not suffer thy foot to be moved; He that keepeth thee will not slumber."

And so the psalm goes on, from this general point of view, to put in two or three different ways the great thought of the perpetual help and all-sufficient presence of the God who is the "Keeper of Israel." "Keeper" and "keeping" occurs half a dozen times in the psalm. Our translators have made sad mangling work of it by their habit, of which they were so fond, of varying the same expression; and they have hidden away from the English reader the beautiful continuity of the psalm. "The Lord that keepeth thee will not slumber." "He that keepeth Israel shall not slumber." "The Lord is thy Keeper." "The Lord shall keep thee from evil: He shall keep thy soul." It is "keep keep, keep," all through: keeping and a Keeper are the two main ideas that lie in the rest of the psalm.

"He will not suffer thy foot to be moved." If the psalm is a pilgrim's psalm, that is beautiful. The one thing that a pedestrian pilgrim wants is a firm, sure foot, that will carry him along the road and not be weary; and here is the promise for him. But at any rate here is the idea of steadfastness against all temptation; the main thought of that first portion of the psalm, as I take it, is the suggestion of the continual guard that this keeping Hand preserves over us. When all the camp slumbers, He is awake; nothing ever breaks the uninterrupted continuity of that Divine protection. Right on through the whole life it runs, never slumbering, never changing.

And then there is another beautiful thing. I am a poor, weak, insignificant unit; can *I* venture to draw down upon my head the thought of that almighty shield and ever-present protection? Yes! "He that keepeth Israel shall not slumber." I may be very small in myself, but I ally myself with the whole body of those whom God loves and cares for. The individual is lost in the Israel. It may be almost too much for me to think that I, if I stood by myself, would get all those blessings, but I will knit myself to the whole company of the faithful in all generations and in all places; and then I shall feel that is not altogether an unworthy thought of God and of His love and mercy, that He is the Keeper of Israel ; and feel that all questions of mine own unworthiness and my own feebleness are lost in the broad thought that I may join myself to that family and society of which God is the Shepherd and the Caretaker.

And now about the "keeping." "The Lord is thy keeper ; the Lord is thy shade upon thy right hand. The sun shall not smite thee by day nor the moon by night." A strange mingling of metaphors. "The Lord is thy shade," is one idea of protection which of course is very much more vigorous than picturesque as a metaphor, when we remember the sunny land from which the psalm comes, than in our own cloudy sunlight. " The Lord is thy shade," that is one; "the Lord is at thy right hand," is another ; but the psalmist, disregarding mere pedantic proprieties, mingles both in order to express the thought that God is at one and the same time doing both things as one and the same act ; by us poor creatures He stands, giving us what we especially need.

We want protection from the evils that threaten us, we want some one to stand at our right hand who shall be our strength as well as our protection. So he places the two ideas side by side, and says :—If ever you want covering from evils that threaten you, you will get it there ; whenever you want companionship from solitude, when you are lonely, of Him you will get it ; whenever you want strength poured into your feeble right hands, to do your work, you will get it there.

The Lord is with thee as thy shade, with thee as the Companion to cheer, with thee at thy right hand. "I have set Him always there, therefore I shall not be moved." And then he enlarges this one idea : "the sun shall not smite thee by day, nor the moon by night." The most bright and blessed things may become full of evil : the very sunshine may slay, the very moonlight may make lunatic, according to the old idea. Whether they be evils which in themselves may be bright and good, whether they be evils proper to the day of the sunshine of prosperity, or whether they be evils proper to the day of adversity, of sorrow and change, the one shade shall be a shade from them all.

And so we come to the last words of the psalm, the expressions that put the idea in its broadest forms, and these are: " The Lord shall keep thee from all evil." "*From all evil.*" As if he felt that he could not enumerate all the things which this presence of the Lord who made heaven and earth, would be ; and so he gathers them all into that one great sentence. Ah! a sentence that no man can receive except by the exercise of a very vigorous and somewhat unusual faith. " The Lord shall preserve thee from all evil."

Then, if anything has smitten you, it is *not* evil. And if He has not preserved me from something that has made my heart bleed and mine eyes to run, it has been because it was for my good. " There shall no evil befal thee," says an old psalm, in the rapture of faith, " neither shall any plague come nigh thy dwelling." So then, brother, let us be sure that the evil in the evil is all taken out of it before it is let fall upon our heads ; that the poison in the arrow has been carefully wiped from its point before He fitted it on the string to aim at our hearts, for He Himself sends the things that we unbelievingly and precipitately are tempted to call evil ; and if He preserves us from all evil, what He sends is good.

Let us set our faces to the unknown future with that confidence in an unseen Helper, who never is remiss nor turns away His eyes from His charge ; in an almighty Helper, who made heaven and earth ; in an ever-loving Helper, who, from His own fulness of love, will guard our lives. " The Lord thy Keeper will keep thee from all evil. He shall keep thy soul." That is the inmost protection, without which all other protections are nothing. It is easy to keep the body, it is nothing to keep that ; it is easy to keep fortunes, it is nothing to keep them, they may come and go as they will ; but no man can keep his own heart, howsoever diligently he may try it.

And there is the one hand that can preserve me, soul and spirit, blameless unto the coming of the Lord Jesus, and that is the hand that keeps from all evil the outward life ; and will also, if we will trust Him, from all sin keep the soul—the most wide and comprehensive, the most unwearied protection.

And lastly : " The Lord shall preserve thy going out

and thy coming in from this time forth, and even for evermore:" a protection which extends to all the activities of life, great and small, and which lasts for ever and ever. So that universal, unwearied, all-comprehensive, eternal, is the keeping of the "Keeper of Israel," who "slumbers not nor sleeps."

"This God is our God for ever and ever: He will be our guide even unto our death."

XXXI. The Captives of Babylon. Psalm cxxxvii. 1–6.

"*By the rivers of Babylon, there we sat down, yea, we wept, when we remembered Zion. We hanged our harps upon the willows in the midst thereof. For there they that carried us away captive required of us a song; and they that wasted us required of us mirth, saying, Sing us one of the songs of Zion. How shall we sing the Lord's song in a strange land? If I forget thee, O Jerusalem, let my right hand forget her cunning. If I do not remember thee, let my tongue cleave to the roof of my mouth; if I prefer not Jerusalem above my chief joy.*"

"By the rivers of Babylon"—by the Euphrates and the Tigris—by waters that were unfamiliar to us,—great, indeed, in themselves, but in their very greatness seeming only to enhance and to deepen our despair. Here is distance—distance from home, distance from familiar scenes, distance that may be measured in many miles. What, then, can there be in a scene like this that can be profitable to us?

I wish to show you that this psalm, though old, is new, and is as true, in its main and substantial features, of ourselves as it was of the captive Jew. We are not distant from our Jerusalem in the sense of measurement. No long miles intervene between us and the place which is to our hearts as Zion. We are in our own house to-day; we are upon our own chosen ground, and our own gates enclose us. How, then, can we know aught of the dreariness and vastness of interposing space which is known as distance from the scene which is most loved and enjoyed?

There is a distance other than that which is measurable

in miles. We may be in the sanctuary, and yet at an immeasurable distance from all things that are holy, heavenly, and pathetic. Distance is not altogether a question of yard measurement. Distance may relate to sympathy, to tone of mind, to the immediate temper of the soul; so that a man shall sit down to his musical instrument, and yet his hands shall have no skill upon the keys, and out of his heart there shall come no sound of melody. I speak, I am sure, to the experience of some, in thus speaking. I have myself again and again closed my eyes, and clasped my hands, and put myself in an attitude of devotion, and yet I seemed to have been at an infinite distance from the altar; and yet, may be, I was speaking words all the time, and devotional words; and people that do not read deeply the inner man might mistake what was said for real sympathy and communion with the Eternal. Now, whilst it was sincere—whilst every word really did come from my heart, and was a cry of want or an utterance of pain, yet the soul itself was not in the sunlight of the Divine Face; and the heart felt that God was at a great distance, and the spirit cried out, "Why standest Thou afar off, O God?" So you may be in Babylon, and yet be in Jerusalem. You may be in the sanctuary, and yet be in the wilderness. Proximity is not identity. You may have an open Bible before you, but no revelation of heaven shining upon the inner eye. If you put these thoughts together, and compare them with your own experience—not perhaps the experience of this particular moment, but an experience with which you are not unfamiliar—you will see that this 137th psalm, a moan of an ancient nation, really expresses, in tenderer and loftier language than you can command, the sorrow that consumes your heart and darkens your eyes.

"They that carried us away captive"—"they that wasted us." Surely, there can be nothing in such words to remind us of aught in our own condition. These tones at all events are ancient. There is a sound of old time here, and no sound in our life conveys such dreary meaning. It is a strain with which we are unfamiliar. We never spoke in language so despairing and sad and mournful. I have spoken in this language. What is captivity? A question of gyves and fetters and plated doors and grating locks?

That is but the very poorest of all captivity. That is but an exercise of mere strength. Babylon says to Judea, "I am stronger than you, and whilst I am stronger I shall hold you here." That is nothing. Babylon is strong to-day, but her strength may be wasted to-morrow, and Judea may be uppermost. That is hardly captivity at all. We only used the word "captivity" for the sake of convenience in describing such circumstances. There is a captivity of the soul. There is a possibility of being at liberty, and yet of being in the deepest dungeon all the time, from which no turnkey can hear our cry. There is a captivity of mind, of memory, of affection, of all that goes out of us, in ordinary circumstances, towards the light of heaven and the morning of immortality. There are times when I come into this house a captive. I can hold up my wrist, and say, "There is no mark there," but many a man has been able to lift up his wrists laden with iron, and to say, "I am free." Many a man has been shut up within strong masonry, and yet has had the enfranchisement of the universe and the liberty of the skies. Captivity is a question of your moral state—of your spiritual condition before God. Are any of us captive to-day? Do we feel a long way from home? And is there a great power that has the upper hand over us? Is there a severe mastery that mocks our endeavours to rise into light and music and joy? Then you will know that this psalm, which you thought a moment ago old and worn out and obsolete, has come up into your English language to say for you, in terms which, perhaps, your limited experience and genius might never have devised, all that is in your heart of a sense of enslavement and limitation and abasement and feebleness.

I do not know that Babylon is to be charged, as at first sight might seem to be natural, in reading these words, with pure mockery and with cruel taunting in the case of the captive Jew. "They that carried us away captive required of us a song; and they that wasted us required of us mirth, saying, Sing us one of the songs of Zion." This verse might be so read as to give us the picture of Babylon pointing the finger of scorn to the oppressed Jews, and crying to them in bitter tones, "Sing us one of your songs, and let us see you laugh now." I am not sure that such would be the correct reading of the spirit of the text. I think I see in these words a hint of clemency—a disposition rather to allure the Jews towards making the best of their circumstances. Babylon says, "Now you are in captivity, make the best of it: be men: make yourselves at home in this distant land: sing your own songs: be as glad as you used to be. You know that you are in our power: you are shut up within our empire. You cannot get away, and, whilst you are here, be as happy as you can. Sing night and day: we shall be quite glad to hear how you do sing when you are at home."

Now, this is an experience that is familiar to us if we have lived honest lives—lives that are many sided and that approach in some degree completeness. People have said to us now and again, in variety of tone and circumstance, "Now you are in our company, make the best of it. You have fallen into society that is not congenial to you, but you are here by force of circumstances. You cannot get your bread in any other place. We all are men of a different mould from yourself. Why should you be groaning and moaning all the day long? Come, come, be one of us, and if you want to sing a hymn or a song, sing it, and we will join you in singing it, perhaps. You are quite at liberty to carry on any practices that will not break up the spirit of this confederacy—that will not rupture the vitality of this relationship. Make yourself happy and comfortable if you can. You are in Babylon, and you want to be in Jerusalem, but you cannot get to your own city, so when you are out make the best of it, and be as genial and sunny as you can." Is there not a temptation to yield to hospitality of this kind? May not a man say, "Well, they are certainly disposed to make large concessions to me: they are not going to shut up my mouth in dumbness. If I wish to speak God's name, and utter God's praise, they are apparently quite willing that I should do so, only I must be one of themselves. I cannot liberate myself from their society, but still I think they are acting as noble a part as they could possibly be expected to act. Well, I will think no more of Zion and home and tender recollections and blessed memories, but, being here, I will just make the best of it." Do not go down so. If you can for a moment receive a concession of this kind from an enemy, and regard it in the light of a favour—if the great birthrights of the kingdom of God should ever come to you in the light of mere human favours or social concessions, and you accept them as such—you have lost something of the volume of your being and the quality of your best nature.

The Jew said, "No, I cannot sing here. The air is heavy; the place is strange. If I have lifted up my voice for a moment, it seems to have fallen back upon me as if there were no outlet heavenward. When I touch the harp it is but plain wood and plain metal. Behold there is no resonance in it; there is no comfort in playing under circumstances so terrible and disastrous." So the Jew, as he must do, entered into covenant, and spoke his soul's feeling in an oath. Old Testament men were wont to do this. It was, "God do so to me, and more also, if——." The Jew was sublime in his oaths, grand in his covenants, and he says, "If I forget thee, O Jerusalem, let my right hand forget her cunning. If I do not remember thee, let my tongue cleave to the roof of my mouth; if I prefer not Jerusalem above my chief joy." Please to observe the beautiful harmony between the speech and the thing which is signified in action. "You ask me to play upon my harp—to take it into my hands, and run over the strings. If I do so, God strike the fingers dead upon the harp-strings, so that they may never move again; and let this right hand and left, in which there is some power of music, forget their cunning if I touch the harp at the bidding of an alien." You see the connection between the speech and the action that was required. "Sing us one of the songs of Zion." "If I do, may my tongue, ere it utter the first note, cleave to my gums, and be a tongue no more,"—the same fine exquisite adaptation between the language of the oath and the thing that was required to be done.

There was constancy. The world is now in need of constant men. There is a great deal too much india-rubber humanity abroad just now—elastic minds, elastic consciences, great power of accommodation to circumstances, marvellous ability to do things that are holy in unholy places and at unholy biddings. What we want is constancy in the Church—not bigotry, not exclusiveness, but constancy to given principles, and to a given faith which has been spoken in love and professed in seriousness. And where such constancy is felt, and is exemplified, Babylon must feel the presence of the Church. It must have been a wonderful thing for Babylon to get hold of a number of men who would not do as Babylon said,—who could be made to bow down simply because the arm was stronger than the individual that was being crushed, but who could not be made to sing or to play upon the harp. There you have no power. You can lay a man down, throw him into the sea, cut him up, burn him, blow his ashes away upon the winds, but you cannot make him sing, or pray, or play upon an instrument before God, and be joyful. There is a region over which you have no power, and the world ought to be taught that, and that was the first great lesson the Jews gave to Babylon. "No, we are taken away by a strong hand and a mighty arm and a cruel power. We abide here: we are your slaves. You may oppress us, but you cannot make us feel at home." Thank God for that home-hungering force that is in the heart,—for that home-hunger which makes us restless even when we are under the happiest circumstances from a social point of view, but at a distance from the loved place. He is not a bigot who loves his home: he is not a zealot who loves his country before all the other countries of the globe: he is not a narrow-minded man who says in the midst of the wilderness, "Would God I had a draught of water from the well of Bethlehem!" God has put these instincts into our hearts, and it is here that we find the strength of patriotism and the glory of the Church—in preferring it to all other associations, and in yielding to it an undivided and loyal homage—in the bending of the knee and the bowing of the heart in all thankfulness and devout love. Have you such feeling as that? I have but little faith in a man who wholly forgets his home, and forgets his friends, and who is just as happy under one church-roof as another. I believe in having attachments to particular places, and particular persons, and particular ways of doing things. There is no occasion for such preference to dwarf itself into narrowness and exclusiveness; but I do believe more in a man who has such preferences than in a man who has them not.

"I love it, I love it, and who shall dare
To chide me for loving that old arm-chair?"

It is possible, I dare say, for some people to have just the same feeling towards all arm-chairs; but that is a better heart—the sturdier, the truer, and the tenderer—that says, "No, it is *this* chair I love best."

> "Would you learn the spell? A mother sat there,
> And a sacred thing is that old arm-chair."

And so the Jew in Babylon was no longer a happy man. He did not say, "I will take down my harp and make the best of it. I have my harp here, and I can play the old tunes over." There was a home-hunger, a home-thirst, a pang that made Babylon millions of miles farther off than it could be according to the mere road. In that constancy you find the element which grows up, when duly watched by prayer and intelligent study, into strength and solidity—into a force that becomes a solid and ruling and reliable power in social life.

Here are men living in memory. Do you know what it is to live in recollection? It is the sweetest of all life. There is a time in a man's days when he comes to think so. There is also a time when to live in hope is the best. That is the young heart's sunny time. I would not shorten it: God forbid I should begrudge it. I like to see the light of hope playing upon the young face, and to hear anticipating words from young lips, but I declare there is something sweeter, tenderer, mellower, richer, in living the old days over again. Not so bright, not so glittering, not such a flashing light, but a calm, subdued, sacred lustre bathes the past. The Jews lived the old times over again. They went back to Jerusalem—walked the old familiar roads, reminded one another of words spoken in the light, and spoken in the darkness. They lived in memory.

> "Oft in the stilly night,
> Ere slumber's chain hath bound me,
>   Sad memory brings the light
> Of other days around me:
> The smiles, the tears, of boyhood's years
>   The words of love then spoken,
> The eyes that shone, now dimmed and gone,
>   The cheerful hearts now broken."

Have you any such recollections? Among all those recollections there will shine, the brightest of the whole, recollections of Christian fellowship, Christian communion, Christian intercourse, bowing together at the altar, struggling together bravely, with a tender, noble heroism, against poverty and weakness and illness and difficulty, and coming up again out of the waters, and shaking them off, and saying, "We shall live yet and see the land again." Oh, we forget the roughness, the rudeness, it may be; we forget all that was merely accidental, and the solemn soul of the past comes to us clothed with a body from heaven, and our yesterdays are more charmful and luring than our morrows.

How then? To-day you are making a yesterday. If you, young friends, live nobly now, you are laying up for yourselves an inheritance incorruptible and that fadeth not away. You do not know the measure of what you are doing now,—its reach and influence and pregnancy of meaning and result. But ten years hence, or twenty, and things will come up again, and the great law will repeat itself—"Be not deceived; God is not mocked, for whatsoever a man soweth, that shall he also reap." Hear it say, "Thou didst give unto me two talents—two little corn-seeds. Here I am a whole ear of corn. Cut me and use me, or sow me again, and I will still bring thee more." If you have once lost the past you cannot make it now. You must be making it as you proceed, little by little, day by day, here a little and there a little; and you cannot tell altogether what you are doing. But things shape themselves—get into order and come back upon a man, and say, "We are yours: take us." I suppose that most of the young people whom I see before me now may confidently, according to ordinary calculation, look on to fifty years of life. What if I conjure you to begin that fifty years' period now by an oath to Heaven—by a vow at the cross—that you will live purely, wisely, nobly, usefully; and then into what Babylon soever of misfortune, adversity, poverty, you be driven in the days that are to come, you will take Jerusalem with you, and the waters of Zion shall flow alongside the waters of Babylon.

Some solemn lessons issue from this pathetic and mournful page that is before us. It will be for our souls' health if we lay them deeply to heart. You may be deprived of religious privileges: you may be withdrawn from the sanctuary: you may be called away from your chosen place, from your delights, and your habitations, and put into circumstances where you cannot hear the old music, or look upon the old relationships, or extract honey from the flowers that have yielded so much sweetness hitherto. We may fall into the hands of mockers. Whilst we are together sitting here, knowing one another and caring for one another, we think all the world is an Eden, and that paradise has regained itself, and that all the earth is more or less under the influence of Christian sentiment. We sit here with our hymn-books, and we sing our psalm-tunes, and read our Scriptures, and hear our favourite preachers preach the gospel to us, and we think things are not, after all, so bad as they are sometimes made out to be. The minister says sometimes, in the heat of his argument, and under the inspiration of his hope, that England is not antichristian. But, O my brother, what if England be anti-moral? Think of the revelations that are coming before us every day of men of position and name and status. What if England be nominally Christian, but really anti-moral,—if under a great profession she is hiding a great corruption? One day, I say, we may fall into the hands of mockers. They may taunt us, and revile us, and take up the holy things, and throw them upon us with violent hands. Are we prepared for that change of thought? We know the value of our privileges best when we have lost them. It is possible to get so familiar with the privilege as to forget it is a privilege at all. It is possible to have so much comfort as to forget that it is comfort. It is possible to see the sun so often as not to know the great work it is doing—that by its own unaided light it is throwing the morning upon many worlds, bringing summer and autumn upon new planets—worlds far away from ours. And it is possible to hear your minister preach until you do not know that he is anything special or particular to you, and you think that you may go into the next house and hear a man who will touch you just as much. You may, or you may not. You may hear one voice so continually that it shall cease to be a distinctive voice to you. They say the bird shows the brightness of its wings most when it is in flight,—that you see the colours upon the wings most vividly when the bird rises, and flies away from you. We may see the beauty of our Jerusalem better when we are in the darkness and slavery of Babylon.

Do cultivate religious attachments. Do not let all things be equally common: do let us have a little enthusiasm about some men, and some places, and some books, and some scenes. Oh, it is not living, to live with a person to whom all places are alike,—who does not know what he is eating, whether it is the very best or the worst. There is no comfort in living with such an individual, on whom the best of your things are wasted. There is no comfort in living with an individual to whom all systems and all Churches and all rituals are alike. Do have your preferences,—not that you may antagonise the preferences of other people, and make yourself unpleasant to those who may differ from you; but do get to love some particular seat in the church, some particular corner. A man cannot go slick down to hell, surely, if he loves one little bit of the sanctuary better than he loves any place else on the earth. Oh, we can surely get hold of him there : we can surely touch him through that one little preference. It is a very poor hold to have upon him, but it is better than nothing. Do you mourn your distance from Zion, and are you unable to sing when you are in far-off Babylon? There is hope for you. One day, the Jew that hung his harp upon the willow shall take it down. One day, the man who prayed that his tongue might cleave to his gums (for that is the true rendering of the passage), rather than he should sing the Lord's song in a strange land, will come out of his captivity. You cannot hold a man like that down always. The pathos that is in his soul means something, and one day he will get the upper hand of Babylon, and will be back again in Zion.

J. P.

XXXII. Isaiah.

ISAIAH is the greatest of all the prophets of the Old Testament in respect both of the style and tone of his prophecy, and of the substance of his witness for God both to his own age and to the ages of the future. I propose to dwell only on the first thirty-nine chapters of his prophecy, without prejudging that question which has been raised as to identity or difference of authorship between this first section of the book and the portion which opens at the fortieth chapter—a question, let me remind you, of profound critical interest, but in no way affecting the authority of this latter part of the book as an integral portion of Holy Scripture. But the question need not be touched upon now, because on any hypothesis there is a distinct separation between the two portions of the book, marking some interval, long or short, of time, and because the former portion, which belongs to the period ending with the establishment of Hezekiah's kingdom, is more than sufficient to occupy all our thoughts to-day. No book of the Old Testament is comparable to the Book of Isaiah in respect of its style and tone. The very language, in its union of freshness with perfection, and of richness with force and vigour, marks the golden age of Hebrew. The variety and fulness of power, uniting pathos with stirring encouragement, bold denunciation of sin with unfailing tenderness, sense of burden and sorrow with predominant hope, and fervent patriotic love of Israel with a clear conception of the higher and wider purpose of God to all humanity which the covenant of Israel served, seems to concentrate on this one book all the elements of prophetic mission and inspiration. Nor can even translation obscure to us the extraordinary wealth of poetic beauty touched by the higher fire of inspiration, both in imagery and in thought. What can exceed the majestic sublimity of the call of the prophet, in the sixth chapter, by the voice out of the glory of the Lord? or the terrible picture, in the fourteenth chapter, of the fall of the king of Babylon, like "Lucifer, the son of the morning," amidst the songs of triumph of the rescued earth, and the taunting welcome of the mighty dead in the realms of hell? Where can we find utterances of tenderer love than in the lamentation of the Lord over His unfruitful vineyard, or the invitation to sinners, whose sins are as scarlet, to make them as white as snow in the stream of the Divine mercy? What exquisite music of peaceful beauty breathes through the description of the wilderness blossoming like the rose along the highway of the redeemed, where they shall move with songs and everlasting joy upon their heads, and sorrow and sighing shall flee away! What psalm of thanksgiving, even in the Psalter itself, is deeper and fuller than that triumphant cry, "God is my Salvation; I will trust in God, and not be ashamed. The Lord Jehovah is my strength and my song"? Or that burst of adoration, "O Lord, Thou art my God. I will praise Thy name. This is our God; we have waited for Him, and He will save us. This is the Lord Jehovah; we have waited for Him; we will be glad and rejoice in His salvation"? But if Isaiah thus stands out pre-eminent in style and tone, how much more in the substance of his prophecy! No prophet ever ministered more effectively to his generation. Through two great crises of his country's history he prophesied to Judah—through the threatening danger of the confederacy of Syria and Israel, in the reign of Ahaz; through the yet more terrible agony of the great Assyrian invasion in the days of Hezekiah, fresh from its triumph over Israel, and threatening to trample out the last spark of national life in Jerusalem. In both it is clear that he stood forth as a very tower of strength—the soul of patriotic resistance and confidence, because the messenger of the light and the grace of the Lord, the witness for the true moral and spiritual strength of the nation, in victory first over sin and faithlessness within, as an earnest of victory over enemies without. Two eras of prosperity he saw: the one at the beginning of his career, in the days of Uzziah and Jotham; the other at the close of this period of his ministry, in the victorious strength and spiritual revival of Hezekiah's reign.

In both we see him raising the thoughts of the people above the blessings of earth to the higher spiritual gifts of which they were the means and the earnest, pleading against the outward hollow service of the worldly heart, and setting forth the devotion of a pure life, and the love of God, not for His gifts, but for Himself. No element of prophetic mission to his own time is wanting to guard the spirituality of the law and the sacrifice, to witness against selfish despotism in the king, and self-reliant trust of the people in material strength. He is, indeed, the true prophet of God to his own age, alike in national sorrow and in national joy, nerving it in the agony of danger, and calming it in the pride of triumph. Yet, of all Old Testament prophets, is he not also the one who looks forward most distinctly to the future, and sends his peculiar message to us whose lot is cast in the kingdom of Christ? As we saw previously, there are two phases of this onward-looking prophecy: the one we called Evangelical, anticipating the teaching and spirit of the Gospel by a foresight of the kingdom of God, in which the free obedience of the spirit should supersede the bondage of the law, in which the knowledge of God should be unveiled, not to a few only, but to all, and in which suffering, sin, and death—those three scourges of humanity—should give way to joy and purity in an eternal life; the other we rather named Messianic, as fixing the eye in strong personal faith on a Saviour and King of the whole world, to come both as the Son of David and as the ruler of the Gentiles, in whom should be at once the perfect exaltation of man and the perfect revelation of God. Some prophets, perhaps, like Jeremiah, are more Evangelical than Messianic; others, like Daniel, more Messianic than Evangelical. In Isaiah both phases of revelation are united in perfect harmony. As Micah in lesser measure, so he in greater, realizes both elements of the great future, with a vividness which in earlier prophecy we have but little trace. Nowhere does the Christ of the Old Testament stand out with such vivid distinctness —whether, as in the Christmas Day lessons, He is looked upon as the Son who is given to us in all the attributes of Divine majesty; or, as in the Good Friday lessons, contemplated as the great Sufferer, "the man of sorrow, and acquainted with grief."

Nowhere else does the unity of spirit between the Old Testament and the New manifest itself so clearly. There is in Him, as it were, a gospel before the Gospel; and the moral and spiritual teaching of Isaiah differs but in degree, though that degree be great, from the teaching of St. Paul and St. John. And what wonder this; for did not Isaiah's prophecy on that famous day in the synagogue of Nazareth furnish the Master Himself with a very description of His own mission—to heal the broken-hearted, to preach deliverance to the captives, and recovery of sight to the blind, "to proclaim the acceptable year of the Lord"?

The ministry of Isaiah is described as extending through "the days of Uzziah, Jotham, Ahaz, and Hezekiah, kings of Judah," a period of at least sixty-two years, even if we reckon, as it seems probable, that his mission only began in the very close of Uzziah's reign, and take no account of the ancient Jewish tradition that he survived to the evil days of Manasseh, and died a martyr, sawn, as says the history, assunder when Manasseh filled Jerusalem with innocent blood. The book which bears his name contains the chief utterances, no doubt, of that long ministry, possibly including in some cases, as in one case we are expressly told that it does include, words of the law spoken long before. As in other prophetic books, it is not always easy to disentangle from one another the separate utterances of the prophet as they now stand, and it may not be always safe to assume that the succession in the order of book corresponds rigidly to the succession in order of time ; but it seems probable on the whole that the order of time is followed ; and in taking only the first thirty-nine chapters, with which we are now concerned, we can discern, after the first chapter, which is a solemn introduction to the whole book, a succession of prophecies belonging to successive epochs in the history of the time. Thus, the first section, from the second to the fifth chapter, may belong to the time of Uzziah or of Jotham, ending as it does in the sixth chapter, which describes the prophet's solemn call in the year that King Uzziah died. Then follows, in the second place, from the seventh to the twelfth chapters, the prophecies of the first great crisis in the reign of Ahaz, when the danger from Syria and Israel that threatened Judah was only averted by the more formidable danger of the Assyrian conquest. Then to this succeeds, thirdly, a series of various burdens on the nations, of which we are told that the first was uttered in the year that Ahaz died, extending from the thirteenth to the twenty-third chapter. Next, the fourth section of the book, from the twenty-fourth to the thirty-fifth chapters, is occupied with the prophecies belonging to the second great national crisis in the days of Hezekiah, when the Assyrian power, before which Judah lay prostrate and helpless, was broken by the arm of the Lord ; and the whole ends, in the thirty-sixth to the thirty-ninth chapters, with a historical narrative, transferred by the compiler to the Second Book of Kings, which tells how Isaiah's prophecy of deliverance was fulfilled in the destruction of the army of Sennacherib, and how the danger from Babylon, though as yet far distant on the horizon, was seen by the prophet's eye, and foretold to Hezekiah in the very hour of his pride. Such in bare outline is this great prophecy. Let us now fill it in, as far as time allows, with some general considerations of the substance of each section.

The first chapter, as I have said, seems undoubtedly a preface to the whole book, containing in brief the very gist of its moral teaching and its prophetic promise. I say its moral teaching, for, much in the spirit of the Lord's controversy in Micah, we find there a picture of a faithless and thankless falling away from God visited by His chastisement, through which "the whole head is sick and the whole heart is faint;" and we hear the indignant rejection of a hollow and outward service of sacrifice, and the loving call for a deep and a true repentance bearing the fruit of righteous life; and I say its prophetic promise, for it declares that all judgment is to be in the true sense a tribulation—a winnowing, that is, of the chaff from the wheat—and that when it is past Zion shall be redeemed with judgment and her converts with righteousness. Then after this preface opens the first section of the prophecy which there is no means of assigning with certainty to any one period, but which, I cannot but think, belongs to the reign of Jotham; for the vision in the sixth chapter certainly seems to me to be the first call of the prophet, and it is fixed in the year in which King Uzziah died. That grand vision itself has impressed itself deeply on the imagination and thought of man. In it we see revealed the unspeakable glory of the Lord of hosts, surrounded by the seraphic worship and hymned in the seraphic song. The terror of the prophet before Him in his consciousness of sin, until his lips are touched by the fire from the altar of God, the call then gladly heard and accepted, the message given telling of wilful deafness to God's voice, and the judgment it should call down, but telling also of the undying life to live still in the faithful remnant, and to shoot forth in luxuriant fruitfulness when the appointed hour is come—must this not be, notwithstanding its position in the book, the first call of Isaiah to his great prophetic office? If so, the first section of prophecy must follow this and precede the utterance in the seventh chapter which belongs to the reign of Ahaz; and it must therefore be referred to the transition period of Jotham's reign, when the people, as we read, did corruptly, although no apostasy like that of Ahaz was dreamed of as yet. This section opens brightly with a future vision of the exaltation of the Lord's house, and of nations gathered round it in a kingdom of peace. Soon it turns to a rebuke of present worldliness and present idolatry on which the hand of judgment is to pass, turning the wisdom of counsel into foolishness, giving to children the rule over men, and scourging the oppressive pride of the princes and shaming the frivolous and luxurious vanity of the women of Israel; but in the end it clears up to the former brightness, once more telling how after chastisement shall come purity, after judgment the love of God manifested as in the cloud and the fire of old to be a tabernacle of rest and of peace. So ends the first great utterance. But in the same section is subjoined to it a sadder prophecy. As iniquity seems to abound, and the coming storm of trouble darkens in it, we hear the famous lamentation of the Lord over His unfruitful vineyard; we listen to the series of woes against rapacity and revelling, against scorn of God's mercy, and the denial of the very principles of goodness; we see in the prophetic vision the declaration of judgments already sent and despised, and the great judgment of invasion and destruction to come clouding the whole heaven of hope and roaring for destruction like the waves of the sea. So ends the warning to Israel in the days of Jotham, when all seemed prosperous and the storm had not yet broken.

In the next section we find ourselves in the days of Ahaz, when the first great crisis of trouble has come. And now the message changes its character to comfort and to hope. The prophet stands before Ahaz in his terror at the combined invasion of Israel and Syria. He bids him be of good cheer; he gives him the promise of deliverance. Ere a child soon to be conceived should " know how to refuse the evil and choose the good," he warns him, although in vain, against the great Assyrian power, which should be to Judah both a greater danger and a heavier scourge; the birth of a child whose name should be, Hasten the Booty and Speed the Spoil, is made the sign of the approaching fall of the great enemies of Judah. The call is given to put aside hollow and dangerous confederacies and trust in the name of the Lord. Then out of the darkness resting on the people was to come the dawn of the bright day of peace, the gift of the child whose name is "Wonderful, Counsellor, the mighty God, the everlasting Father, the Prince of Peace." So he speaks to Judah; and then on the traitorous ally of Syria—the rebellious kingdom of Israel—he utters a fourfold woe. Judgment succeeds judgment, and the ominous words are repeated again and again, "For all this His anger is not turned away, but His hand is stretched out still."

Then the eye of the prophet rests on the Assyrian himself—the rod of God's judgment—falsely deeming the victory to be wrought by his own strength, and to be used for his own purpose. With a stern joy, Isaiah tells how in God's hand that terrible rod shall be used and broken, how he shall serve the Divine purpose, and then for his own sin be swept away; for there rises now before the prophet's eye the bright vision of the kingdom of the true Son of David, "on whom the Spirit of the Lord shall rest in its sevenfold gifts, whose reign shall be in righteousness and His government in peace. Then shall the earth be filled with the knowledge of the Lord as the waters cover the sea; then shall the captives of the Lord return, and all enemies shall perish in a deliverance like the great deliverance of Egypt in the days of old." What wonder that this utterance is welcomed with a burst of exultant thanksgiving—"Behold, God is my salvation; I will trust and not be afraid; with joy shall ye draw water out of the inexhaustible well of salvation. Cry out and shout, thou inhabitant of Zion: for great is the Lord in the midst of thee." How striking it is that the same voice which spoke in solemn warning in the days of prosperity should now tell the tidings of comfort and hope in the dark days of trial; and how unmistakable is the tendency by which, through the growing trials and dangers of the present, the prophetic thought is borne onward more and more to the completeness of the great future glory of Israel!

But now to this succeed—beginning at least in the year in which Ahaz died—a series of what are called the burdens on the nations, and working out with a magnificent fulness that idea of God's universal rule over the kingdoms of the earth, of which in our study of prophecy we have heard but little or nothing since the first simple utterance of the prophecy in the opening of the book of Amos. Through the whole there runs the twofold idea of the exclusiveness of the law, and the catholicity of the Gospel—the view of the heathen nations, simply as related to the chosen people of God, and judged of enmity or friendship to them; and as being themselves also a part of God's kingdom, having blessing, probation, and judgment at the hand of the Creator of all things, who hateth nothing He has made. First, there is that magnificent vision of the judgment to come upon Babylon, to which I have already alluded. Then the prophecy turns to the nearer lands of Palestine and Moab, to the northern kingdoms of Damascus, to the coast of the south of Ethiopia and Egypt, for which, by strange symbolic action of the prophet, is prefigured a captivity of shame in Assyria; to Edom and Arabia; and, lastly, to Tyre, the great queen of the sea, that harlot of the world's merchandise and luxury—a grand survey from the watch-tower of prophecy of all the kingdoms of the earth far and near, claiming all as the field of righteousness and mercy, of the Divine government, and all, as in different degrees, willingly or unwillingly, working out the glory of the Lord.

These utterances we may suppose, I think, to belong to the interval between two great national crises—when the first danger had passed away of ignoble vassalage to Assyria, and before the yet greater storm of danger which Isaiah then foresaw as bursting in the future upon Judah.

Now, in the next section, more varied and broken in character than the former, full, I think, of a greater power of intensity, both of joy and of sorrow, we have the utterances of that terrible time when the full wrath of Assyria, blaspheming in the very greatness of its pride, was turned on the little realm of Hezekiah. These prophecies fall, I think, into two chief groups, the one from the twenty-fourth to the twenty-seventh chapters, and the other from the twenty-eighth to the thirty-fifth. The first of these groups opens with a passage making a link of connection with the burdens of the nations. The prophet looks forth, and sees the time of widespread trouble and distress upon all the earth, probably from the cruel and oppressive power of the great empire of Assyria; but out of it he sees shall come the establishment of the chosen Kingdom of Zion. "O

Lord, O Christ, Thou art my God. I will exalt Thee, I will praise Thy name. For all nations He shall spread the spiritual feast in His holy mountain; He shall take away the veil from all the people; He shall swallow up death in victory. Lo, this is our God; we have waited for Him, and He will save us; we have a strong city indeed; salvation is its walls and its bulwark. Open the gates that my righteous nation which keepeth the truth may enter in. The Lord Jehovah is our everlasting strength." "Only," he cries, "let us listen to the word of the Lord; let us see His hand; let us bear the pains of travail; let us wait patiently for Him until the day of trial is past. If we do this, then life shall rise out of death; the earth itself shall disclose her blood, and shall no more cover her slain." How marvellously in this grand prophecy does Isaiah show himself the prophet of an undying hope!

Then follows, in yet more broken and varied strain, a series of isolated prophecies. In one chapter we hear of a woe on the two great empires of Assyria and Egypt, between which Judah lay; in another a denunciation of destruction on the drunken revelry of Samaria, then tottering to its fall, and chastisement on the proud, worldly-minded statesmen who ruled Judah; in a third there is a woe against Ariel, the lion of God as in Judah the city of David, because of its smooth hypocrisy; in the fourth and fifth there is a noble witness in the hour of terror against flying to the desert, against alliance with Egypt, against base submission to Assyria—there is a cry at once of patriotism and prophetic warning to trust in the might of the Lord and the might of the Lord alone. Then in mingled strain we hear tell of the kingdom and the righteousness which should be, of the worldly confidence and indulgence which marred it in effect and which clouded its blessings with judgment; and finally, in magnificent prose, there is a call to all nations to behold the desolation which shall pass on the enemies of the people of God, and the final revelation of His kingdom in all its phases of blessings—the fruitfulness in which the wilderness shall blossom like the rose, the comforting of weakness, the healing of disease, the opening of the lips of the dumb, the highway of holiness stretching plain and straight through all the dangers of life, and the end to which it leads, when the ransomed of the

Lord shall return to Mount Zion with "everlasting joy upon their heads," when "they shall obtain joy and gladness, and sorrow and sighing shall flee away." Wonderfully magnificent is this last prophecy, of which I can but give you the very slightest sketch. In it, as in all that goes before, we have surely the very loftiest strain of the prophecy of the Old Testament to be the support of the ancient people of God in their time of sorrow and of trial; but although time fails for any adequate description, I cannot but remind you now, in conclusion, how constantly in this wonderful book the vision of that Messianic hope which we have inherited in possession comes out again and again. With what true instinct, from the earliest days, has the Church drawn from the Book of Isaiah her chosen lessons of Christian prophecy! In some places, notably in the great prophecy of the seventh chapter, "A virgin shall conceive, and bear a son," there must clearly have been some fulfilment at the time typical of the greater fulfilment of the future, and it may well be that to the prophet's eye the type and anti-type blended in one; but it is notable that in every section of the book at which we have glanced there is, as it were, an involuntary rise to the glory of a great future hope, now of a universal kingdom, now of a Divine King. In the first section, the prophecy of the days of Jotham, we have the exaltation of the Lord's house to be the centre of the kingdom over the world; we have the expectation of the Branch of the Lord to be beautiful and glorious in the restored glory of Jerusalem; in the second, the comfort that shall come in the great crisis in the days of Ahaz. And here we have three great utterances: "Behold, a virgin shall conceive, and bear a son, and shall call his name Immanuel"—God with us; "Unto us a child is born, unto us a son is given; and the government shall be upon His shoulder; and His name shall be called Wonderful, Counsellor, The Mighty God, The Everlasting Father, The Prince of Peace;" "There shall be a rod of Jesse; and the Spirit of the Lord shall rest upon it, the spirit of knowledge and understanding, the spirit of ghostly strength, and the earth shall be filled with the knowledge of the Lord as the waters cover the sea." Allow as you will for poetical and Eastern hyperbole, what can have satisfied such prophecies as these by any mere human kingdom? What son of man can rise to the greatness of that destiny who is not also the Son of God?

And in the next section, of the days of Hezekiah, we have the declaration of the revelation which shall gather all nations with the unveiled eyes of faith to Jerusalem, to One who shall swallow up death in victory, and wipe off all tears from all faces.

And the last section rises to the glorious climax of that description of the kingdom of peace and holiness of which in one kingdom alone there can be even any approach to fulfilment. Yes, my brethren, as it were by a spiritual necessity the end of every vista of thought, of every utterance of joy or mourning, of judgment or blessing, is in Christ Himself. The visions of Isaiah here have in some measure been fulfilled already in His kingdom, in some points wait still for fulfilment; and in the knowledge of Christ they catch the very spirit of His Gospel of grace and mercy until they almost seem to be a link between the Old Testament and the New, and speak to us with even deeper and fuller meaning than when from Isaiah's lips, touched with the fire of God, they were a light in darkness and a comfort in sorrow to those who, with him, inherited the blessings of the old covenant with David.

A. B.

XXXIII. The Cry of the Creatures. ISAIAH vi. 1–3.

"In the year that King Uzziah died I saw also the Lord sitting upon a throne, high and lifted up, and His train filled the temple. Above it stood the seraphims: each one had six wings; with twain he covered his face, and with twain he covered his feet, and with twain he did fly. And one cried unto another, and said, Holy, holy, holy, is the Lord of hosts: the whole earth is full of His glory."

THE vision of Isaiah is in many ways remarkable. First, because of the time in which the vision came, and that time brings to us all in passing a lesson. It happened, as you know quite certainly, because the prophet leaves no doubt about it, in the year that Jotham came to reign on the throne; after the reign of a man that had been most distinguished for three characteristics which followed one after the other as a natural consequence. He distinguished himself for pride, pride quite naturally was followed by presumption, and then, as a necessary consequence, by sacrilege. He had begun, like other men since, in even modern times, by thinking himself rather better than God; he had gone on to presume on the awful image of the Eternal; and he ended by disregarding the very House of God, and by thinking that while his palace ought to be adorned with splendour of decoration, the House of God might be anything under the sun; that anything, however ugly or contemptible, was quite good enough for God. There have been plenty of Uzziahs in ancient and modern times. He died, and as he died, and Jotham his son came to the throne, immediately a great change took place. Why? As long as there is, just as long as there was, pride, presumption, sacrilege, there is no vision; God's laws do not change, He is not moved although we forget it. The unchanging laws of His love are the same, and if people are proud and presumptuous and sacrilegious they will get what they like; for Uzziah had been filled with pride, presumption, sacrilege, and there had been no vision. There followed, as you remember, the accession to the throne of Jotham. And Jotham is one spot of blue in the sky, in the long line of kings. No sooner had the spotless king come to the throne and the sacrilegious one gone, "in the year that King Uzziah died I saw the Lord." The revelation was remarkable: and let us remember that the way to see God is first to come to Him, and then with confidence based upon His promises, which is no presumption, and takes away your sorrow, you get a sense of His presence which teaches you that there is nothing in worship or in offering, external or internal, too good for God. That is the meaning of the vision. But then the vision of Uzziah was remarkable for a another reason, because it marks a change in the life of the prophet, it cuts across that life with a most splendid chasm. Before that, Isaiah was a prophet of things of comparatively little interest, but afterwards he prophesied of the kingdom of Christ. But the vision is remarkable for a third reason. It points out, first, a revelation, the unveiling of Him from whom we come, and to whom we go, in whom we live and move and have our being. It points out to us the nature of Him upon whom we trust, every pulse that throbs, every thought that flashes across the brain, every affection that warms the heart teaches us His nature, and that is important; it reminds us very distinctly of the duty of the creature when he is face to face with the Creator. It reminds us also of distinguishing characteristics of the Church of God, as distinct from all religions or half-religions that have taken up a sort of appearance of being the tabernacle of the Eternal. For that reason the vision is quite interesting; and therefore let us gaze upon that vision for a few moments and try to learn some of the lessons that are in it.

The one great refrain of the prophet's vision, if you bring it up to its final result, is that which ought to occupy your thoughts and mine. God! God! Well, I would remind you that it is always well, in the great mercy of our Creator, that times like this should come upon us, when we are lifted, whether we will or not, out of that which is apparent into that which is real. Let me speak upon a theme too large to dwell much upon. We are living, I speak with all sincerity, in a world of appearances. We are carried away by the appearances of the moment, we are borne away from the present; the necessities of life, the anxieties of business, the demands of the moment, the cry of man around us, the awful sorrows of the poor, the splendours and the troubles of increasing civilization, our own needs, thoughts, intellectual characters, these things are borne in upon us, are they not? from moment to moment. We are crushed by appearances, we forget what is real. Oh! is it not good for God to call us by what we call circumstances, to remember that appearance is one thing and life is quite another; to remember that there is a real world around us; and that the prophet's vision is not a pretty picture like Raphael's picture of Ezekiel's vision in the galleries of Florence, not a pretty poem like Milton's Paradise Lost, but is a revelation, the most awful and beautiful, the most real that we can contemplate. When, for a moment, we come out of the world, when we contemplate God as He is, we shall be His people.

The vision of the prophet puts before us first, in a very awful manner, God. We can apprehend, we cannot comprehend that. The mind can strike it, and it can strike the mind, but it cannot grasp so great a thought. But there is a thought about it which the mind can grasp. As the prophet paints them in his vision there were creatures in the temple of God that spread their wings, two of them to cover the face, two to cover the feet lest they should touch the soil, two with stretched-out wings that they might do Him service. But, whatever they did else, they did with great ecstasy of soul :—" Holy, holy, holy is the Lord of hosts." They did that which the Church does or ought to do, they did that which precisely, at the highest level, you and I are bound to do, and which one day, please God, we shall do.

The creatures were, in the first place, engaged in the exercise of an intellectual satisfaction. There is about what they did, not the outcome of a beautiful, prophetic, inspired enthusiasm, not the outcome of a mere enthusiasm at all. It lay upon a fact, that was a thing, and is what is helpful to us now. Facts are the only reliable certainties; dreams, visions, theories, all other physical aspects will vanish, scientific theories will go, while facts stand. A man that denies or ignores a fact is a man that dashes his head against a wall; in plain English, he is a fool. And so when we come face to face with the creatures, we shall see that their cry is a cry of intellectual satisfaction, based upon a fact, a quiet restrainedness which is worth our attention.

Human nature is always the same, and man is frail, and in modern times religion has sometimes taken the form of a wild rhapsody. Now rhapsody is a kind of ecstatic poetry, as in the rose-coloured light of dreams. Sometimes it is beautiful, sometimes attractive; but there is always this distinguishing sorrow about it, that when it is past, flitted across your brain like a dream, there is nothing left like the basis of fact: a wild religion, like that of the middle ages in a large part of Southern Germany, and like a certain amount of religion in modern times amongst some who strive to do good, therefore we wish them well, but a religion made up of rhapsody and enthusiasm, and unlike the religion of the Crucified.

Believe me, a religion of rhapsody, a religion strongest when the nerves are weak and the body is excited, when we take such a religion into the world, standing face to face with awful changes, with terrible accident, with dreadful death, then that religion fails. There is nothing at all, as I submit, of rhapsody about the cry of the creatures. It is the cry of an intellectual satisfaction. There is an actual truth built upon it, a splendid consequence, the going out of a lofty intellect; a sweet restrainedness, a wise moderation. Ah! believe me that restrainedness and moderation never die down into that which carries a mere majority. They are always akin to truth.

There are rocks in the Atlantic far too high ever to be touched by the most lofty spray. And there are thoughts too lofty ever to be washed by the spray of mere empty words, and so the cry of the creatures is the cry of intellectual satisfaction. They are dealing with a fact, and I should like you to remember that fact: "Holy, holy, holy is the Lord of hosts: the earth is full of His glory." We deal with a serious fact, and it is quite possible to contemplate it by the intellect. You know that there are intellectual men of great note in the intellectual world, who think that our religion, and small blame to them, considering the way in which it has been put before them, —they imagine that our religion is a rhapsody. And there are many faults in our religion—judging by the voices of many politicians—but there is, at any rate, one sin that cannot be laid to the charge of the Church, at any rate she cannot be charged with rhapsody. No, no! rather the other way; and after all, is it not a sacred and a wise way?

The cry of the creatures is not only a cry of intellectual satisfaction but an act of spiritual life. Suppose you ask, "What is man?" The Church answers, and the materialists join their voices in answering, "Man is an animal, man will die, dissolve into dust, pass away into gases, disappear. But supposing you ask the question again, the cry of the materialists will be silent, but the voice of the Church of Christ would be loud, "Man is a spirit." The cry of the creatures was a spiritual act. The Church speaks truth, and if we are spirits we can understand it. What is it? There is one act of the spiritual life that to me is most true, and I can describe it in no better word than that the cry of the creatures is an aspiration. We have all felt aspiration some time or other. The boy is ever hoping for manhood, the man struggles on to middle life; yes!

and when he reaches the confines of old age there is still hope in him, kindled within in some dying embers of the fire of the past. We are ever looking to the future, aspiring always; there is a poetry about even the lowest and the basest if we can only get at it through the medium that surrounds him, as mediums surround all of us—conventionalism, fear of other people, pretence, respectability—that wrap us all around unless we keep near to God.

There is always the aspiration, the hope for better things. You read your newspaper each morning, as an ordinary English citizen, and take note of this or that advantage, amused sometimes when you see through the motive for doing the things you see done. You go to your prayers five minutes after, and think about what you have read as a Christian—the disasters, the sorrow that prevails everywhere, the struggles of passion, jealousy, self-seeking, misery that make up human existence and human history; and if you have a heart within you or a mind to think of it all in the light from beyond the confines of time, and you hope for something better than we dream of, you aspire for the coming of a moral world when all the crime and sin will be gone, when the scientific and commercial life shall be purified. The act of a spirit is aspiration. We have known what it is

"To rise on stepping-stones of our dead selves to higher things."

We have known too—and the Lord help us—more self-seeking, less lofty views, less pure determination as well as higher purposes. Our path begins in hope; possibly we have gone on to a middle life, and the path is strewed with dead leaves; but there yet may be within us a rising of hope, that is the first whisper of the hope of the glory, that there is a higher life, a better future, where not the lowest possessions but the highest faculties of man may find their satisfaction. That is an act of a living spirit. Now, most certainly the cry of the creatures was an act of spiritual life—to see, to understand, in some measure, the vision of Him who is the Beginning and the End of us all. Therefore, as they gazed aspiring and yet satisfied, satisfied and yet aspiring, rising more and more into the high thoughts of perfect brightness, goodness, holiness—and the beauty and the truth is lofty as the heavens and deep

T

as the deeps—they rose, as you and I may rise, day by day into better thoughts, more responsible power, more determined intention, purer, sincerer purposes; they were overwhelmed by the vision of His majesty, and they cried, "Holy, holy, holy, is the Lord of hosts." They lost themselves in Him, and that is what the Christian may do by His grace; they lost themselves in aspiration towards God.

There is only one more act of the creatures that I should like to notice. It was not only the exercise of an intellectual satisfaction, nor yet only the act of a spiritual life. No! it was that which touches us more closely, the cry of a warm embracing affection, of the heart of the creature to the Heart from which his life came.

Ah! surely none of us have sunk so low in lust or selfishness, or contemptible love of the world, as to have lost the sense of affection. Surely each of us knows something of what it is to love, to love others, and if we love others, to rise into the love of God. Well, if we do that we have got a kind of whispered thought of that eternal life, that view which is brought before us in the vision. It was an act of affection that loved God. It is like a picture of the human heart when it stands face to face with the dear dear friend, and remembers the future when it watches some strange vision in an open grave, and hopes for a resurrection. It is like a picture of the human heart in its better moments, its higher resolves, its sweeter visions; and like the cry of affection it teaches us, "O Lord! Thou art Holy, holy, holy! The whole earth is filled with Thy glory."

Now let us ask ourselves are there any lessons to be drawn from this, first about the soul, then about the Church?

First about the soul. Let us learn that a human soul, do what it may, can never do without God. Never in the long run. All the intellectual processes of scientific investigation, I may add all those imaginations of scientific poets which they sometimes put in place of fact, all the dreams of the scientists lead up to one distinguishing conclusion, that there is one great cause that they, the scientists do not quite understand. They cannot quite do without God. We cannot do without Him intellectually. Oh, believe me, the best way to find that out is to try it as the mathematicians try a problem, as we lads used to do at school. Where does your intellectual criticism land you if you try to do without God? Where? One of the Latin poets, the greatest of any age, to my mind, tried it. He put his striving doubting thoughts into poetry, he acknowledged that he had to forget the vision of the life and the death; and he landed himself in philosophic despair, where intellectual men have often since followed him. There can be certainly no other end to your argument of no God, but first despondency and then despair.

Try it where wealth and commerce and progress abound, in its highest circles as in its lowest. Oh, I am afraid we have, sometimes, practical testimony; I am afraid it lands you in pure materialism, which is only the hard language of earth to earth, ashes to ashes, dust to dust. It will only condemn your spirits' aspirations to confusion, dismay, corruption. There is something dignified in intellectual despair; there is nothing but what is debasing in materialism.

Try it another way. Ask yourselves what this great world would be without God—who impels the stately procession of the stars, who measures the circles of the winds, who watches the changing of the seasons? Try to reason to yourselves what is the reason and origin of the universe; ask yourselves, "How am I to admire all this beautiful *Cosmos*, this Order, this—what the old Greeks used to call God?" It lands you into the sense of an awful and prevailing force of pitiless laws, the crushing power of Everlasting Movement without a meaning, and the human will is crushed under the machinery of the universe. And you stand, like a lonely orphan creature, looking at the merciless mechanism, how it would snap your fingers off, tear you to pieces; for you have dismissed its Master—God.

Intellectual, scientific, material—none of these can do without Him. And if you cannot tell the reason for it, there is the intellectual satisfaction, the rest of the aspiration, of the creature, the object of the heart's affection; and it is all to be found in One, in whom is no spot, no blemish, across whom there passes no cloud, in whom is no darkness or shadow of turning, a Friend that never changes, a Father with loving tenderness, a Heart on which we may always rest, a dear Companion to whom we can always speak a word, One that leads us in commonplace work to higher things, that Saviour is the One that sustains us though we forget Him, the sweet, kind, gentle Nature who brings pardon and peace. Every one that gains faith to go to Him in His revelation in His own dear Son finds that He is holy, that "the whole earth is full of His glory."

There is material glory in the flashing heavens, there is moral glory in a good man's soul, there is supernatural glory in the mysteries and the acts of the Church, of the undying Mother Church.

Now what are the marks of the true Apostolic, historical Church? First, the reality. The creatures saw a real God, and they really worshipped Him. The Church always loves the reality. There is another mark of the true Church, and it is that she never talks about a supernatural Word, as if it were supposed to be sometimes interesting, sometimes useful or profitable, but that there is nothing real about it—as if there were a doubt about it, sometimes holy and sometimes not. Your principles are not those at all. The Church is definite when she teaches, like her Master. The life and the words of Jesus were definite, not like so-called modern Christianity.

If we have the certain belief in the existence of an immortal spirit, quite definite though invisible, each with joys and sorrows of our own, we can realize that justice is not done in this world, and that therefore there must be a better country; each of us knows that love has no frontiers and that there must be an Eternal City; and that the Church, like the cry of the creatures, points to the future. "The whole earth shall be filled with His glory"; but it does not always show its light, it is also full of darkness; the creatures were speaking of a future as if it were accomplished, for they were gazing upon the coming glory.

Ah! remember your God! your relation to Him. The tones of your Church must be like the Old Testament harmonies of the Church. And remember, it is quite practical work when you are at church, or at your prayers, commemorating the sacrifice of Calvary, listening to the words of truth, worshipping God. And when you are doing that you are not wasting time. What are called practical men,—that is, materialistic men,—think they waste time if they are with God.

Remember, the moments that you spend in prayer, in contemplating Scripture, in worship, are fruitful for eternity. You must not be contented with doing this for yourselves. You must be apostles, you must get others to love God, to perform duty, to seek to fulfil your conviction. That is *living* God. That is climbing up to the love of God; and remember that as the creatures could gaze on His glory, you and I can gaze on His humanity. Jesus, the founder of the Sacraments, the Friend of humanity, the Author of the Bible, the Builder of broken hearts, the great Sacrifice for our iniquity,—He is the Revealer of that awful vision.

Why? He loved lost women, and saved them; little children He loved, and He saved them; despised not the rich man, but corrected him. He gathered young and old to Him by the beauty of His goodness. He was always young although growing old, always fresh although the centuries have travelled on. And you and I look at Him in the midst of our sins, weakness, sorrows; you and I lean on Jesus with our breaking hearts and our despairing fancies; you and I follow His example, trying to do our duty, to fulfil our vocation, to be kind and tender and true and faithful, large of heart, generous, forgiving, patient. You and I are doing, are we not? something like that. We see the Godhead then when we look at Him and worship Him. Oh! live for God; make your church worthy of Him; make your offerings worthy of God; try to follow the example of God in Christ; then you will feel your own unworthiness, your own misery in life and in time. But you will feel this certainly and assuredly, that you can look up, with the creatures, in intellectual satisfaction, with the spirit's aspiration, with the love of the heart of the creature, on Him the Creator. You may cry, "O my God! my Saviour! Thou art awful and holy, but Thou art a Man and a Brother, a Friend, a Helper. I am broken-hearted, sin-stricken; help me to come to Jesus, to persevere in following Him, to attain to Him; that we may each attain to His blessed side." And when we wake up with Jesus, after this world of weary conflict, we shall indeed be satisfied in Him.

W. J. K. L.

XXXIV. The Vision of the Dry Bones. EZEK. xxxvii. 3. *"And He said unto me, Son of man, can these bones live? And I answered, O Lord God, Thou knowest."*

THOSE who have read the book of the Prophet Ezekiel—and it is perhaps less read than any other book in the Old Testament—will remember this vision of the dry bones. Like many other visions before and since, it is partly shaped by the circumstances of the times. The horrors of the Chaldean invasion, which had resulted in carrying away the Jewish people into Babylon, were still fresh in the memories of men. In many a valley, on many a hill-side in Southern Palestine, the track of the invading army as it advanced and retired would have been marked by the bones of the unoffending but slaughtered peasantry. In a work written some years ago, Mr. Layard has described such a scene in Armenia, an upland valley, covered by the bones of the Christian population who had been plundered and murdered by Kurds. Such a scene may well have suggested to Ezekiel that the vision was so shaped as to express a truth which Israel needed to know. Ezekiel, wrapped in a spiritual ecstasy, was set down in a valley that was full of bones. He was gazing upon them round about, he marked their great number, he marked their dryness. They were the bones of a multitude of men who had been slain long since. He was asked by the Divine Being, with whom he was the while in close communion, "Son of man, can these bones live?" Ezekiel knew that nothing was impossible with God; he knew too, that what was possible might be forbidden by necessities, by laws of which he knew nothing, and he reverently answered, "O Lord God, Thou knowest," and forthwith he was made the instrument through which the question which had been put to him was answered. "He said unto me, Prophesy upon these bones, and say unto them, O ye dry bones, hear the word of the Lord. Thus saith the Lord God unto these bones; Behold, I will cause breath to enter into you, and ye shall live: and I will lay sinews upon you, and will bring up flesh upon you, and cover you with skin, and put breath in you, and ye shall live; and ye shall know that I am the Lord." And then Ezekiel continues: "So I prophesied as I was commanded: and as I prophesied, there was a noise, and behold a shaking, and the bones came together, bone to his bone. And when I beheld, lo, the sinews and the flesh came upon them, and the skin covered them above: but there was no breath in them." That was the first stage of the revival; it was still incomplete, something more was needed, something which the prophet goes on to describe. "Then said He unto me, Prophesy unto the wind, prophesy, son of man, and say to the wind, Thus saith the Lord God; Come from the four winds, O breath, and breathe upon these slain, that they may live." Then he continues: "So I prophesied as He commanded me, and the breath came into them, and they lived, and stood up upon their feet, an exceeding great army." That was the second stage of the revival, and it is followed by the explanation or purpose of the vision.

But let us at this point ask ourselves the question, what are we to understand by the dry bones of the vision of Ezekiel. The dry bones of Ezekiel's vision are doubtless, to begin with, the bones of human bodies, bones from which all the flesh had been completely stripped or decayed away through exposure to the air. Ezekiel beholds the working of God upon these bones, he sees them again clothed with flesh, with sinews, and finally the breath comes into them, and they live, they stand on their feet. This is plainly a picture of a resurrection, not, indeed, of the general resurrection, because what Ezekiel saw was clearly limited and local, but at the same time it is a sample of what will occur at the general resurrection, and on this ground the passage is regarded by the Church as a proper lesson for Easter Tuesday. It may be urged that this representation is presently explained to refer to something quite distinct—namely the restoration of the Jewish people from Babylon, and, therefore, that what passed before the prophet's eye need not have been regarded by him as more than an imaginary or even impossible occurrence intending to symbolise a coming event. But if this were the case, the vision, it must be said, was very ill adapted for its proposed purpose. The idea of the restoration from Babylon was humanly, or politically speaking, sufficiently improbable already, without heightening its existing improbability by what is then supposed to have been a greater improbability still. Men do not learn to accept difficult or unfamiliar truths through the assistance of truth still more unfamiliar, still more difficult. The fact is, that the form of Ezekiel's vision, and the popular use which Ezekiel made of it, shows that at this date the idea of the resurrection of the body could not have been a strange one to religious views. Had it been so Ezekiel's vision would have been turned against him. The restoration from the captivity would have been thought more improbable than ever if the measure of its improbability was to be found in a doctrine unbelieved in as yet by the people of revelation. We know, in fact, from their own Scriptures, that the Jews had had for many a century, glimpses more or less distinct of this truth. Long ago the mother of Samuel could sing that the Lord bringeth down to the grave and bringeth up; and Job could be sure that though worms destroy his body yet in his flesh he would see God; and David, speaking for a Higher Being than himself, yet knows that God will not leave His soul in hell, nor suffer His Holy One to see corruption; and Daniel, Ezekiel's contemporary, or nearly so, foresees that many who "sleep in the dust of the earth shall awake, some to everlasting life, and some to shame and everlasting contempt;" and later on the courageous mother of the seven Maccabean martyrs cries to her dying sons that "the Creator of the world, who formed the generations of men, and thought out the beginning of all things, will also of His mercy give you life and breath again, if you regard not yourselves for His sake." Undoubtedly there was among the Jews a certain belief in the resurrection of the body, a belief which this very vision must have at once represented and confirmed. Men shrink from admitting the idea that there will be a resurrection of the dead, on the ground mainly that it involves an exertion of Divine power to which nothing exactly corresponds within the range of everyday experience. Whether it is quite right to make the range of our experience the measure of what God can do may be more than questionable, but at least the doctrine of the resurrection of all men from the dead involves no greater difficulty for a thoughtful man than that which he already encounters, if he believes seriously in God at all. For belief in God involves as a necessary part of itself a belief in the creation of the universe out of nothing. However you may multiply the centuries during which man is supposed to have existed on the surface of this planet; however vast may be the common tracks of time which you may demand as theoretically necessary to fill up the interval between some primary chaos and man's first appearance on the scene; say what you will about the date of the solar system, or of the fixed stars, or of the presumable history of their evolution, still in the last resort, in the rear of these theories amid which the scientific imagination may run such splendid riot, the question of questions awaits your answer, it cannot be ignored, it cannot be eluded—how did the original matter out of which all that we see around us itself took shape, how did this originally come to be? That is the question into which all others ultimately resolve themselves, and upon the answer which is given to it depends no less an issue than belief or disbelief in the existence of God. For if you say that original uniform unevolved matter always existed, then you deny the existence of the Being whom we call God. God is nothing if He is not alone everlasting, if He is not the source of all else that is, if He is not in His essence altogether spiritually immaterial. If there existed an everlasting side by side with God, a something which you call matter which is not Himself, which is in its essence distinct from Himself, which did not owe its existence to Him, and which, as being itself presumably eternal, contradicts the first law in nature as the source of all that is besides Himself, then God the Creator of all things has no existence. But if, having on dependent grounds a clear and strong belief in God, you deny as you must deny the eternity of matter, then you must trace the origin of the raw material out of which this universe has been fashioned, in whatever way, back to God. How did it come from Him? If it escaped from Him,—and what would be this escape of matter from the immaterial?—if it escaped from Him without or against His will, then He is no longer master, not merely of His creation but of Himself.

Being God, He must have summoned it into being by the free act of His free will. There is nothing out of which to frame it and therefore He must have summoned it out of nothing. There was vacancy, and He bade the rude elements, of matter to begin to be. It was something to fashion man out of the existing dust of the earth, but to give existence to the dust of the earth when as yet there was nothing, was an infinite exercise of power. Think, my brethren, think what this means, creation out of nothing, that act which every thinking and sincere believer in God must necessarily credit Him with, and then compare it with the relatively puny difficulties which we are told ought to arrest the hand of the Great Creator on the day of the general resurrection. It is not for us to trace His methods of procedure by audacious guesses, or to say how He will restore to each human body such of its proper materials as may have drifted away into subtle connection with other forms; but this I take it is certain to any reasonable man, that no difficulties about the resurrection of the body can seriously suspend our belief in it if we do believe already in God as really God, that is as the Creator, and believe further that He has told us that He will one day raise the bodies of all men from the dead.

Ezekiel's vision, then, may remind us of what Christ our Lord has taught us again and again in His own words of the resurrection of the body. But its teaching by no means ends with this. For the dry bones of Ezekiel's vision may well represent the conditions of societies of men at particular times in their history, the condition of nations, of Churches, of less important institutions. Indeed, Ezekiel as we have seen was left in no kind of doubt about the divinely intended meaning of his vision. The dry bones were pictures of what the Jewish nation believed itself to be, as a consequence of the captivity in Babylon. All that was left of it could be best compared to the bones of the Jews which had been massacred by the Chaldean invader, and which bleached the hillsides of Palestine. "He said unto me, These bones are the whole house of Israel: behold, they say, Our bones are dried, and our hope is lost: we are cut off." Certainly, in the captivity little was left of Israel beyond the skeleton of its former self. There were the sacred books, there were royal descendants of the race of

Jacob, there were priests, there were prophets, there was the old Hebrew and sacred language not yet wholly corrupted into Chaldean, there were precious traditions of the past great days of Jerusalem,—these were the dry bones of what had been earlier. There was nothing to animate them, they lay on the soil of heathenism, they lay apart from each other as if quite unconnected. The form of the representation changes as the explanation succeeds the vision. They now lay buried beneath the soil, beneath the thick layer of Pagan life, of Pagan worship, of Pagan oppression, of Pagan vice, which buried them out of sight. To the captive people Babylon was not merely a valley of dry bones, but socially and politically it was fatal to the corporate life of Israel—Babylon was a grave; accordingly the prophet was desired to address his countrymen: "Thus saith the Lord God; Behold, O my people, I will open your graves, and cause you to come up out of your graves, and bring you into the land of Israel. And ye shall know that I am the Lord, when I have opened your graves, O my people, and brought you up out of your graves." And this is what actually did happen at the restoration of the Jews from Babylon. Each of the promises in Ezekiel's vision was fulfilled. The remains of the past history, its sacred books, its priests, its prophets, its laws, its great traditions, its splendid hopes, these once more moved in the soul of the nation as if with the motion of reviving life. They came together, they were readjusted into an harmonious whole, they received the clothing of bone and sinew which originally belonged to them. And the nation, thus reconstructed in the days of its captivity, was lifted by the Divine power out of its grave, and restored to the upper air of its ancient Temple in Palestine. It was a wonderful restoration, almost if not altogether unique in history. We see it in progress in the 119th Psalm, which doubtless belongs to this period, which exhibits the upward struggle of a sincere and beautiful soul at the first dawn of the national resurrection, and we read of its completion in the books of Ezra and Nehemiah; it was completed when the Temple, the centre of the spiritual and national life, was fully rebuilt, and when the whole life of the people in its completeness was thus renewed in the spot which had been the home of their fathers from generation to generation.

And something of the same kind has been seen in portions of the Christian Church. As a whole, we know the Church of Christ cannot fail, the gates of hell shall not prevail against it; but particular Churches may fail in their different degrees,— national Churches, provincial Churches, local Churches. These, like the Seven Churches in Asia, which stands as a warning for all the ages of Christendom, these may experience their varying degrees of corruption and ruin and the moral insensibility which precedes death. So it was with the Church of Rome long ago even as the tenth century. Those who know the history of that century know that no man could ever have violated the spirit and the law of Christ more flagrantly than did the rulers of the Roman Church in that dark and miserable age, and yet this age was succeeded by a striking moral and religious restoration. And so it has been, though in a somewhat different sense, with the Church of England, and more than once since the Reformation.

When John Keble entered upon the work of his life, the Church of England was to a considerable extent in the condition which answered to Ezekiel's vision of the valley of dry bones. She had succeeded to a splendid inheritance, but she understood her privileges very imperfectly. In large numbers of people the higher and nobler sides of the Christian life, its pathos, its fulness, its risks, its strength, its capacities for heroism, its capacities for sacrifice, its great power derived from communion with the unseen, and its magnificent prospects had dwarfed down to insignificance—all that lifts above the eye of sense—these had been forgotten. Then the kingdom of heaven had come to the Church almost as one of the kingdoms of this world. The episcopate was merely a form of Church government approved of by the State in this part of the Empire; the sacraments were old ceremonies, pleasing as a religious sentiment, but very far indeed from being necessary to salvation; the Bible was a most venerable book, but nobody knew what presently would be said of it; and as for the Prayer-Book, it was described as a human compilation just three hundred years old. Think of the case of a soul which might hope from the echoes of the Gospel reaching down the centuries, when a home had been found for it on earth—a home in which its sorrows may be consoled and its aspirations encouraged, and then wending its way into the Church which had so largely forgotten its first love as this. There are those still living who can say what has happened to such souls in that dreary period; but it was the high privilege of the man whom we are thinking of, more perhaps than any other man, to bring the remedy. Not from any position which of itself commanded attention, but as relying on the native course of duty and majesty of truth, he published a collection of poems, unwillingly enough, which has had more effect than a thousand volumes of a more pretentious character. Nobody could think less highly of "The Christian Year" than did its humbleminded author; and it was, in the judgment of very competent judges, inferior as poetry to other works of his pen, it was merely fugitive, it was careless of finish, it was indistinct, it was hard to be understood by those who had not the key to understand it. It was eminently a book which was not made, but grew, and it was marked by the rude irregularities of growth as distinct from the polish and the finish of mere manufacture. But underneath its language, above and beyond its literary faults, whatever they were, there was a subtle, fine, penetrating, I may almost dare to say a Divine spirit, which told of the religious genius of the spirit of its author, and which has renewed the face of the Church of England. It breathed through this book upon the dry bones around it, it clothed once more the chief pastors of the Church in the garb of Apostles, it traced beneath the Sacraments an inward grace which unites to Christ, which supplied the point of view for reading the sacred Scriptures intelligently, yet as an inspired whole and with a constant sense of their profound and unfathomable meaning. It lighted up the Prayer-Book as a beautiful relic of the past work of the Primitive Church, upon which the sixteenth century, while removing blemishes and corruptions, has after all only lightly laid its hand. It did this after such a fashion that at least we can understand it. Even yet we are too near the date of the publication of this book to take the correct measure of all that it has done for the Christian Church, but we can see enough to be sure that through it breathed the breath of Heaven by which dying Churches are renewed, by which the dry bones of past ages of faith and love are again clothed upon with the substance of life.

And some of us may have noted a like resurrection in some institution, neither as defined as a Church nor yet so broad or inclusive as a nation, in a school, a college, a hospitable, a charitable building, a company. It is the creation, it is the relic of a distant age, it is magnificent in its picturesqueness, it lacks alone nothing but life. It persists in statutes that are no longer observed, it observes ceremonies and customs which have lost their meaning, it constantly holds to a phraseology which tells of a past time and of which the object has been forgotten. But certain it is in each year its members meet, they go through the accustomed usages, they signalise their meeting it may be by splendid banquets, by commanding oratory, but in their heart of hearts they know they are meeting in a valley of dry bones. The old rules, usages, phrases, dresses, these are scattered around them like the bones of Ezekiel's vision, a life which, once animated and clothed, has long since perished away. They lie apart, without connection with each other, without attempt at arrangement, without the decencies of order, and the question is, who shall bring them together, who shall restore to them movement and power, who shall clothe them with flesh and blood, and make them once more what they might be? But we can think, it may be, of cases where a man has appeared who, instead of contemptuously sweeping away all that the past has left, sets himself to arrange, to combine, it may be to reconstruct, sets himself, above all, to invoke that Divine Spirit, life, and grace which alone can restore life to the dead and inaugurate a moral and social resurrection. Before he began his work the thought came, "Can these bones live?" but believing in God who is the resurrection as well as the author of life, whether moral or physical, he went forward. It was enough for him to say, "O Lord God, Thou knowest," and he heard not long after the Divine voice saying, "Son of man, prophesy unto the breath, and say, O breath, come into these bones, that they may live."

Lastly, the dry bones of Ezekiel's vision may be discovered, and that not seldom, within the human soul. When the soul has lost its hold of truth or grace, when it has ceased to believe or ceased to love all the traces of what it once has been, do not forthwith despair. There are survivals of the old believing life, fragments and skeletons of the old affection, bits of stray logic which once created phrases that express the feeling which once won to prayers ; there may remain amid the arid desolation of every valley full of dry bones the aspirations which have no goal, the actions which have no real basis, no practical consequences, the friendships which we feel to be holy and which are still kept up, the habits which have lost all meaning ; we meet with writers, with talkers, with historians, with poets whose language shows that they have once known what it is to believe, but for whom all living faith has perished utterly and left behind it only these dried-up relics of its former life. Such may be the case—partially at least—of some who hear me, such a case must suggest the solemn question—" Can these bones live?" Can these phrases, these forms, these habits, and these associations which once were part of the spirit life, can they ever again become what they were? Is it worth while to treasure them? Were it not better, were it not more sincere, to have done with them altogether, to disavow what we no longer mean, to abandon habits of devotion which have become for us only forms, to break with practices of piety or benevolence which are only due now to the surviving force of habit? Why keep up this charnel place of the past? why not clear it out and begin afresh with some such new life as may now be possible? Brethren, it is better now, believe me, to respect the dry bones, though they are only the dry bones, for they have their value in that they witness to the living past, for they have their value in that they point to a possible restoration in the future. It is easy enough to decry religious habit as only habit, as motiveless, soulless, unaccepted service. Doubtless habit which is only habit is not life, but it is better, I dare say, than nothing at all, better if not in itself, yet surely for the sake of that which it may lead on to. A man may have ceased to mean his prayers, his prayers may now be but the dry bones of that warm and loving communion which he once held with his God; but do not let him on that account give them up, do not let him break with the little that remains of what once was life. It is easy enough to decry habit, but habit may be the scaffolding which saves us from a great fall, habit may be the arch which bridges over a chasm which yawns between one height and another on our upward road ; habit without motive is sufficiently unsatisfactory, but habit is better, better far, than nothing. Some of us it may be, surveying the shrivelled elements of our religious life, cannot avoid the question which comes in upon us from Heaven, "Can these bones live?" they seem to us, even in our best moments, so hopelessly dislocated, so dry, so dead; but to this question the answer must always be, "O Lord God, Thou knowest." Yes, He does know ; He sees, as He saw of old into the grave of Lazarus ; He sees as He saw into the tomb of the Lord Jesus ; so He sees into the crypts of a soul of whose faith and love only these dry bones remain, and He knows that life is again possible—ay, that it is much more than possible, that the Word of His power may again clothe with form and with flesh, the breath of His Spirit may again impart animation, warmth, movement, life, the quickening power of Christ's Resurrection, from which all recovery, whether moral or social or physical, must go forth,—this may assert itself victoriously in that desert soul, so that, like as Christ Himself was raised up from the dead in the glory of the Father, even so this soul shall walk in newness of life.

H. P. L.

XXXV. Nebuchadnezzar. Daniel iv. 37. "*Those that walk in pride He is able to abase.*"

THESE are the words of King Nebuchadnezzar on his restoration from the deepest fall, from the most fearful exile, that ever befel one of the children of men. The chapter which records it is one of the most eloquent, one of the most pathetic chapters in the Bible. There is inspiration in the sound. If it were an allegory, if it were a parable, if it were a poem, it would still have the breath of God in it. We believe it to be history. We are not of those who think lightly of the testimony of the Bible till it can bring profane evidence to corroborate it. Well may it be said of many of the records of the Old Testament Scriptures, "If these should hold their peace the very stones would cry out." Again and again the stones have cried out, to an incredulous generation, in proof of a discredited Bible and a forgotten God. Inscriptions of which the very language had been lost for ages have yielded themselves to the patient toil of modern discoverers, to the laborious induction of modern philologists, and have confirmed the Word of God in Scripture by an unsuspicious and unquestionable voice from the deserts and ruins, from the very dens and caves of the earth. If it has not yet been quite so with the particulars of the mysterious eclipse and new splendour of the magnificent king, whose destiny it was, in so many ways, to cross the path of the theocratic people, and thus to secure for himself unawares a share in the immortality of the Bible, we can still believe that somewhere in the hidden archives there may exist such a confirmation to be revealed in due time of Him with whom "a thousand years are as one day;" and if not, the Bible record, alone and unsupported, shall suffice for us: the dream and the interpretation, the proud boast from the palace roof, and the voice from heaven sentencing it, the alienation and aberration of the reason, the banishment from the society of men, till humiliation has had its perfect work, at last the return of the understanding, and with it of the glory of the kingdom, and the tribute paid by the despot and the polytheist to the supreme power of the King of heaven, all whose works are truth, and His ways judgment, whose hand none can stay, nor say to Him, "What doest Thou?"

A man of great name in the Church of England, whose recent departure, in the fulness of days and of good works, has been the signal for an outburst of promiscuous and somewhat indiscriminating panegyric, from a wider circle than that of his own party and following, chose this book of the prophet Daniel some twenty years ago, to quote his own words, as the subject of his contribution against that tide of scepticism which a particular publication had, in his opinion, let loose upon the young and uninstructed In his preface to that volume of lectures he used one expression with which I think we shall all be in sympathy. "This has been," he says, "for some thirty years a deep conviction of my soul—that no book can be written in behalf of the Bible like the Bible itself. Men's defences are men's words: they may help to beat off attacks; they may draw out some portion of its meaning; the Bible is God's Word: through it God the Holy Ghost speaks to the soul which closes not itself against it. Let us hear that Word in one of its most searching, humbling utterances: "Those that walk in pride God is able to abase."

I. *Pride and vanity.* In one of our famous English universities an annual sermon is preached on "Pride." No one will say that once a year is too often for a congregation, young and old, to be bidden to meditate on that thesis. I propose it to you to-day, not being so presumptuous as to think of preaching it in a formal manner by definitions and divisions more suitable to the lecture-room, but proposing to draw one or two reflections upon it from the history here opened before us, and to ask of you that spirit of self-application, without which, on such a subject, we speak and we hear in vain.

We see introduced abruptly, for it seems to be the turning point of the whole, that appearance of the great king walking in his palace of Babylon, and saying, whether to himself or in the hearing of his courtiers does not appear, "Is not this great Babylon, that I have builded by the might of my power, and for the honour of my majesty?"

Many learned things have been said and written upon the nature and essence of pride. Probably none of them could equal in depth and impressiveness this account of pride-speaking, this repeated pronoun, the personal and the possessive: "Great Babylon, that *I* have builded by the might of *my* power, and for the honour of *my* majesty." Whatever other definitions may be given of pride, certainly this is true of it, that it is the contemplation of self, a concentration in self, the having self in the throne of the being, as the one object of attention, of observation, of consideration, always, everywhere, and in all things.

It is often assumed that this attention given to self is of necessity the contemplation of supposed excellence, that it is therefore, so far as it is characteristic of pride, of the nature of self-complacency, or self-admiration, and yet some of the proudest of men have been at the very antipodes of self-satisfaction.

It is the very consciousness of their own deformity, moral or physical, of their own inferiority in some prized or coveted particular of birth, gift, or grace, which has driven them in upon themselves in an unlovely and unloving isolation. Self-complacency is not the only form of pride. It is doubtful whether that self-complacency does not rather belong to the very different title of vanity. A beggar may be proud; a cripple may be proud; failure takes refuge in pride—even moral failure, the experience of perpetual defeat in that life-battle with which no stranger intermeddles. Pride is self-contemplation, but not necessarily self-admiration; self-absorption, but not necessarily self-adoration.

It is not quite evident from the words of King Nebuchadnezzar whether his besetting sin was pride or vanity. Something may turn upon the unanswerable question whether he thought or whether he spoke the " Is not this great Babylon?" I think that vanity always speaks. I doubt if the vain man ever keeps his vanity to himself. I am sure that pride can be silent; I am not sure that pride as pride ever speaks. If I would ascertain which of the two was Nebuchadnezzar's failing, I should look rather to the hints dropped first in the judgment upon him, and then in the account of the recovery. From the one I learn that what he had to be taught was that "the heavens do rule;" from the other I learn that he then first praised and honoured Him that liveth for ever. This decides me that, however pride and vanity may have mingled (if they ever do mingle) in his composition, pride was the differentia; that pride which contemplates self as the all in all of life and being, not necessarily as beautiful, or perfect, or happy; not necessarily as satisfactory, either in circumstance or in character, but as practically independent of all above and all below it—the one object of importance, and interest, and devotion; knowing neither a superior to reverence, nor an inferior to regard. Vanity, though, or perhaps because, a poorer or meaner thing, is also a shallower thing, and less vital. Vanity may still be kind, a charity. Vanity may stil love and be loved. Vanity, I had almost said, and I will say it, vanity may still worship. Vanity does not absolutely need to be taught the great lesson that "the Most High rules in the kingdom of men," or "does according to His will in the army of heaven." Pride and vanity both ask, " Is not this great Babylon?" but vanity asks it for applause from below, pride asks it in disdain of One above.

But in all this, brethren, we may not have found our own likeness. There may be some, there may be many, here present who are not by natural temperament either proud or vain ; and yet when I think once again what pride is, I doubt whether any one is born without it. We may not dwell complacently upon our own merits. Certainly we may not be guilty of the weakness and the bad taste which would parade those supposed merits before others. Pride itself often casts out vanity, and refuses to make itself ridiculous by saying aloud, " Is not this great Babylon ? "

But the question is not whether we are self-admirers, but whether we are self-contemplators ; not whether we are conceited in our estimate of gifts or graces, in our retrospect of attainments or successes, in our consciousness of power, or our supposition of greatness ; but whether, on the contrary, we have constantly in our remembrance the derivation and the responsibility, and the accountableness of all that we have and are ; whether there is a higher presence and a diviner being always in our view, making it impossible to admire or to adore that self which is so feeble and so contemptible in comparison ; whether we are so in the habit of asking ourselves the two questions: "What hast thou which thou hast not received?" and "What hast thou for which thou shalt not give an account?" as to maintain always the attitude of worship, the attitude of devotion within, and this superscription ever upon the doors and gates of the spiritual being, "Whose I am and whom I serve."

II. *God's judgment on pride.* We have formed now from the history perhaps some idea of pride. We have heard what pride says to itself in the secrecy of its solitude. The same history shall suggest another thought or two about it, and the first of these is its penal, its judicial isolation. "They shall drive thee from men." We are not going to explain away the literal, or at least the substantial fulfilment of this prophecy. Though it would be untrue to say that medical history furnishes a complete illustration of the judgment threatened and executed upon King Nebuchadnezzar, yet medical history does afford a sufficient likeness of it to render the fact, not credible only, for that its being written in the Bible would make it, but approximately intelligible. Some grievous forms of insanity in which the sufferer finds himself transfigured, in imagination at least, into an irrational creature, of which he adopts the actions and gestures, the tones and the habits, under which, in that harsh and cruel treatment of madness, from which even kings down to our own age were not exempt, the dweller in a palace might find himself exiled from the society and companionship of men. Something of this kind may seem to be indicated in this touching and thrilling description, and the use now to be made of it requires no more than this brief and general recognition of the particulars of the history from which it is drawn. He was driven from men: the Nemesis of pride is isolation. The proud man is placed alone in the universe, even while he dwells in a home. This is a terrible feature; this is the condemning brand of that self-contemplation, that self-concentration, that self-absorption, which we have thought to be the essence of pride. The proud man is driven by his own act, even before judgment speaks, if not from the presence, if not from the companionship, at least from the sympathy of his fellows. This isolation of heart and soul is the Cain-like mark set upon the unnaturalness of the spirit which it punishes. No sooner is self made the idol, than it shuts the windows of the inner being alike against God above and man below. "They shall drive thee from men." Thou hast driven thyself from God!

Another thought comes to us out of the history. Mark the words describing the recovery: "Mine understanding returned unto me; my reason returned unto me." What was the first use of it? "I blessed the Most High; I praised and honoured Him that liveth for ever." It is deeply interesting to notice, and it fully accords with the observations of medical men, that the return of reason is here prefaced by a lifting up of the eyes to heaven as though in quest of reconciliation and recognition. Yes, prayer is no stranger to the hospitals and asylums of the insane. Very pathetic is the worship offered within the the walls of those chapels which modern humanity and modern science have combined to append everywhere to the once disconsolate homes of the disordered and deranged intellect. "I lifted up mine eyes unto heaven, and then mine understanding returned to me."

Our moral is, the pride which will not worship is of itself

an insanity. Worship is the rational attitude of the creature towards the Creator. Pride, dreaming of independence; pride, placing self where God ought to be; pride, telling of the Babylon which it has builded; refusing to recognise any being above or below external to it, yet possessing claims upon it, is a non-natural condition. Before it can recover intellect it must look upward. The first sign of that recovery will be the acknowledgment of the Eternal.

We have yet one word, and it is that of the text itself: "Those that walk in pride He is able to abase." Nebuchadnezzar puts it into his proclamation of thanksgiving: "Now I Nebuchadnezzar praise and extol and honour the King of heaven, all whose works are truth, and His ways judgment: and those that walk in pride He is able to abase." King Nebuchadnezzar knew it by experience: he had lived in ignorance, he had lived in defiance of it, he had reaped as he had sown, he had walked in pride, he had been driven from men. "Seven times had passed over him." Not till he lifted his eyes to heaven, not till he knew that self was not all, did reason return to him. Honour and brightness came back with it. His counsellors and his lords sought him. We in England know, by tradition at least, what the rejoicings are when a monarch recovers his understanding, though there may have been no judgment in that insanity which was the calamity and the sorrow of an earlier generation of Englishmen. Nebuchadnezzar may have meant only to enthrone the God of heaven as one God, though the chief God, of the crowded Pantheon. That is nothing to us now. We can read his words and put our own construction: "Those that walk in pride He is able to abase." Solemn, awful, terrible confession; verified day by day in history, not modern only, but of to-day! How often in our experience has a proud man, quite apart from act or deed of his own, found himself under a treatment but too nicely calculated to humble him! How often has a rich man, building his house on the winnings of chance or of speculation, found to his discomfiture that he has built it upon the sand! How often has a selfish man, having but one tender spot or two in his whole moulding and making, staked his very life, we will say, upon two well-beloved sons, and then found, to use the Scripture similitude, that he has "laid the foundation of his prosperity in the first-born and set up the gates thereof in the younger," to see them cut off successively in the very moment of triumph by sharp sickness or by sudden accident! How often has a professional man, on the eve of the last step to greatness, developed some fatal symptoms of palsy, or consumption, which made him bid farewell to all his glory, and betake himself to his last gloomy home! How often has a statesman, brought by the last turn of the wheel of politics to the very summit of his ambition, been laid low by the importunate stroke of a jealous and envious rivalry, and compelled to exchange earth for the melancholy Pantheon of posthumous fame!

But, brethren, these are great cases, illustrious examples. Let us descend to our own level. "Those that walk in pride" are of all ranks, and the possible abasement also has all ranks for its victims. Who shall tell the mortifications of pride which befal it? Every day of pride is a day of disappointment. The thousands and tens of thousands who are living without God in the world, self-contemplating, self-concentrating on the smallest and most microscopic scale, offering to their idol, self, the poorest and humblest of oblations—the mere chance invitation to dinner, or supper, of the mortal creature man or woman that is but one half-step above them on the social ladder, or the hollow, unmeant compliment of one whose blame would have been more honourable ; what a life of abasement is theirs, themselves almost being the judges! How many slights for one salute! How many rebuffs for one recognition! What a life! Abasement is the word for it, even in its triumphs. That climbing itself is grovelling—that pushing is itself repulse.

But instead of dwelling upon the shame and contempt of all this, let us think rather of the merciful design which works in it. This king, this lord of the world's empire that then was, is thrust down from his throne, driven from men, made "to eat grass like the ox till seven times pass over him." You would call this a cruel and pitiless fate for him. You would say that there was nothing but punishment, nothing but judgment in it. But so did not he. When his reason returned to him, he praised and blessed God for his humiliation. He knew now that "the heavens do rule." Men and women walking in pride, having self for your aim, and self for your idol, pray God to break that idol in pieces before your face. Pray God to make you know and feel that "the heavens do rule." That is humility, the opposite and antithesis of pride, not to think abjectly of self, but to have a loving consciousness of One greater, and better, and nobler.

Is not that a lesson worth any sacrifice, or any suffering in the learning? What would earth be if each form of flesh and blood were self-centred, and self-absorbed, elbowing its own way to the rewards, and luxuries, and the honours of earth? Where, then, would be either piety or charity, where the sweet harmonies of souls at peace with God, where the gracious influence of hearts, loving and loved? Let us not resent, let us rather invite that abasing which brings back the walker in pride to a truer understanding of himself and of his position. What hour of earth is comparable to that in its sense of reality, and in its consciousness of safety, which has made us feel that all we have and all we are is of God alone, and that He of His infinite love and mercy has taken us for His forgiven children in Jesus Christ, all our sins laid upon Him, and an inheritance of joy and glory reserved for us in heaven?

Brethren, one depth of uttermost abasement there is before each of us. It is the hour of death; it is the day of judgment. The very approach of that hour is humiliation; the gradual decay of the brightness of the intellect, the slow recollection, the faltering speech, the growing tardiness of step and motion, at last the absolute helplessness, the stretching forth of the hands for another to guide, and then the being bound hand and foot by another with graveclothes, the being carried forth stiff and stupid, and laid with our forefathers to see corruption. How shall mortal man be proud for whom this is the last exit? But oh, to wake up in a world unrealized, amidst countless generations clad in bodies, not natural but spiritual, to find ourselves face to face with a Saviour never before known, or capable of being known, in His glory, who is now ready to confess or deny us according as we in that former state of being have confessed or denied Him! How shall mortal man be proud before whom lies this dread ordeal? Happy is he who has so accepted here the Divine abasing that he may receive there the benediction which has all honour and all exaltation in it, "Blessed are the poor in spirit, for theirs is the kingdom of heaven."

C. J. V.

XXXVI. Daniel among the Lions. DANIEL vi. 22.
"My God hath sent His angel, and hath shut the lions' mouths, that they have not hurt me."

Try to realize old Babylon. Try to spirit your thoughts from this place to that, from this time to that. That great and glowing wonder we can hardly believe was ever alive when we wander with step or with thought over the secrecy and the silence and the darkness of the spot where the glory once lived. But now, forget familiar faces and familiar voices, and live back in that Babylon, and try to feel as if you were there at the time when Daniel was alive.

If you are making that effort of imagination, if you are ready, I ask you now to go with me first into a royal palace there and watch the workings of a strange conspiracy; in the next place, I would ask you to go to a private house there, to see the object of that conspiracy; and next I ask you to go look at the lions' den, to see the end of that conspiracy.

I. The conspirators. First go to the palace. Who is the king? An old forgotten king. I say forgotten, for he would not be owned now if he had not happened to keep lions, and if there had not happened to be present near him some who wanted to make those lions terrible instruments of death to Daniel. He was a most mean king. He was nothing in himself. There was no nobility; there was no kinghood in him. He was only circumstantially conspicuous; he was essentially obscure. His little name comes down the stream of time on the raft of Daniel's story. Crown though he wore, and a sceptre though he wielded, he was only an incidental creature—a tool, not an agent; a thing, not a man. Why, we are not even sure that his name was Darius. There is no unanimous and absolute certainty of vote on that subject, for

Darius is not the name of an individual; it is not a personal name, but an official name. We just know from historical notices of him that he was a sensualist, and nothing stamps the spark divine out of a man like sensuality. There was once an epitaph written—a "Sybarite Epitaph." It was said of a man that he could eat well, and drink well, and sleep well, and he died. That might have been his epitaph. I will not dwell upon him. It seems that just at this time Cyrus was the real ruler, but he was away. Just after the Medo-Persian work of conquest, Cyrus was the real ruler, and this old man called Darius was the uncle of Cyrus, and he was left in charge. Now remember that you are still in the palace where this Darius lives. You will see coming into the palace an influential deputation, a great number of satraps, governors, and princes, speaking to the king with falsetto tones of simulated reverence. They ask him to make a law to this effect—that no man shall within thirty days make a request to God or men save of the king; that if he should do so, he be cast into the den of lions. What an enormous extravagance! If the sun should burn the land, there must be no request made to the Lord of the elements for rain. If pestilence should blast the people, there must be no request of Him to send powers of healing, or to come between the living and the dead for the plague to be stayed. If a fire should break out, there must be no request to a man to help to put the fire out. If a person were to be ill, there must be no request to a physician to prescribe. If a person should be drowning, there should be no request to the man on the shore to fling a rope and help the sufferer out of the water. If any wrong had been done, there must be no request for forgiveness. If the mysterious spirits supposed to dwell in stone should thunder and lighten at any suspense to their worship, there was to be no request, even then, that these gods should wait with patience until the time was up.

Now, he is just like the man I have described. There is no hesitation, no word of inquiry, no word of surprise, no word of resentment; they catch the fly in their web. He seems to say in spirit, "Let me alone. Do what you like, only let me be quiet." That was the very spirit of the man.

II. In the next place, leaving this palace and those who were making this conspiracy, let us go into a private house in Babylon and mark the object of the conspiracy. Who is it? Daniel. And what is it for? It is difficult to say—impossible to say—with any clearness of reason, or with any show of right. They hated him; but it was said of Jesus, "They hated Him without a cause." It is in the nature of the carnal mind ever to hate God; and so it hates that which has God in it. They hated this man on account of his faith. Amidst the rabble of deities, gods and goddesses, with all their splendour and all their circumstantial authority, in Babylon, he was true to his worship of the one living God; true to Jehovah, and true to the covenant; true to the counsel of God, which was then working under all events, and from time to time flashing up through all secrecies, giving hints of what was understood to be when Christ Himself would come; and the mighty spirit of revelation rose in the soul of Daniel. While he was believing, he was lifted up in thought to an immense height, commanding a view of after ages; and surely he, like Abraham, saw Christ's day, saw it afar off, "saw it and was glad." If you look at some of the passages in the 9th chapter of Daniel, you will find that he used words about the coming Christ such as Paul himself might have used. He was coming "to make reconciliation for transgression," coming to "make an end of sin," coming to "bring in everlasting righteousness." So Daniel was hated for his strange, holy, eccentric faith; he was hated for the life that sprang out of faith. Men did not like that life. When that life is the life of wealthy or influential or scholastic Christians, they put up with it; they speak with respect of the wealth or the influence or the scholarship, and they put up with the grace of God working through these.

Now, in all ages it has been just so. There was in Daniel's life nothing that ought to have excited hatred; even amongst human immoralities it was irreproachable; there was no fraud; there was no bribery; he was abstemious; he was righteous; he was courteous, living like one who lived at court—the court of the King of kings, where every Christian ought to live and ought to show the influence of atmosphere, the nameless grace of patrician calmness and patrician influence, of lovely winning manner that comes of a heart that belongs to God. It was so with Daniel, and it was so in the time of his early youth. He was the child of a very poor family, and the pride of his father and mother—ripe, beautiful, bounding—when he was snatched away from them—taken away right into Babylon, for them never to see him more; and now he was an old man, very old, like a shock of corn fully ripe; and all throughout he had maintained his steadfastness of holy life; and they hated that holy life. They hated him also because he was a man of rare gifts; they sickened with envy at the sight of those rare gifts. He was remarkable for his wisdom when young, so that Ezekiel, when speaking of Dives personified, said ironically, "Thou art wiser than Daniel." He belonged by presidency to the Magi—not to the sacerdotal, but to the scientific order. He was a thinker; he was gloriously educated; he was an influential man, naturally, supernaturally, and educationally. They hated that; they hated the distinctions and gifts of one who eclipsed them; they hated him, too, for his supremacy in office.

You may read in this chapter how Darius divided the empire. I believe 120 provinces were parted out, and there were three presidents over these. Daniel was the president of the presidents—not a native noble; he was higher than the native nobility; and they reared their stately crests; they were haughtily proud; they resented this altogether; they looked right and left, in and out, for something which should be fatal in its discovery and presentment, fatal to Daniel. They could find nothing. He was not violent; he was not cruel. There was no defalcation; the accounts were all right. There was perfect stainlessness as to bribery; but there was this one thing—he prayed. And it was an open prayer. Every one knew it, for he threw his windows open every day three times. He was most methodical in his prayers, and he turned towards Jerusalem. I think he built his house with his windows that side on purpose. Jerusalem was the place of the mercy-seat; Jerusalem was the place where the footsteps of God's glory had been seen, where the voice of His love had been heard. It was the scene of his prophecies. He turned that way, and that was his way of expressing his faith in that great sacrifice and that exalted Saviour who was typified by all that was done from age to age at Jerusalem; and because of this they invented this remarkably ingenious conspiracy, a conspiracy that was sure to catch this man. He was sure to pray.

In the next place, notice the effect of this conspiracy. The effect of this conspiracy in the first place was to bring out Daniel's confession. My subject is a Hebrew confessor. This is one of the grand Hebrew confessors who, lifted up above the mists of time, are for you to see, living in this Christian age, and who are to be conspicuous as our examples to the very end of time. He knew that the writing had been signed. What then? Was he politic? There are many things that I think you might have said if you had been there. I wonder what the effect would be if such a law as this could be possible in any land where you live. Would it make any difference to the prayer meetings? I am afraid not much. I think it would make some difference, however, if your habit of prayer had been in form like that of Daniel's. He might have said, "Well, I shall pray, but I shall shut the windows." That mere question of open and shut as to the windows has nothing to do with the question of prayer or no prayer. "I shall pray, but I think not in that room." There are other rooms not so conspicuous. Prayer in a cellar will be just as acceptable to Him who is on the throne of thrones as prayer in the most splendid apartment. He said, or he would have said, or might have said, " I will pray, but I need not pray with the lip. God looks not at the lip, but at the life. It is not what we say, but what we mean.

> "'Prayer is the burden of a sigh,
> The falling of a tear,
> The upward glancing of an eye,
> When none but God is near.'"

Or perhaps he might have said, "I will pray, but not with such order, such method." Now, apply this to your own circumstances. You who are young Christians, I beseech to make a good confession in this respect. I know that in early life, when you are in the early stages of a profession or trade, or when you are at school or college, you may have even to carry on your private prayer in the view of others, and I know what young life is. I know who has the majority of votes; I know the tendency to scorn that which is Christian, and that which is outspoken in Christian life; and I fear for some of you. I fear lest you should be laughed out of your prayers. I am speaking as plainly as I can, for I want every one to understand me —every child who is not yet in public life or school. I want every one to get ready; and although prayer is not a matter of form, although it is a thing of the life, although you may pray when you say nothing, I beseech you not to let go prayer. Not only do I say you must not let go the spirit, but do not let go the form; do not let go the method and the rule; for in this life we are such creatures of rule and form and method, that it is dangerous to give way in these outworks and these machineries; for much that is vital is connected with much that is external, and I pray you to be like Daniel. Stand to it, and show that you are like Christ not only by joining a Church, but being steadfast and immovable, always abounding in prayer at the right time. Never give up; keep on praying, and pray without ceasing in spirit. But, besides that, have special definite terms, and times, and forms. Keep on with your confession and your prayers till you win. Daniel did so. Was he a man that would alter his conduct towards God in consequence of the conduct of an insect towards himself? Oh, but he is great. He keeps on, whatever may be said about him. And do not we see amidst the great movements of the actual world, symbols and emblems of what I want to assert now? You find that the sun shines whether you look or not. He never waits for your approbation, never asks for your praise. He shines on, whether you open your eyes or shut your eyes. The sea rolls on in tranquil majesty, without waiting for you to look or not look; and the great peaks and mountains of the world rear their heads in wintry grandeur crowned, whether you look or do not look. And so the great spirits, men of great principle, do the same. They are not waiting to know what man thinks. Daniel did not wait to ask who was looking. What did he care about that? There was no ostentation; there was no bluster; there was no saying, "Now, I have determined to stand my ground and assert my principles. I am determined to say, and do, and die and I care nothing about these creatures of a day, these reptiles of a court. I shall still hold on my way, and I know I shall wax stronger and stronger." But there was no such boast; there was no boasting at all; there was no effort about it. He simply kept on with his confessorship.

Passing on to the issue of this conspiracy, to tell you fully, I must tell you further. See Daniel, in consequence of this confession, thrown to the lions. In the heroic age of Christianity, when in all likelihood to be a Christian meant to be some day a martyr, Christians were often seen to drop on the red sawdust at the stroke of a lion. Once (it was in the days of Diocletian) there was a youth named Pancratius who had in the beginning of life vast and romantic possibilities of earthly greatness, but he became a Christian, and that implied the probability of soon being flung to the lions. It might have been said to him, "What a pity you should do so! You will be so rich, and you will do so much good. Think of your usefulness, think of what you are throwing away, think of your mother, think of your father, think of the Christians whom you might serve if you kept your Christianity still for a while. No doubt it is right in the abstract to be a Christian; but you will not throw your life away for an abstraction. It is right in itself to be baptized, but baptism is only a sign; Christ is the thing signified. You may have the thing signified without the sign. It is, all things being equal, right to make a confession before men of your faith in Christ, but Christ looks not at what you say or at what you are; He judges not by the label, but by the life. No doubt it is right, when all things are equal and fair, to come out, as you propose to come out; but oh! say nothing now! say nothing now; be still, hold your faith in the dark; the time will come when it may appear in the light." But Pancratius saw in the clear daylight of truth that he was to believe, and then that he was, as a matter of course, to confess that faith. So he believed and did confess, and he was sentenced to the lions. There came a day when a hundred Christians were sentenced to the lions, and this young Christian was to come last. See him! oh! look at him, the little, slim youth—for he was only a youth; see him there standing in the amphitheatre, with some

25,000 people all round him, like one scared. There they are, ring above ring; there they are, all round him when he stands there; and presently there is a great rattle in the far distance, and out from that cage springs a lion, and he slips and wanders about. At last he sees the youth; he seems at once still as a stone; he burns, as it seems, into terrible beauty; then he drops on to the sand, and looks at him at a distance—looks and looks at him; then he trails, and trails, and trails, gets nearer, and nearer, and nearer, walks round, and round, and round, and stops; round again—stops; and then, with a bound and a blow, and a flash of black lightning, down he drops on to that quivering young life; there is a moment's paralysis, and then "the sacred, high, eternal noon."

We ought not to think of our lions: they are chained. Would you be ready, if the call were to come forth to the lions for Christ's sake, would you be ready? There is none of us feel ready now; but if we do trust Christ, we who do trust Him now, we shall be ready whenever that call shall come. Daniel was ready for the lions that were set about him; and to the lions he was hustled, to the lions he was flung.

Now, under this last head, one more remark. Think of the night Daniel had with the lions—the night and the morning. The night! Did you ever dream of such a thing as that? Night is the time for rest; day is for action. If in the day we court peril, in the night we seek repose; if in the day we like to be abroad, at night we like to be at home; in the day our Heavenly Father, whose other name is Love, surrounds us with light, vivacity, and movement, and everything that can inspire thought, rouse activity, and stimulate the Divine; but when the night comes, He hushes the sounds, puts the lights out, stops the songs of birds, draws the curtains of tender darkness, and says, "Hush!" and with a love beyond all conception, more exquisite and tender than ever love was that ever rocked a cradle or sang the cradle's song, He gives us and all His "beloved sleep." Nights we have heard of have been spent in fasting and amidst the incongruities. We have heard of a night passed amidst the silence and shadows of Westminster Abbey; we have heard of a night passed alone on a spar in the sea; we have heard of a night passed by one who was lost amidst the snows of Salisbury Plain; we have heard of a night passed amongst the lions—amongst these terrible lions. But God sent His angel to stop the lions' mouths; and you may imagine their bland, caressing movements, as John Foster has it, round Daniel just as they used to be round Adam in Paradise. So in the morning when the cry came, "Daniel! Daniel! servant of the living God, is He able—the God whom thou servest continually—to keep thee alive, to keep thee from the lions? are you alive?" You know what the answer was. My text is the answer—Daniel lived. Daniel lives now,—lives in heaven, lives in this Book, and lives for you. You are not placed in similar circumstances, but every one of you is tried sometimes to the fullest extent of your powers. You have lions of some kind to face; and oh, I beseech you, open your windows towards Calvary, open your windows towards the great sacrifice. Look to the Lord Jesus; let your hopes be there; draw your light from thence. Be real Christians, making the solemn vow of consecration, first alone, and giving yourselves right up to Jesus when no one sees you. Then come out—come out from the world, out from the laughers, out from those who are making their way and getting their fortune and their influence, perhaps, by compromise; perhaps by indefiniteness. Be distinct; be decisive; let every one who sees you know what you are, and know what Christ can do for you. You know that He whom you serve is able to give, able to teach, able to sustain, able to console, able to do above all that you can ask or think.

C. S.

INDEX OF SUBJECTS.

Abraham, 25.
Abraham's Death, 30.

Balaam, 63.
Barak's Faith, 89.

Captain of the Lord's Host, The, 82.
Captives of Babylon, The, 248.
Cry of the Creatures, The, 268.

David, 101.
Daniel among the Lions, 297.
David in the Psalms, The Preaching of, 217.

Elijah's Faith, The Failure of, 111.
Elijah's Flight, 121.
Enoch, 1.

Isaac, 39.

Jacob at Bethel, 45.
Jacob's Death, 50.

Job, 155.
Job, The Book of, 166, 175, 184, 194, 202.
Joshua, 75.
Josiah, 146.

King Conquered, The, 134.

Marah, The Waters of, 58.

Nebuchadnezzar, 288.
New Year, A Song for the, 242.
Noah, 9.

Penitence, 224.
Psalm, The Second, 211.

Ruth, 96.

Trust and Waiting, 229.

Vision of the Dry Bones, The, 278.

Waiting, 237.

INDEX OF TEXTS.

GENESIS.	PAGE
v. 21–24	1
xxv. 7, 8	25
,, 8	30
xxxv. 1	45

EXODUS.	
xv. 23–25	58

NUMBERS.	
xxiv. 11	63

DEUTERONOMY.	
xxxiv. 9	75

JOSHUA.	
v. 13–15	82

JUDGES.	
iv. 9	89

RUTH.	
i. 22	96

2 SAMUEL.	PAGE
xii. 7	101

1 KINGS.	
xix. 13	111
,,	121

2 KINGS.	
vi.	134

2 CHRONICLES.	
xxxv. 21	146

JOB.	
i. 8, 9	155
Book of, 1	166
,, 2	175
,, 3	184
,, 4	194
,, 5	202

PSALMS	
ii.	211

	PAGE
xxvii. 8	217
li. 5	223
lxii. 1, 2	229
,, 5, 6	237
cxxi.	242
cxxxvii. 1–6	248

ISAIAH.	
Book of	257
vi. 1–3	268

EZEKIEL.	
xxxvii. 3	278

DANIEL.	
iv. 37	288
vi. 22	297

HEBREWS.	
xi. 7	9
,, 20	39
,, 21	50

STANDARD RELIGIOUS BOOKS.

The Clerical Library.

THIS SERIES of volumes is specially intended for the CLERGY, STUDENTS AND SUNDAY SCHOOL TEACHERS OF ALL DENOMINATIONS, and is meant to furnish them with stimulus and suggestion in the various departments of their work. Amongst the pulpit thinkers from whom these sermon outlines have been drawn are leading men of almost *every* denomination in Great Britain and America, the subjects treated of being of course practical rather than controversial. The best thoughts of the best religious writers of the day are here furnished in a condensed form and at a moderate price.

Five volumes in crown 8vo are now ready (*each volume complete in itself*). Price, $1.50.

NOW READY—FOURTH EDITION.
300 OUTLINES OF SERMONS ON THE NEW TESTAMENT.

By **72** Eminent ENGLISH and AMERICAN CLERGYMEN, including

Archbishop TAIT.	Canon LIDDON.	Rev. Dr. H. CROSBY.
Bishop ALEXANDER.	Canon WESTCOTT.	Rev. Dr. Pres. McCOSH.
Bishop BROWNE.	Rev. Prin. CAIRNS.	Rev. Dr. M. R. VINCENT.
Bishop LIGHTFOOT.	Rev. Dr. M. PUNSHON	Rev. Dr. JNO. PEDDIE.
Bishop MAGEE.	Rev. Dr. W. M. TAYLOR.	Rev. Dr. C. T. DEEMS.
Bishop RYLE.	Rev. PHILLIPS BROOKS.	Rev. C. H. SPURGEON.
Dean CHURCH.	Rev. Dr. R. S. STORRS.	Rev. Dean STANLEY.
Dean VAUGHAN.	Rev. Dr. W. G. T. SHEDD.	Rev. Dr. A. RALEIGH.
Canon FARRAR.	Rev. Dr. T. L. CUYLER.	*And many others.*
Canon KNOX-LITTLE.	Rev. Dr. J. T. DURYEA.	

OUTLINES OF SERMONS ON THE OLD TESTAMENT.

AUTHORS OF SERMONS.

G. S. BARRETT, B.A.	J. OSWALD DYKES, D.D.	Canon LIDDON.
Dean E. BICKERSTETH.	E. HERBER EVANS.	J. A. MACFAYDEN, D.D.
Bishop E. H. BROWNE.	Canon F. W. FARRAR.	ALEX. MACLAREN, D.D.
J. BALD. BROWN, B.A.	DONALD FRASER, D.D.	Bishop W. C. MAGEE.
T. P. BOULTBEE, LL.D.	J. G. GREENOUGH, B.A.	THEODORE MONOD.
J. P. CHOWN.	W. F. HOOK, D.D.	ARTHUR MURSELL.
Dean R. W. CHURCH.	Bishop W. BASIL JONES.	JOSEPH PARKER, D.D.
E. R. COUDER, D.D.	JOHN KERR, D.D.	Dean E. H. PLUMPTRE.
T. L. CUYLER, D.D.	Canon EDWARD KING.	JOHN PULSFORD, [D.D.
A. B. DAVIDSON, D.D.	Bp. J. B. LIGHTFOOT.	W. MORLEY PUNSHON,
ROBERT RAINY, D.D.	WM. M. TAYLOR, D.D.	M. R. VINCENT, D.D.
ALEX'R RALEIGH, D.D.	S. A. TIPPLE, B.A.	W. J. WOODS, B.A.
C. P. REICHEL, D.D.	H. J. VANDYKE, D.D.	C. WADSWORTH, D.D.
CHAS. STANFORD, D.D.	Dean C. J. VAUGHAN.	G. H. WILKINSON.
Dean A. P. STANLEY.	JAMES VAUGHAN, B.A.	Bp. C. WORDSWORTH.
W. M. STRATHAM, B.A.		

Sent on receipt of price, charges prepaid.

A. C. ARMSTRONG & SON, 714 Broadway, New York.

THE CLERICAL LIBRARY—(Continued).

OUTLINES OF SERMONS TO CHILDREN.

With numerous Anecdotes. Crown 8vo. Cloth, $1.50. (Being the 3d vol. of the CLERICAL LIBRARY.)

"*These sermons are by men of acknowledged eminence in possessing the happy faculty of preaching interestingly to the young. As an evidence of this, as well as of the character of the teaching, it is only necessary to mention such names as those of* WILLIAM ARNOT, THE BONARS, PRINCIPAL CAIRNS, JOHN EDMOND, D.D., Drs. OSWALD DYKES *and* J. MARSHALL LANG, *besides many others.*"—*Canada Presbyterian.*

"This book contains a very high grade of thinking, with enough illustrations and anecdotes to stock the average preacher for many years of children's sermons."—*Episcopal Register.*

"They are full of suggestions which will be found exceedingly helpful; the habit of using apt and simple illustrations, and of repeating good anecdotes, begets a faculty and power which are of value. This volume is a treasure which a hundred pastors will find exceedingly convenient to draw upon."—*N. Y. Evangelist.*

PULPIT PRAYERS BY EMINENT PREACHERS.

Crown 8vo. Cloth, $1.50. (Being the 4th vol. of the CLERICAL LIBRARY.)

The British Quarterly says: "*These prayers are fresh and strong; the ordinary ruts of conventional forms are left and the fresh thoughts of living hearts are uttered. The excitement of devotional thought and sympathy must be great in the offering of such prayers, especially when, as here, spiritual intensity and devoutness are as marked as freshness and strength. Such prayers have their characteristic advantages.*"

London Literary World: "Used aright, this volume is likely to be of great service to ministers. It will show them how to put variety, freshness and literary beauty, as well as spirituality of tone, into their extemporaneous prayers."

Anecdotes Illustrative of New Testament Texts.

With **600** Anecdotes. Crown 8vo, **400** pages. Cloth, **$1.50**. (Being the 5th vol. of the CLERICAL LIBRARY.)

London Christian Leader says: "*This is one of the most valuable books of anecdote that we have ever seen. There is hardly one anecdote that is not of first-rate quality. They have been selected by one who has breadth and vigor of mind as well as keen spiritual insight, and some of the most effective illustrations of Scripture texts have a rich vein of humor of exquisite quality.*"

The London Church Bells: "The anecdotes are given in the order of the texts which they illustrate. There is an ample index. The book is one which those who have to prepare sermons and addresses will do well to have at their elbow."

N. Y. Christian at Work: "AS AN APT ILLUSTRATION OFTEN PROVES THE NAIL WHICH FASTENS THE TRUTH IN THE MIND, THIS VOLUME WILL PROVE AN ADMIRABLE AND VALUABLE AID, NOT ONLY TO CLERGYMEN, BUT TO SUNDAY-SCHOOL TEACHERS AND CHRISTIAN WORKERS GENERALLY."

N.Y. Observer: "A book replete with incident and suggestion applicable to every occasion."

Sent on receipt of price, charges prepaid.
A. C. ARMSTRONG & SON, 714 Broadway, New York.

STANDARD RELIGIOUS WORKS.

TALKS WITH YOUNG MEN.

By J. THAIN DAVIDSON. 12mo, in handsome cloth binding, illuminated cover. Price, $1.25.

"These talks are direct, practical and pungent, such as young men like to hear. They are crowded with points of counsel and direction; they will be invaluable to any young man, and all so plainly and forcibly told, and so fully illustrated, that one can but pursue the reading of them to the end. The graphic descriptions of human nature, and sharp laying open of motive in worldly and selfish living, show an unusually keen sense of observation and understanding of the human heart. It should have a wide circulation."—*N. Y. Evangelist.*

Rev. Mr. SPURGEON says: "*The author gives young men fine advice—full of grace and thought—enlivened by story and proverb, fresh with sympathy, and on fire with zeal. These short talks are just what they should be, and all that they further need is to be largely distributed among the crowds of our advancing manhood.* **TO BEGIN TO READ IS TO BE BOUND TO CONTINUE; THE TALKS ARE SO SENSIBLE THAT NO ONE WISHES TO SILENCE THE TALKER—BY LAYING ASIDE THE BOOK.**"

N. Y. Christian Advocate and Journal says: "This volume will find readers wherever it is known. The talks are fervent and **DIRECT APPEALS TO THE HEART. THE STYLE IS ANIMATED AND PICTURESQUE, AND THE BOOK WILL BE READ BY ALL WHO BUY IT.**"

The Parabolic Teaching of Christ.

A Systematic and Critical Study of the Parables of our Lord. By Rev. Prof. A. B. BRUCE, D.D. 1 vol., 8vo, cloth, 527 pp. Price, $2.50.

"A work which will at once take its place as a classic on the Parables of our Saviour. No minister should think of doing without it."—*American Presbyterian Review.*

American Literary Churchman says: "We recommend this book with the most confident earnestness. It is a book to be bought and kept; it has both depth and breadth and minute accuracy; it has a living sympathy with the teaching of the Parables and with the spirit of the Master."

ENGLISH NOTICES.

"Prof. Bruce brings to his task the learning and the liberal and finely sympathetic spirit which are the best gifts of an expositor of Scripture. His treatment of his subject is vigorous and original, and he avoids the capital mistake of overlaying his exegesis with a mass of other men's views."—*Spectator.*

"The studies of the Parables are thorough, scholarly, suggestive and practical. Fullness of discussion, reverence of treatment, and sobriety of judgment, mainly characterize this work."—*Christian World.*

"Each Parable is most thoughtfully worked out, and much new light is thus thrown on the difficulties which surround many of these beautiful and suggestive examples of Divine teaching."—*Clergymen's Magazine.*

"This volume has only to be known to be welcomed, not by students alone, but by all earnest students of Christ's oracles. On no subject has Dr. Bruce spoken more wisely than on the question why Jesus spoke in parables. The one end the author sets before himself is, to find out what our Lord really meant. And this he does with a clearness and fullness worthy of all praise. **Familiar as we are with some of the best and most popular works on the Parables, we do not know any to which we could look for so much aid in our search after the very meaning which Christ would have us find in His words.**"—*Nonconformist.*

Sent on receipt of price, charges prepaid.

A. C. ARMSTRONG & SON, 714 Broadway, New York.

STANDARD RELIGIOUS WORKS.

New and Enlarged [4th] Edition, in Cheaper Form,
OF

CHARLES L. BRACE'S GESTA CHRISTI.

A HISTORY OF HUMANE PROGRESS UNDER CHRISTIANITY. With New Preface and Supplementary Chapter. 540 pp., cloth.

Price reduced from $2.50 to $1.50.

"It is especially adapted to assist the clergyman and religious teacher in his struggles with honest, thoughtful infidelity."

"*It presents a storehouse of facts* bearing on the influences of Christianity upon such important topics as the paternal power, the position of woman under custom and law, personal purity, and marriage, slavery, cruel and licentious sports, and all matters of humanity and compassion, etc. THE THOUGHTFUL READER WILL HERE GATHER INFORMATION WHICH COULD ONLY BE OBTAINED FROM LIBRARIES OR MANY VOLUMES."

Rev. Dr. R. S. STORRS says: "*IT IS A BOOK THAT DESERVES THE VERY WIDEST CIRCULATION FOR ITS CAREFULNESS AND CANDOR, ITS AMPLE LEARNING,* its just, discriminating analysis of historical movements as initiated or governed by moral forces, and for the fine spirit which pervades it."

"'The skill and industry with which Mr. Brace has gleaned and sorted the vast accumulation of material here gathered together, the better to show forth the power and influence, direct and indirect, of Christ's teachings, is not only praise-worthy, but even in a certain sense wonderful. He has a complete mastery of his subject, and many chapters in the book are of exceeding value and interest."—*London Morning Post.*

A NEW and REVISED EDITION, with NEW MAPS and ILLUSTRATIONS,
OF

STANLEY'S SINAI AND PALESTINE.

In Connection with their History. By Dean A. P. STANLEY.
With 7 Elaborate and Beautifully Colored
Maps, and other Illustrations.

Large Crown 8vo Vol., Cloth, 640 pp. Price reduced from $4 to $2.50.

The late Dean Stanley published a new and revised edition of his "SINAI AND PALESTINE." In it he made considerable editions and corrections, giving the work the final impress of his scholarship, taste and ability. This edition has been carefully conformed to the last English edition—including the new maps and illustrations, and is herewith commended anew AS THE MOST READABLE AS WELL AS THE MOST ACCURATE WORK ON THE SUBJECT IN THE ENGLISH LANGUAGE.

Rev. Dr. H. M. Field, Editor of "*N. Y. Evangelist,*" says of Stanley's "*Sinai and Palestine*": "We had occasion for its constant use in crossing the desert, and in journeying through the Holy Land, and can bear witness at once to its accuracy and to the charm of its descriptions. *Of all the helps we had it was by far the most captivating.*"

Sent on receipt of price, charges prepaid.

A. C. ARMSTRONG & SON, 714 Broadway, New York.

STANDARD RELIGIOUS WORKS.

A MANUAL OF PREACHING.

Rev. FRANKLIN W. FISK, D.D., Professor of Sacred Rhetoric in *Chicago Theological Seminary.* Crown octavo vol., cloth. $1.50.

This work sets forth and illustrates the principles and rules of Homiletics in a brief and practical manner. Although chiefly designed for theological students and young ministers, it is believed that the treatise will be of service to older pastors. Reference is made to the most recent literature, both of the pulpit and of works on Homiletics. The method followed in the volume is, first, to take a sermon in pieces and inspect its principal parts, and then to show how to gather materials and form a sermon. The aim has been to make the work, in a brief and practical way, as helpful as possible to the preacher.

"Many will welcome this manual for its clear, logical and thorough presentation of the whole subject."—*N. Y. Independent.*

Chicago Interior says: "The book is precisely what it claims to be—a practical manual of Preaching. Its style is simple and perspicuous, and just what the author commends in the sermon. On every page the meaning stares the reader full in the face."

Presbyterian Review: "Back of this modest manual lie twenty-five years of diligent study and valuable experience. The volume carries on every page the characteristics that we should expect to find in it. *It is unpretending, direct, honest, manly.* Its pages are full of references to authorities and illustrations."

REVIVALS: HOW AND WHEN?

By Rev. W. W. NEWELL, D.D. With steel portrait. 1 vol., 12mo. $1.25. (3d thousand.)

This is no ordinary book on the subject of Revivals of Religion. It does not commend great excitement followed by depressing apathy. It favors a religious quickening and an ingathering of souls every passing year. It does not commend a theory. It is eminently practical. It gives the exact experience of persons who, in the greatest variety of seemingly hopeless conditions, have been taught of the Lord just how to secure a spiritual blessing. It shows how the Revival has been secured and conducted in the Church, the Household, the Bible Class, the Sabbath School, the Missionary and the Temperance circle.

ARCHBISHOP LEIGHTON'S BIOGRAPHY.

With Notes and Selections from his Writings. By WILLIAM BLAIR, D.D. Handsomely bound in white parchment, gilt top and side. $1.25.

"The memoir is admirably composed, . . . the general contents include various rare spiritual treasures, in which the mind of Leighton was so fruitful."—*New York Churchman.*

NEW WORK BY REV. W. M. TAYLOR, D.D., LL.D.

JOHN KNOX.

With a fine Steel Portrait. Engraved by HOLL, from a Painting in the possession of Lord Somerville. 12mo, cloth. $1.25.

This work gives a vivid, comprehensive and accurate account of the life and work of the great Scottish Reformer. It includes a careful and well ordered summary of the career of Knox in England, as that has been brought to light by the recent investigations of Lorimer and others. Particular attention has been given to the course of events in Scotland during the last thirteen years of the Reformer's life, and his interviews with QUEEN MARY, as well as his work in the reconstruction of the Scottish Church, are described with fullness of detail and independence of judgment. The story is admirably told, the interest being maintained from first to last, so that the book will be at once delightful to the young and instructive to those of maturer years.

Copies sent by mail, post paid, on receipt of price.

A. C. ARMSTRONG & SON, 714 Broadway, New York.

REV. DR. WM. M. TAYLOR'S WORKS.

Contrary Winds and Other Sermons.

Crown 8vo Volume, Cloth. $1.75. 3d Edition.

"This work touches on numerous phases of life and thought and experience, showing that the author has lived through a vast deal and has been made the richer and stronger by it. It leaves the impression of wisdom that comes from actual experience, dealing with life rather than speculations, and so comes home to the heart and conscience. IT SHOWS A WIDE RANGE OF READING AND CLOSE GRAPPLE WITH THE DIFFICULT PROBLEMS OF OUR TIME. Such preaching is tonic and invigorating. It strengthens the heart and fortifies the will to overcome trials and conquer temptations and achieve victory."—*N. Y. Christian at Work.*

The Congregationalist says: "Its variety of theme and the never-failing intellectual power which it illustrates, the author's reverent positiveness of faith, his broad and intimate knowledge of human nature, and the richness of his personal spiritual experiences—never obtruded but always underlying his words—render it a volume of rare and precious value to the Christian believer, and A CAPITAL SPECIMEN OF MANLY, BUSINESS-LIKE DISCUSSION TO ALL OTHERS WHO CARE TO READ WHAT A CHRISTIAN HAS TO SAY FOR HIS RELIGION."

N. Y. Churchman: "Sermons practical in their nature, full of deep thought and wise counsel. They will have as they deserve a wide circulation.

Now Ready—4th Edition of
THE LIMITATIONS OF LIFE
AND OTHER SERMONS.
By WM. M. TAYLOR, D.D.

WITH A FINE PORTRAIT ON STEEL BY RITCHIE. CROWN 8VO VOL., EXTRA CLOTH, $1.75.

"In variety of theme, in clearness and penetration of vision, in distinctness of aim, in intensity of purpose, in energy and well-directed effort, etc., this volume is perhaps without its equal in the language."
—*The Scotsman.*

Providence Journal: "The directness, earnestness, descriptive and illustrative power of the preacher, and his rare gift for touching the conscience and the heart, are fully exemplified in these eloquent discourses."

N. Y. Evangelist: "They have the noble simplicity and clearness of the truth itself, and which, fixing the attention of the reader from the beginning, holds it to the end. It is impossible to read them without the constant sense of the personality of the author."

Copies sent on receipt of price, post-paid, by
A. C. ARMSTRONG & SON, 714 BROADWAY, NEW YORK.